MASTER OF THE BIG BOARD

Bill Carey

MASTER OF THE BIG BOARD

THE LIFE, TIMES, AND BUSINESSES OF JACK C. MASSEY

BILL CAREY

CUMBERLAND HOUSE
NASHVILLE, TENNESSEE

Published by
Cumberland House Publishing, Inc.
431 Harding Industrial Drive
Nashville, TN 37211-3160

Cover design: Gore Studio, Inc.
Text design: John Mitchell

Library of Congress Cataloging-in-Publication Data

Carey, Bill, 1965–
  Master of the big board : the life, times, and businesses of Jack Massey / Bill Carey.
    p. cm.
  Includes bibliographical references.
  ISBN-13 978-1-58182-471-1 (hardcover : alk. paper)
  ISBN-10 1-58182-471-8
  1. Massey, Jack C., 1904-1990. 2. Businessmen—United States—Biography. 3. Capitalists
and financiers—United States—Biography. I. Title.
  HC102.5.M27C37 2005
  338.7'6'092—dc22
                                                                              2005022687

Printed in the United States of America

1 2 3 4 5 6 7—10 09 08 07 06 05

To the members of the Massey family,
in this and successive generations,
to enhance their knowledge of the legacy
of Jack C. Massey

CONTENTS

THE TEN GREATEST THINGS JACK MASSEY EVER SAID ABOUT BUSINESS

"If you just have an ambition to make money, you are going to neglect a lot of things that are necessary to do it. You have to plan, you have to be patient, and you don't do that overnight. Just working for money doesn't get the job done. You have to work for success, and with success you will get the money. Money is a side effect; it's not the main thing."

"Nothing is bought. Everything is sold."

"My advice to anyone going into business is to get the best lawyer you can get, get the best banker you can get, and get the best accountant you can get, and put them all together and tell them that you are going to start a business and need them in on it from the beginning. And tell them that you need them to tell you things before they happen, not after they happen."

"If you want to start your own business, you have to have an 'I Will Not Fail' attitude. That is what you have got to do, and you have got to work toward it. If you see that things are going wrong, do something about it. Work harder. Go out and get business. Communicate."

"I knew that I had arrived the first time I borrowed a million dollars."

"The real key to success or to leadership in any endeavor, be it business, professional, social, personal, or whatever, is the ability to recognize an opportunity and the willingness to invest the time, money, and effort that it takes to capitalize on it. . . . There is a Senegalese proverb that says, 'The opportunity that God sends does not wake up he who is asleep.'"

"Work is and should be a major part of a person's life. It will be one of the most rewarding and fulfilling things that you do. But alone, financial success is not a life, but only one part of it. Without family happiness, good physical and mental health, social acceptance, religious faith, and a commitment to serve your fellow human beings, you will not be a whole person."

"When you go public, you build your 'house of glass,' and the shades will never again be drawn."

"A man has got to have a commitment to what he wants to do. He has to be able to risk something. We wouldn't look for five minutes at a man who won't put his own money in the business. He should put in everything he's got, except his family."

"I never was tempted to give up. I sold my automobile and rode the streetcar, but I never was tempted to give up."

FOREWORD

Jack Massey's friends were beginning to think he'd gone mad.

A couple of years earlier he had sold the business he had spent his entire life building—a surgical supply company that sold equipment to doctors and hospitals throughout the South. In exchange for it he had received 16,754 shares of stock in Brunswick Corporation, worth about $1.6 million in cash the day the deal was signed. Most of Massey's friends thought that sounded like a pretty good deal.

Fifty-nine-year-old men who work too hard and sell their companies generally retire, and that's what everyone expected Jack Massey to do. He tried. Massey had a place down in Fort Lauderdale, Florida, and he moved down there and gave retirement his best shot. But it didn't take.

"I went there and stayed about two months and found out that you can't play golf and loaf and be happy when you've been working all your life," he said.

All of Massey's friends knew that he was a straightforward man, a good conversationalist, a chronic gin rummy player, and that he liked to wager on trivial things. "He was the kind of guy who would bet you as to which bird would fly off the fence next," a friend once said. What many of his friends didn't know about Jack Massey was that he was a real venture capitalist.

A board member of Nashville's Third National Bank, Massey loved the meetings where they went through all the small business loans, and he especially liked to hear about the new businesses. His part-ownership in a pesticide firm called Rigo Chemical was one of the best-kept secrets in Nashville. Massey liked "the game" so much that even after he sold his surgical supply business he continued to operate a small equipment leasing business—another well-kept secret.

Now it was February 1964, and Massey was going around town talking up a company that he was on the verge of buying. It made perfect sense, Massey was telling everyone. It was a simple business that had proven profitable just about everywhere it had gone. A fabulous company that operated in limited parts of the country that could be spread to new markets. A company that had been taken as far as its founder could take it. And it was time for that founder, a quirky fellow named "Colonel" Harland Sanders, to retire.

Massey told a lot of people about this business, and he did so with the enthusiasm that made him a great salesman. But most people he talked to were less than eager to take him up on his offer to buy stock. After all, the original contract in which Sanders agreed to sell Massey and a partner the business was scribbled on a yellow note pad, and it was signed at the Covered Wagon Motel in Salt Lake City, Utah. No one knew Massey's partner in the venture, a young lawyer from Kentucky named John Y. Brown Jr.

Besides, Massey had never owned or run a restaurant before in his life—let alone a chain of restaurants. In fact, he couldn't even cook. So what made him think he had any business buying an operation called Kentucky Fried Chicken?

Clyde Moon operated a small chain of Nashville drugstores in which Jack Massey owned a minority interest. Years later Moon told his daughter that Massey had told him he was on the verge of buying Kentucky Fried Chicken. Moon's reaction to the news was typical of almost everyone in Nashville. "My father told Mr. Massey that it was the stupidest thing he'd ever heard," Kitty Moon Emery said years later.

Stockbroker James C. Bradford Jr. also remembered the way people first reacted to Kentucky Fried Chicken. A couple of years after Massey and Brown bought the company, they took the business public using J. C. Bradford & Company as one of their underwriters. Many of Bradford's investors didn't know what to make of Kentucky Fried Chicken when their stockbrokers called.

"Now there are companies franchising everything," Bradford said in 2004. "But back in those days there weren't many companies out there that had something franchised. The biggest was Coca-Cola, but hell, Kentucky Fried Chicken was no Coca-Cola. People thought these were just a bunch of chicken stands on the side of the road."

It may very well have been that Jack Massey didn't have a clue as to what he was doing. But it is a good thing that he didn't err on the side of conservatism or listen to the advice of people who told him he was nuts to buy a fried chicken company. A good thing for Massey, a good thing for Nashville, and a good thing for the American economy. Thanks to Massey and Brown, Kentucky Fried Chicken did well. Not only did it make its investors happy, but it also created a wave of franchise stocks that helped make the stock market a good place to have one's money for a couple of years.

About the time KFC peaked, Massey was so confident in himself and in the economy that he helped start another business that also had its skeptics: a for-profit chain of hospitals called Hospital Corporation of America. HCA became Massey's second company on the New York Stock Exchange. There would also be a venture capital company and investments in other companies and real estate deals here and there. And he would eventually take a third company, called Winners Corporation, to the New York Stock Exchange—thus becoming the only person to ever, as chairman, take three unrelated companies to the so-called "Big Board."

None of this would have happened if Jack Massey had let anyone talk some sense into him back in February 1964.

MASTER OF
THE BIG BOARD

1

DELIVERY BOY

S ANDERSVILLE IS A SMALL COMMUNITY in southeast Georgia known more for its mud than its people. Today the town proudly proclaims itself the "Kaolin Capital of the World," in honor of a type of clay mined there. A hundred years ago its economy was dominated by cotton, its culture by the Baptist Church, its transportation by the railroad. And it was here, on September 7, 1904, that Jack Carroll Massey was born.

Jack's father, Harris Benton Massey, had been raised on a small cotton farm in the nearby community of Tennille, where a little-noticed county road still bears the Massey family name. H. B. Massey, as he was frequently referred to in the written vernacular of the time, was a well-liked, outgoing man who was elected clerk of the Washington County Court in 1902. Re-elected in 1904 and 1906, he was thus one of the more prominent citizens in turn-of-the-century Washington County, Georgia.

Jack Massey's mother, whose maiden name was Jodie Louise Brown, was born and raised in Tennille. A well-educated young lady person by the standards of that time and place, she received a graduation certificate in 1892 from Shorter College in Rome, Georgia. Jack Massey had two older brothers, Harry (four years older) and Joe (two years older). The family lived in a respectable Victorian-era house on Sandersville's main drive. It still stood a century after Jack Massey's birth.

Prominent or not, life could be hard in turn-of-the-century small-town Georgia. In 1906 Jodie Massey gave birth to her fourth child, a boy named Alex. He was not healthy, and twenty months later the infant Alex Massey died of "stomach trouble," according to the *Sandersville Progress*. As devastating as this event must have been to Jodie Massey, things didn't improve.

Three months after the death of her youngest son, her husband followed him to the grave. "For the past four years Mr. Massey had been in failing health, and nothing could be done for his improvement," the local paper reported. "He realized the hopelessness of his illness and had several times told his friends that he knew that he did not have long to live. Everything possible was done for his relief, but to no avail."

Whatever the cause of Harris Benton Massey's death, it left Jodie the sole responsibility of raising three boys. The family's meager income was derived from the rented farm; as her eldest son later put it, "She made do." By the standards of the time Jack Massey's family was not poor. They could, for instance, feed themselves, and each boy was able to finish high school under his mother's support. But there were no luxuries of any kind. And in an era before welfare, the boys were completely dependent on Mrs. Massey and extended family members.

Given the situation, it is no wonder that the Massey boys revered their mother. It is also easy to understand why the brothers, especially Harry and Jack, had a deep-seated desire to succeed in business and help their mother get by. "I was always very conscientious about my mother's living and income, and always felt that it was my responsibility to help," Jack Massey later said.

When he was still in elementary school, young Jack heard that a cotton mill in a nearby town was paying good wages. A few days later he wrote a farewell note and slipped out of the house in the middle of the night, heading in the general direction of the mill. In the morning, when his mother found the message, she sent Harry to fetch his brother.

Like many other people of his generation, Jack Massey later emphasized how hard his childhood was, and it certainly was austere compared to what most American children of later generations experienced. Jodie Massey was active in the First Baptist Church's Women's Missionary Society and the Women's Christian Temperance Union, and she was not a pushover by any stretch.

"She neither smoked nor drank, and none of her boys ever smoked or drank in front of her either," her granddaughter Barbara Massey Rogers said many years later. Another grandchild would later describe his Sandersville grandmother as taciturn. "I really didn't like going to visit her because she did little to accommodate us," Joe Massey said. "She had no toys. The only thing we had to play with when we visited her were Fiddlesticks."

Nevertheless, Jack Massey was apparently happy and playful, and he liked doing things that children of every generation loved to do. In 1920 he wrote a letter to his brother Joe and talked about dancing, basketball, and other pastimes. "Write me and tell me how much money I must send you so you can bring me a lots [sic] of fireworks and what kind u [sic] can get," he wrote, demonstrating a lack of attention to written grammar in correspondence which would remain with him for a long time.

Massey also preferred working to studying. "I had a lady principal in high school, and I carried her books home for her in the afternoon and we fell in love; she was ninety and I was twelve or fifteen or seventeen, you know," he told a reporter many years later. "We became good friends, and she realized that I wanted to work. I didn't like school. I didn't feel that I needed it . . . so she let me skip a grade and graduate a year early."

With his father gone, the most important adult male in Jack Massey's life was his uncle Alex Brown, who owned a drugstore in Tennille. The Massey brothers spent much of their childhood at the Tennille Drug Company; it was, after all, a good way for them to stay out of trouble. When Jack was twelve years old, Uncle Alex gave him a job there as a delivery boy. Like most drugstores of that era, it had a soda fountain, and young Jack began to set his sights on operating it one day. But soon his ambitions grew higher, something that would happen throughout his life.

Jack loved to watch his uncle fill prescriptions. Standing by his side, listening to him as he worked, the boy picked up bits of knowledge about being a pharmacist. He learned what the more common prescriptions were; he learned the basic composition of some of them; he learned how the pharmacy was arranged. Jack was so eager that he took a correspondence course to become a pharmacist. Eventually, under the watchful eye of his uncle, he began to fill simple prescriptions.

Uncle Alex taught Jack many things about running a drugstore. One day, when it was crowded and Jack was helping at the soda fountain, he tossed a woman's change across the counter and hurried to serve someone else. His angry uncle took him aside. "Never treat a customer the way you treated that woman!" he said. "Give her the change—don't throw it at her. Thank her for coming in. Ask if there's anything else you can do. And only then turn to the next customer. Is that clear?"

Other things about the store intrigued Jack. The local pharmacy and lunch counter were the nerve centers of the community. Massey spent hours listening to men discuss the news of the day.

"In a small community in those days, the local druggist was a civic figure of major proportions," Massey told an audience at Harvard University in 1977. "The drugstore was a social center for the town where the leaders of the community gathered to enjoy the products of the soda fountain and discuss the issues of the day. The druggist, almost always called 'Doc,' was a wise and kindly professional who dispensed medicines, concern, and advice from his lofty position behind the prescription counter. In his spare moments he mingled with the sages and thinkers of the town at a table near the soda fountain and added his wisdom to the topic of the conversation, whether it was fishing, politics, or the local flu epidemic.

"I wanted to be a man like that."

The experience of listening to grown men discuss the country, its future, and its policies taught Massey more than business skills; it made him realize what it meant to be an American. Many years later, a fifty-five-year-old Massey wrote to his daughter and told her about her duty. "Hope you are going to be a good American and vote," he wrote. "If you have not written, as I advised you previously, for your absentee ballot, please send an air mail letter immediately so you can get it."

Eventually, Massey's ambitions grew beyond the soda fountain and also beyond the idea of just being a pharmacist. "I found I loved the drugstore business in general," he said years later. "Even then, little by little, I developed a resolve to someday own a drugstore of my own. I even promised myself to achieve that goal by the time I was twenty-five."

After graduating from high school at the age of seventeen, Massey found work at the Beeson Drug Company in the small town of Wauchula, in northeastern Florida. In a letter written to his grandfather on April 13, 1922, Massey said he didn't have much free time except on Sundays.

"I like this place I'm working fine, and Mr. Beeson and my boss are both mighty fine men," he wrote. "I have to do lots of work tho [sic]. Mr. Beeson says if they work me to [sic] hard to let him know and he would come and work for me while I rested [sic]. He also told me that if I got homesick to tell him and he'll take his car and run me up for a few days."

In that same letter, Massey said he thought Florida was quite pleasant. On one occasion he borrowed someone's car and took a sightseeing drive through several nearby towns such as Lakeland, Bartow, and Auburndale. "The only thing I couldn't get used to was this sulfur water," he wrote. "The odor and taste is awful."

Mr. Beeson took a liking to young Jack Massey and gave him plenty of responsibility. Soon after the young man went to work there, Beeson got sick and Massey spent several weeks as the acting pharmacist. "That didn't create a problem because Mr. Beeson was secretary of the state board of pharmacy, and nobody ever checked," Massey later said.

Beeson soon gave Massey some advice that would change the young man's life.

"Still planning to own your own store?" he asked Massey one day.

"Absolutely."

"Well, take the advice of an old hand who has watched many a young feller get ahead or stumble. Go to college. Get a pharmacy degree. Get a license. Otherwise, you'll spend the rest of your life as a clerk or soda jerk."

The advice might seem obvious several generations later, but it was hardly so then. In 1922 the world of pharmaceutical training, much like the world of medical training, was hardly formalized in the rural South. Not only did a pharmacist not need formal schooling or a license, a doctor didn't need formal training or a license either. In fact, when Massey went to work for the Wauchula drugstore, the state of Florida didn't even have a public pharmacy school yet; it was in the process of being organized.

Massey saved enough money to pay his tuition. And in the fall of 1923 he left Wauchula for Gainesville, registering to be a member of the University of Florida's brand-new pharmacy school and finding a room in a local boarding house. Massey apparently loved college and everything about the collegiate experience. He even joined the Alpha Tau Omega fraternity.

Only a few weeks after classes started he felt so confident about his situation that he made plans to take a train to Atlanta with several of his classmates to see the Florida-Georgia Tech football game. But he then had a harrowing experience that in some ways robbed him of collegiate innocence.

When he arrived in Gainesville, Massey had deposited his life savings ($100) in the Florida Bank & Trust Company. On October 1 he wrote a check to the University of Florida for his tuition and other expenses, which he knew would reduce his account to nearly nothing. A day or two later he heard that the bank had failed, which he assumed meant that he had lost his deposits.

"I picked up the paper and read it for myself and now I'm ruined," he wrote to his mother. "I had a balance of $100 at the Florida Bank & Trust Company here and it's gone. Now what am I going to do? I have about five dollars in my pocket and a hundred is gone. My board will be due soon and it will take all I've got for that most [sic]."

Massey said many people in the university community were affected by the bank failure. "My roommate lost $170 and he's afraid he'll have to go home. . . . He's been working and had just a little money and his folks aren't able to sent [sic] him [money]. He wired his brother who is married and has several children and is a druggist and his brother wired money for him to stay, that he would see him through some way. . . . The lady I'm staying with lost several hundred; it's terrible, this town is all excited. Might as well not have tried to have school today; as I said before, 90 percent of the students and teachers lost [money]. Some several thousand, some several hundred, and some less, but it sure has thrown a gloom around here."

The eventual impact on Massey of the failure of the Florida Bank & Trust was a mystery eight decades later. According to the letter Massey sent to his mother during the days in which the bank began to fail, the president of the bank noticed Massey's check and made certain it cleared (taking steps that were probably illegal).

"Now talking about a real friend," Massey wrote, "that's what I call one after they've paid a check they are not supposed to."

However, in a 1978 interview Massey said that he had, in fact, lost his money in the bank failure. "I transferred the money I had saved into a bank in Gainesville, Florida, and about two weeks after I entered school, the bank went broke and I lost my money," he said. "Although the president and the vice president were put in jail for embezzlement, I didn't get my money back. However, I had made a good friend at Wauchula who was president of a bank, and he loaned me enough money to finish school the first year."

Regardless of how the incident played out, it is important that Massey did not distrust banks for the rest of his life, as so many people did because of that era's many bank failures.

Academically, Massey did well during the rest of his first year at pharmacy school. The following summer he was staying with his brother Harry, who had gone to work as a car salesman in Macon, Georgia. On that visit Jack read in a newspaper that the Georgia State Board of Examinations for Pharmacists was about to give its annual test. Jack decided to take the test, mainly for practice.

When he arrived to take the exam, the secretary who was conducting it asked him how old he was. Massey said he was nineteen. "The minimum age for a license is twenty-one," she said, according to Massey's recollection. "I suppose you could put down you're twenty-one. That's up to you. It won't make any difference anyway. With only one year in school, you won't be able to pass."

Massey took the test and went back to his summer job. A few weeks later he received an official communication from the State of Georgia. Massey had made the second-highest grade among all the candidates, and the State of Georgia had issued him a pharmacy license.

Many years later Massey described his thoughts after he got the test results: "Should I have returned that license, confessing I was not twenty-one? Should I have treated the whole thing as a joke? Maybe. Those are the kind of thoughts that come a lifetime later. In those days my reasoning was simpler. In spite of my age, I clearly had all the qualifications for a license. I also had a few years of experience of working in drugstores. So why shouldn't I make the most of my knowledge? What difference could a year or so make?"

Two considerations probably weighed heavily on Massey's mind. One was that in that era, when the vast majority of all pharmacists had no formal training, Massey was already more qualified than most. The second thing was the cost of tuition. Massey had no scholarship and had already endured the horrifying experience of nearly losing his life savings. Why not save money and leave school now?

Massey left college. After making inquiries throughout Georgia, he accepted an offer to be the pharmacist and manager at the smaller of a chain of two drugstores in Columbus. "The salary was disappointing," Massey later said. "I had hoped to get more. But the man made an additional offer that interested me, really challenged me."

According to Massey, his prospective employer told him that he would give him a bonus if he could increase the amount his store was earning. "It sounded very good, a real opportunity. So I took the job. Maybe I was a bit cocky at the age of nineteen, but I was sure I could boost the earnings."

Massey went to work in Columbus and did a good job running the store, treating his sales clerk with the kind of respect he had grown to appreciate as a young employee. "That clerk and I got along well because I knew exactly how he felt. I did what he would appreciate—made him feel he was an important associate," Massey said. "Anytime he had a good sales idea, I listened."

Massey also paid attention to details, using merchandising tactics he had picked up from his uncle. He paid special attention to doctors who patronized the store, a habit that would pay dividends throughout his career. Most important of all, Massey worked hard and made certain that the store owner saw him working hard.

"He told me that when he got his first job, he used to always get to work before the owner and leave work after the owner," Jack Massey's nephew Joe Massey said years later. "If you do that, he used to tell me, the owner will pretty soon find you to be indispensable."

After a year of working twelve- to fourteen-hour days, Massey saw that his store's sales numbers had increased significantly. He broached the matter of the promised bonus with his employer, and learned a valuable lesson about life in the process. "Jack, you're too young to earn that much," the man reportedly said, reneging on his verbal agreement to give his young manager a bonus.

Jack Massey quit immediately and wrote to the regional manager of the Atlanta-based Liggett drugstore chain. Within a few weeks he was offered a job there.

Having lived in small towns all his life, Massey found Atlanta to be a real change of pace. Nevertheless, his new position was in some ways a step down, since he took a job as "third assistant manager" for one of Liggett's four Atlanta stores. "You might say I was low man on the totem pole," he said. "But it was a fine place to get big-city experience."

Massey moved to Atlanta either in 1927 or 1928 and, once there, lived in the Bellevue Apartments at 110 Fifth Avenue. It was during this time in Atlanta that young Jack had a rather exciting experience. As his uncle Alex had taught him many years earlier, one of the keys to running a profitable drugstore was to keep an eye out for thieves. At one point during Massey's stint in Atlanta, a man bounced a check in his drugstore and came back a few days later.

"I had him arrested," Massey said. "And he broke away from the sheriff and ran down to the drugstore and hit me in the head—and I think I still feel a knot up there where he hit me. He knocked me into a cigar case, and we had a box full of baseball bats. Well, I came up with a baseball bat, and I knocked him in the head."

After this fight, Massey's boss at Liggett said that he didn't mind what had happened too much. "Coca-Cola pays for its advertising, and I'm getting mine free and I love it," his boss said, apparently referring to newspaper coverage of the incident. "But the next time you get ready to fight someone, you'll call me so I can come down and watch you."

Massey did well in Atlanta and earned rapid promotion. In 1929 he was slated to become the manager of a Liggett store in Birmingham, Alabama. Then, at the last minute, the company changed its mind because of the city's economic situation.

"All the steel mills closed, and everything went bad in Birmingham," Massey said years later. "All the city of Birmingham was absolutely without any business; it was the first city in the South to really feel the depression in a big way. So instead, my friend, the district manager, transferred me to Nashville, where there was a good store—not the biggest store, but a good store."

Massey packed his belongings into his second-hand car and headed northwest toward Nashville, with no idea that he was on his way to what would become his permanent home.

Jack Massey arrived in Nashville during the most fascinating era in the city's history. In the 1920s more interesting things were happening in Nashville than in probably any other Southern city. Thanks to several locally owned banks, insurance companies, and brokerage houses, Nashville was rightfully regarded as the Wall Street of the South.

The largest of the banks was the Fourth & First National Bank, headed by the venerable James E. Caldwell, a proud, formal man with a white beard who made such an impression that people would clear a path for him when he walked down the street. Nashville's largest insurance company, the National Life & Accident, had only a few years earlier invested in a new radio station, giving it the call letters WSM (short for the insurer's motto, "We Shield Millions"). To the surprise and dismay of its owners, the station quickly became known for a Saturday night show first called the *Barn Dance* and later known as the *Grand Ole Opry*.

The most important financial institution in Nashville was a municipal bond house called Caldwell & Company, headed by James E. Caldwell's son, Rogers. Rogers Caldwell was regarded as the J. P. Morgan of the South. His business not only sold bonds that financed government buildings and high-rises all over the region, but it also bought and sold everything from factories to newspapers. In 1928 Rogers Caldwell was at the peak of his career; the assets of the companies controlled by

Caldwell & Company were almost $500 million. The flamboyant Caldwell was, for the moment at least, one the great heroes of the South, comparable to Huey Long in terms of stature.

Fascinating things were happening on other fronts as well. Vanderbilt University, the city's most prominent academic institution, had just moved its medical school to a massive building on Twenty-first Avenue, at that time the only medical school and hospital under the same roof in the South. The school had the best football team in the region and was in the middle of a cultural revolution led by a group of literary-minded students known as the Fugitives.

Meanwhile, the business migration to the suburbs was still a generation away; downtown was still where everyone in Nashville worked, shopped, and viewed movies. And the Liggett Drug Store at 530 Church Street was the heart of downtown Nashville.

When he got to Nashville, Massey rented a room at a boarding house on West End Avenue, a graceful boulevard with a streetcar track running down the middle of it that connected downtown to the Vanderbilt area. At the time Massey moved into his new quarters, Nashville's replica of the Parthenon, just across the street from the rooming house, was less than a year old. Vanderbilt's football stadium, the first stadium built south of the Ohio River, was two blocks away.

It must have been a heady time for young Jack, being the manager of a drugstore in a new city where so much was happening. Nevertheless, as his twenty-fifth birthday came and went, Massey remembered the goal he had set for himself a few years earlier.

In July 1930 Massey heard that a small drugstore was up for sale. Known as Young and Thompson, the store was located on the bottom floor of the Tulane Hotel at 718 Church Street. One day Massey slipped out of Liggett to inspect the place. He found the store small and dingy, but the location had potential. Massey went in and negotiated with the owner. After a few conversations he had worked out a deal under which he could buy the store by selling his car and borrowing money from Third National Bank, a two-year-old financial institution that was already beginning to develop an image as a bank friendly to small business owners.

"He was completely frank with us," Third National banker Webb Johnston recalled. "He told us exactly how little he had, how much he owed in notes, what he proposed to do. I think it was his candor as much as his self-confidence that appealed to us."

Massey quickly made friends with just about everyone else at Third National, including a recent Vanderbilt graduate named Sam Fleming. In a 1997 interview Fleming recalled, vaguely, that Massey paid five hundred dollars for the store.

An unfinished account of Jack Massey's life written in the 1980s also claimed that he got financial help from his eldest brother, Harry, when he purchased that first drugstore. This certainly makes sense; by this time Harry's career as an automobile salesman was taking off, and he was well on his way to a remarkable career that would eventually make him the owner of the largest Buick dealerships in the country.

No one is exactly certain exactly when Massey took over the former Young and Thompson Drugstore. But in September 1930, a newspaper advertisement listed Massey's store at 718 Church Street as one of two dozen or so places where people could buy tickets to the county fair. Massey Drugs was described in the ad as being "previously known as Young and Thompson," which makes it likely that the store had only recently changed its name.[1] A few weeks after taking over the store, Massey closed it temporarily to clean and remodel it, doing virtually all of the work himself.

Meanwhile, Jack Massey found time to socialize. Being a good-looking, slender, dapper young man with obvious prospects, he didn't have a hard time attracting young ladies. During his first year in Nashville he had a blind date with a young lady named Elizabeth Frances Polak. Miss Polak was a music student specializing in piano and pipe organ at Ward-Belmont College, an all-girls school located on the grounds of the old Belmont mansion south of town. Her father, Charles Francis Polak, was a bookkeeper for the Nashville Waterworks and had been a practicing lawyer in Nashville during the 1920s.

About the same time that he worked out the deal to buy the drugstore, Massey proposed to Elizabeth and she accepted. A few weeks later, while he worked around the clock to get the store in shape for its grand re-opening, he penned a short note to his bride-to-be: "I appreciated your coming back last night very, very much," he wrote. "Am working all night and am having the ceiling and woodwork cleaned. . . . Please remember you have a luncheon engagement with me Friday at twelve sharp. All my Love, Jack."

Jack and Elizabeth's wedding announcement appeared in the September 28, 1930, *Nashville Tennessean*. The story listed several social affairs planned for the bride-to-be, including a tea, a breakfast, a luncheon, a buffet supper, two bridal parties, and five bridge parties.

Young Jack Massey was so thrilled at the idea of becoming the husband of Elizabeth Polak that he tried his hand at writing, wit, and romance. A few weeks before their wedding, he sent his wife a box of candy with a note attached that looked like a telegram.

The bill was rendered "For the balance of your natural life. This account is due in full Oct. 18. If not paid prior to this date it will be necessary to serve papers upon you requiring that you appear at 5:30 p.m. at Wightman Chapel, Scarritt College, and therefore receive sentence before the Honorable G. L. Stewart for a lifetime of suffering—and it will be the subscriber's pleasure to suffer with you. Devotedly, Jack."

After the wedding, the couple drove to Hot Springs, Arkansas, for a honeymoon. But it wasn't a long trip because

Massey had plenty of work to do back home. Having shut down his drugstore temporarily, he had a goal of reopening it concurrent with the opening of the Paramount Theater across the street. This he accomplished, and Massey Drugs reopened on November 14.

"The building has been completely remodeled and rearranged, in order to meet the demands of the modern downtown drugstore," the *Nashville Banner* reported. "It will cater especially to the theater trade, serving lunches and offering a complete fountain service. Its prescription service will be maintained. Six clerks will be employed to care for the trade. . . . In celebration of the opening, a cut-price sale will be held and a wide variety of articles will be offered at especially low prices. In addition, favors will be presented to all visitors."

Jack Massey, age twenty-six, had a wife and a drugstore. He and his young bride moved into a place of their own at 2405 Belmont Boulevard.

*J*ack Massey frequently gave advice on how to make a business successful: Work hard. Expand the areas in which you are making money. Be bold enough to take risks when you have to.

Another important part of business, Massey used to say, was to keep an eye out for employees who steal from you.

In the 1930s Massey became convinced that one of his employees was pilfering. He asked the man how many cold medications he thought there were on one shelf, and when the employee said he didn't know, Massey said that there were exactly eighty-seven. When the employee declared that there was no way there could be that many, Massey asked him to count them, and sure enough, there were exactly eighty-seven.

The employee went away shaking his head, amazed that his boss kept up with stock quantities so well. Of course, Massey had just counted the cold remedies a few minutes earlier; his little exercise was staged to frighten his employee into never stealing from the store again.

Massey also used to recount an anecdote about how, during the 1930s, a Nashville doctor asked him to examine the operation of his chronically indebted practice.

"While I was waiting to see him, I watched a lady come in and pay cash to his secretary," Massey said. "She [the secretary] didn't put the money in the cash drawer; she put it over to one side and left it there, and in a few minutes she dropped a piece of paper on top of it. So I knew she was putting that money in her pocket.

"When I went in to see him, I told the doctor about it. He didn't believe it at all, and just got real mad at me because he said she was too good a girl, that it was impossible.... But she was stealing. That sort of thing was going on in a lot of places because the doctors were relaxed."

2

BALANCING THE TILL

NOVEMBER 1930 WAS A BIG month for Jack Massey, but few people noticed his early achievements. The week the Massey Drug Company reopened, the Great Depression hit Nashville.

In fact, on the very day that the *Nashville Banner* carried a short article on page 16 about Massey's new drugstore, a front-page headline announced the "merger" of Nashville's two largest banks—Paul Davis's American National Bank and James E. Caldwell's Fourth & First National Bank. The paper, seeing it as its civic duty to downplay bad business news, lied about the transaction and said it took place after long negotiations. Truthfully, the merger between Nashville's largest and second-largest banks was a last-minute deal arranged by national banking officials in an attempt to withstand a rumored "run" on the Fourth & First.

Also on the *Banner*'s front page that day was a story announcing Caldwell's "retirement" after an illustrious career, as a result of the bank merger. James E. Caldwell was really forced out, and he would spend the rest of his life arguing that he and the Fourth & First's shareholders were wronged by the sudden merger.

In other words, the *Banner* that day contained a story about the end of the career of one of the greatest businessmen in Nashville history (Caldwell), plus another story about the beginning of the career of another (Massey).

Things changed fast. After a full year in which Nashville's civic leaders and newspapers had tried to convince citizens that the New York stock market crash would have only limited impact on a city so far away, there was no way anyone could kid himself about the events of early November 1930. Local stock prices collapsed. Lines formed around several banks, as panicked citizens tried desperately to withdraw everything they had deposited.

Announcements about soup kitchens began to make their way into the paper. At least one bank failed: the Liberty Bank & Trust. Its president, R. E. Donnell, checked into a nearby hotel on November 28, removed a shoestring, and strangled himself with it. When police found him, his vest pocket contained a watch and chain in an envelope bearing the words "to Ridley E. Donnell Jr. from Daddy."

Tough times for Nashville were harbingers of things to come for the entire South. The biggest single story in this regard was Caldwell & Company. Its collapse the first week in November precipitated the merger between American National and the Fourth & First.

The following weeks brought the closure of about 120 Southern banks, many of them in some way linked to Caldwell & Company or institutions affiliated with it. The darkest day was November 17, when an incredible fifty-one Southern banks closed their doors to customers.

Jack Massey was just as bewildered as everyone else while this Greek tragedy was taking place in board rooms and bank lobbies throughout the city. A young man with limited connections, a small business to run, and a young wife to worry about, he remembered the latter part of November 1930 much like everyone else of his generation. "Mr. Caldwell went broke, and so did the city of Nashville almost go broke," Massey said later.

Massey understood one thing for certain: business was terrible. Within a few weeks he had to dismiss his other pharmacist and his secretary and could no longer pay his rent. "I was broke and I owed a lot of money," he said many years later. "The banks and everybody told me to take bankruptcy, and I refused. I said, 'No. If you put me in bankruptcy, you will lose everything. But if you leave me alone, I'll pay you off.'"

Massey said he had real trouble paying his vendors. "I think I owed Johnson & Johnson twenty-five hundred dollars. So I sent them a check for five dollars, and I said it was evidence of good faith. I told them I can't pay them any more right now but every month I'll send you a check. Well, as time went on, I finally paid everybody off. But had I taken bankruptcy, I wouldn't be here today. In those days bankruptcy was a disgrace."

Massey survived the depression by working seven days a week and, by his own estimate, more than eighty hours a week. He didn't always sleep through the night.

"During the depression, on Thursday nights, I never slept for a couple of years because I would wake up and start thinking about where I'm going to get the money to meet payroll the next day," he said. Massey later said that his employees were incredibly loyal during this period.

"I guess 1933 was the worst time I had," he later recalled. "I met a young lady by the name of Mary Ella Flowers. I needed a secretary very bad but couldn't afford one, and this girl came to see me and asked for a job. I told her I'd like to hire her, but I couldn't afford her. She said, 'Well, I'm fresh out of school. I've just graduated from business college, and I need a job.' I said, 'Well, I wish I could give you one.' She said, 'Well, give me one anyway. I'll work for nothing just to get some experience.'

"So I started her to work, committing no salary, but she was a good gal and very efficient, and so at the end of the first week I paid her ten dollars. For a while she worked at ten dollars a week." Flowers, whose married name was Purdom, remained an employee of Massey's for more than thirty years.

Massey said that many of his employees would work every other week during the depression. "That was the only way to keep the store open," he said. "None of them quit because there was not another job they could get anywhere. They were a very loyal group of people."

He also learned to renegotiate his lease during hard times. In a story he told many times, Massey said he once told his landlord that he couldn't afford to pay the rent, and that he suggested the man allow him to pay 10 percent of revenue instead. "He said, 'Well, you'll just have to pay it, and if you don't do it, I'll take the store.' I said fine, and I took the keys and threw them on his desk and said, 'The drugstore belongs to you,' and walked out. That afternoon he came over and brought the keys back and said, 'You've got to lock up tonight. I'm not going to run this drugstore; I don't know how.'

"It was a gutsy risk," Massey said. "But I had to do it. I couldn't pay the rent."

The depression forced Massey and his bride to whittle down to the bare necessities. A few months after they married, the couple moved in with Elizabeth's parents. Without a place of his own or a way of getting himself around town, Massey didn't have much to his name except a lot of debts.

"I rode the streetcar every day," he later said, "but I never was tempted to give up."

Young wife Elizabeth didn't give up either. "She loved and supported him her whole life," daughter Barbara Massey Rogers later said. "She worshiped the ground he walked on."

Jack Massey's ability to survive the Great Depression eventually instilled in him a confidence in his own business acumen. It also gave him the foundation of one of his most important pieces of business advice. "If you want to start your own business, you have to have an 'I will not fail' attitude," he said several years later. "That is what you have got to do, and you have got to work toward it. If you see that things are going wrong, do something about it. Work harder. Go out and get business. Communicate."

Massey's confrontation with his landlord may have been a turning point, because it got him looking at other locations. In 1933 he bought another drugstore. This one was apparently on the verge of bankruptcy; it was located a block east on Church Street, on the bottom floor of a relatively new office structure called the Bennie Dillon Building.

Massey, who always seemed to be able to see a business opportunity before it occurred to other people, was well aware of the importance of this site, because most of the building's tenants were physicians and dentists. Nevertheless, he could hardly afford a second store.

"Not having enough money to pay for it, I gave them post-dated checks, so much a month for twelve months," Massey later said. He soon shut down his store in the Tulane Hotel.

Somehow Massey held on. And as he made it through the worst parts of the depression, it occurred to him that he could sell his fellow tenants more valuable things than band-aids and aspirin. As Massey met and talked to these doctors he became convinced that he could make more money by selling them surgical supplies such as syringes, stethoscopes, and other specialized products. So in 1937 Massey started a sister company, called Massey Surgical Supply, which was at first co-located with his drugstore in the Bennie Dillon Building.

Breaking into the business was not easy. At the time, Nashville's surgical supply business was dominated by two companies which, according to Massey, resorted to dirty tactics to keep him from getting off the ground. "These two men, presidents of these two companies, would interfere with my purchasing," Massey later said. "They would tell the companies [pharmaceutical wholesaler Merck and Company, for instance] that if they sold to me, they would quit buying from them."

Massey got a lawyer. The two men went to visit the head of one of the surgical supply companies and demanded that they stop the practice. "We had built up a lot of information . . . and he just laughed and said, 'We'll run our business and you run yours,'" Massey said. "So we told him we were going to sue him for a hundred fifty thousand dollars in damages, and walked out."

A few hours later, Massey's attorney received a call from a lawyer representing the head of one of the other surgical supply companies. He said that his client had agreed to stop putting pressure on suppliers not to sell to Massey.

Massey later said his surgical supply company got a boost from this early attempt to keep him out of the business. "I made friends by telling people what they had done to me," he said. "So the hospitals and doctors became my best friends."

One of those early doctor friends was a cardiologist named Dr. Thomas Frist Sr., who met Massey when he was a junior at Vanderbilt medical school in 1931.

"He gave me my first stethoscope," Frist said many years later. "You see, he gave away stethoscopes to many medical students, because he knew that the medical students would be buying supplies from him when they settled down to practice only a few years later."

Because the Massey-Frist partnership eventually became such a high-profile one, people have always assumed that Frist was one of Massey's biggest customers. Not true.

"I think I equipped his first office," Massey said in 1978. "He was in an office with his brother-in-law, and I don't think they bought much equipment. It was a little bit of a disappointment that he didn't buy and spend a little bit more money than he did. But the answer was, 'I don't have it.'"

Most physicians at the time bought on credit. "I did not have anything but a family and a 1934 Plymouth," said L. C. (Lawrence) Jackson, who set up a practice in Dickson at the height of the depression.

"I tried to borrow money at the bank, and of course I had no collateral and they refused me. So I went to Nashville and met Jack Massey. He agreed to furnish all my office furniture, all the equipment and supplies and everything, and have them in the office on July 1, and I wasn't to make the first payment until October. Jack was just a prince of a fellow to do this, and I never deserted him."

Massey's relationship with Jackson paid long-term dividends, because Jackson's younger brothers William and Jimmy followed his footsteps to medical school and to private practice in Dickson. They, too, became customers of Massey Surgical Supply.

Years later, the Jackson brothers pooled their resources and developed a fifty-bed hospital in Dickson called Goodlark. They hired a young Nashville architect named Donald Cowan to design and equip the hospital and told him to buy as much as possible from Massey. Cowan asked why.

"He [Jackson] told me that he had come from a very poor family in South Pittsburg, Tennessee," Cowan said. "When he got through medical school, he was looking around for a place to set up shop and ended up in Dickson. But he had no idea how to get his doctor's office furnished, and the local pharmacist in Dickson told him to come to Nashville to see this fellow called Jack Massey.

"So [Jackson] went into see Massey. And Massey said to him, 'I tell you what, you look like a nice fellow. I'll tell you what you do. You bring a truck up to Nashville and load up whatever you want, and you pay me whatever you can.' And that is exactly what L. C. did. He loaded up an examining table and an examining light, probably a few pieces of furniture for the waiting room. And L. C. told me that because of that, he was able to help to pay his brother's way through medical school and his brother was able to pay the next brother's way through medical school. And they felt like they owed a lot to Jack Massey."

As doctors became bigger customers, Massey learned more about their businesses. Some physicians simply came through the door and paid for their products at the end of the month. Others needed Massey to extend somewhat lengthy credit contracts to them. But in some cases Nashville physicians actually asked Massey to audit and organize their practice.

"One man owed me about six thousand dollars," Massey remembered years later. "He gave me a note and was going to pay it off [at] so much a month. . . . [But] he would keep that thing revolving around from year to year, and it would grow a little bit every year, and so it just reached the point that it wasn't possible to do it. . . . He just had so many people to pay he just couldn't make ends meet."

Massey took a look at the doctor's books and ended up helping him consolidate all his debts into one bank. "When we got a good bookkeeper in there and got to collecting his bills and running his business as it should be, he paid it off in two years," Massey said.

The vast majority, but not all, of these physicians were white males. But Jack Massey said that one of his customers in the early 1950s was Dorothy Brown, who had graduated from Meharry Medical College in 1948. Brown was not only the first black female surgeon in the South, but she also later became the first black woman elected to the Tennessee legislature.

"He always told me that he extended to her the same rates and credits as he did to all the white male doctors, and he always said that she paid him right on time," Elizabeth Queener, Massey's sister-in-law, said several years after his death.[2]

In the 1930s, as was the case seventy years later, the key to doing business with a physician was to have a good relationship with his staff. In 1939 a pediatrician named James Overall had an office in the Bennie Dillon Building, and he had a nineteen-year-old lab technician named Dorothy Schiffman. Interviewed sixty-five years later, Schiffman (whose married name was Dorothy Kottler) said she remembered only a couple of things about Massey's drugstore and surgical supply business. One was the fried apricot pies and chocolate sodas they served at the soda fountain. Another was the fact that Massey gave her a small Christmas present.

"He gave me a set of cosmetics at Christmas, and for the life of me I can't remember why, because I didn't know Mr. Massey at all," Kottler said. She added that it was very possible Massey gave gifts to many people who worked for doctors as a way of ingratiating himself to the staffs.

Meanwhile, Massey became somewhat accustomed to pushing the financial envelope himself. A vendor who frequently called on Massey in the late 1940s was Hunter Woods, a salesman for the Abe Plough pharmaceutical company. "I got along with him pretty well and got some business out of him," Woods said.

Woods, who later went to work for a Massey-owned company called Rigo Chemical, said it was hard to get an appointment with Massey because he stayed too busy. He also said it could be hard to get him to pay up.

"I remember a couple of times Massey Surgical would make an order and my credit manager would tell me that they weren't going to send what they had ordered because they hadn't paid for the last order," Woods said. "So I'd go back down there again and I'd say, 'Mr. Massey, you haven't paid the last damn bill.' And he'd say, 'Oh, I have. I remember signing the check.' And then I'd walk out to Miss Sattler [Massey's secretary, Omega Sattler], and she'd be sitting there holding the check in her hand, grinning. And the check would have been signed a month or two earlier—he had signed it; he just hadn't mailed it.

"Massey was hard to collect off of, but he was just operating on your money, and this kept him from having to borrow as much. But I got along with him good, and he liked me and I liked him. And he wasn't the only person who did us that way."

Later in Massey's career there were scores of people who became rich and prominent because of their connection to him. Perhaps the first person to whom this happened was Max Goodloe. Goodloe first got Massey's attention in the 1940s, when he worked at a dry-cleaning store Massey frequented. Massey was impressed with Goodloe's eagerness and offered him a job at his surgical supply business. Goodloe became one of Massey Surgical's best employees, and a few years later he started a surgical supply business in Richmond, Virginia,—with Massey's help, of course.

"Just being around Jack helped me immensely," Goodloe later told a *Forbes* magazine reporter. "It's amazing, but he can talk to someone for five minutes and tell exactly what kind of guy he is and how to motivate him."[3] Massey's ability to size up people is something many others would notice throughout his life.

Massey didn't live with his in-laws long. By the time Nashville's 1933 *City Directory* was published (after a three-year hiatus), Jack and wife Elizabeth moved into a small house in the city's Belmont section, where they would remain for more than a decade.

After four years of marriage Jack and his young wife, Elizabeth, were beginning to think there was no way they could have children of their own. In 1934 they adopted an infant son and named him Don. Four years later, to the couple's happy surprise, Elizabeth became pregnant and gave birth to a daughter, Barbara.

When America entered World War II, the thirty-seven-year-old Massey was not drafted for military service. He stayed home, took care of his two children, and tried his best to turn a profit with his drugstore and surgical supply business. It was, in hindsight, the quietest period of his life; years later, he frequently told anecdotes from other time periods, but not from World War II.

During these years he was making contacts and making a name for himself as an outstanding businessman and organizer. This would pay dramatic dividends to his bank and church immediately after the war. The Massey family also frequently moved during this period—once into rental property and once into an apartment—as they built a new home on affluent Overton Lea Road south of Nashville.

Jack Massey could be a playful father, and he took very good care of his family. As soon as he could afford it, Massey bought a houseboat. Later the family started a regular routine of taking an annual two-week vacation to Florida. Jack Massey's nephew, Joe Massey, said that his earliest memories of his uncle were from those vacations.

"He would come through town [Macon, Georgia] once a year on his way down to Florida," Joe Massey said. "I remember that he was always in a hurry, and he was always worried about how long it was going to take him to get there and whether he could get there faster this year than last year."

Massey was a kind but firm father who had high expectations for his wife, son, and daughter. "He didn't tolerate laziness; he didn't tolerate dishonesty; and he expected a lot from us," his daughter, Barbara Massey Rogers, said. "For example, one of the things I remember about my childhood was that he made us come up with New Year's resolutions every year. I would write them every year and sign them, 'From Your Trying-to-be-Somebody-Daughter.'" She also recalled that her father didn't allow her brother, Don, to leave the house wearing blue jeans.

Barbara reacted well to her father's paternal philosophy and expectations, and she adored her father his entire life. Older brother Don did not fare so well. In what is without question the saddest aspect of Jack Massey's life, he and his son eventually grew very much apart. Maybe Don Massey felt that he couldn't please his father; maybe he felt bitter because he was adopted and his sister was not.

Don Massey was never a healthy person. During his senior year of high school he was struck with ileitis, an intestinal disorder that caused him to miss five months of classes and resulted in the removal of a large portion of his intestines. From that point on, Don was not supposed to eat roughage or drink alcohol, and on the occasions when he did so, he sometimes had seizures and passed out.

After graduating from high school in 1952, Don did not finish college, but he did marry a young nurse named Yvonne White, who was loved by everyone in the family. That marriage later ended in divorce, as did Don Massey's second marriage. In the 1960s Don worked for the Shoney's restaurant chain for a while and served on its board of directors. But around 1970 the relationship between Jack Massey and his son deteriorated to the point where they could no longer be in the same room together.

Don Massey died in 1979 in a one-car accident.

*J*ack Massey liked to play golf; he liked to watch sports; he liked to travel. But there was nothing in the world he liked more than gin rummy. Just about everyone who knew Massey played gin with him at least one time, and many people played with him regularly. There are dozens of Massey gin rummy anecdotes, and there are themes common to all of them. Massey always played for money (although small amounts). And he played to win.

Winfield Dunn, who met Massey when he successfully ran for Tennessee governor in 1970, said he frequently played gin rummy with Massey but rarely won. "Jack had an incredible capacity for remembering every card that had been played," Dunn said. "I just wasn't as good as he was. But when I did, just by virtue of the luck of the draw, win a little money, it would just disgust him terribly. He had one of the most competitive attitudes of any man I've ever met in my life."

Tom Cummings, who had many personal and business connections with Massey, recounts how one day he and Massey were flying back from New York on a private plane. "We played gin rummy the whole way," Cummings said. "Normally he beat me, but on this day the cards were running with me like you wouldn't believe. I had him down pretty good, and this was the first time ever, and, man, I was just ecstatic about it. Then I looked out the window and we were circling Nashville. You see, he had the pilot orbiting Nashville to give him time to get the game turned around so he could get his money back."

Clarence Edmonds, who first met Massey in 1961 and went to work for him full-time in 1969, says he saw his boss pull a similar stunt many times. "The pilot's name was Walter Dube, and I many times saw [Massey] turn around and say to him, 'Go around one more time, Dube,' when it came time to land," Edmonds said.

A veteran of hundreds of gin rummy games with Massey, Edmonds said Massey generally didn't make him pay his gin rummy debts because of the financial disparity between the two men. "But then, one day, I was in his office telling him how I had recently won some money in a golf game," Edmonds said. "And after I told him this, he opens his desk drawer and pulls out a sheet of paper and told me that I owed him twenty-eight dollars or something like that. It turns out that he had been keeping score all along."

Massey's most frequent gin rummy companion was Dr. Thomas Frist Sr. There is no telling how many times Massey and Frist played gin rummy together. But many people who knew the two men said they kept a permanent running score between them.

Gin rummy was clearly for fun, but Massey believed it was an educational hobby. A couple of years before Massey's death a reporter asked him how it felt to have taken three companies to the New York Stock Exchange. Massey shrugged it off as luck.

"But don't you make some of that luck?" she asked. "Yes, indeed, you make it all," he answered. "It's like a gin rummy game; there's no luck in it. It's skill. And if you don't believe that, play me a game."

3

THE HOSPITAL ORGANIZER

I N THE FALL OF 1946 Jack Massey was appointed to the board of Nashville's Third National Bank. At the time he was the youngest director in the bank's history.

This was a turning point in Massey's life. By this time, of course, he had demonstrated that he knew how to work hard, run a business, and believe in himself even in tough times. But he was still operating in a relatively small circle of customers and business acquaintances. The board appointment gave Massey regular exposure to some of Nashville's most important business figures, such as banker Sam Fleming and National Life & Accident Chairman Edwin Craig. It also gave also gave him a free education in the world of bank finance.

Massey's position on the board also provided him with much more access to capital, and it is not coincidental that Massey Surgical Supply began to grow rapidly at about the same time he became a bank director.

In 1946, in anticipation of a citywide move from downtown to the suburbs, Massey moved his operation into two buildings located near the corner of West End and Twenty-first avenues, a location near many of Nashville's hospitals (Vanderbilt, Saint Thomas, and Protestant). He built a new headquarters for his surgical supply business at 2110 West End Avenue and a new drugstore at 2026 West End Avenue, taking out a big bank loan in the process.[4]

After the move Massey became convinced that others in the Nashville medical community would soon follow him, which is why he bought several other houses along that stretch of West End in the process. "I bought four houses for sixty thousand dollars [total]," Massey said many years later. "I was thinking that I could move some doctors out there close to me and it would help my business."

Sure enough, Massey convinced one doctor to do just that, which is why he was able to sell Dr. Thomas Frist the house at 2104 West End for sixteen thousand dollars. "I sold it to him for exactly what my cost was, including interest and taxes," Massey said.

The expanded business achieved profitability faster than he realized it would. By 1950, when Massey was well on his way to paying off his debt for the new surgical supply headquarters and drugstore on West End, he expanded again. On the surgical supply side, he moved into Knoxville, opening a new showroom at 411 West Main Avenue. An illustrated ad for the Knoxville office pointed out that Massey Surgical rented hospital beds, mattresses, wheelchairs, walkers, ultraviolet lamps, and infrared lamps.

The Knoxville division was later followed with divisions in Chattanooga and Kingsport. By 1960 the company's sales territory included Tennessee, North Carolina, Georgia, Alabama, Virginia, West Virginia, and Kentucky.

On the drugstore side, Massey leased space in Vanderbilt's new Medical Arts Building and opened his third store at that location in 1955. By standards of the time it was a superstore, containing a pharmacy, camera department, and florist.

Always looking for a profitable niche, Massey started side businesses that produced things for his drugstores and surgical supply businesses. One was a brace shop at 1925 Broadway. The other was a business called Massey Laboratories, which bought over-the-counter medications in quantity, bottled them, and labeled them as generic medications.

Massey expanded his business fast, but he didn't spend money on luxuries for his West End Avenue headquarters. Interviewed in 2004, architect Donald Cowan said he vividly remembered his first trip to Massey Surgical Supply when he was designing and furnishing Goodlark Hospital in Dickson in 1957.

"I remember that the place was not very well designed or attractive," Cowan said. "It was very banal; the walls were gray, and there was very little color about the place.

"I walked in and the first person I met was this fairly small man called Ray Goff. And I told him who I was and what I was doing, and he told me I should meet Mr. Massey. So we go to the back of the shop, and in the left-hand corner was a small room. In the far corner of the room was this gray metal desk that was catty-corner, and sitting behind this desk was Jack Massey. It was the first time I ever saw him. He had this wide face and big glasses and a kind of a benign sort of look that I later came to realize was not the way that he really was."

Some people who knew Massey during this period describe him as always busy and always in a hurry to move onto his next task. But he apparently found time to mentor someone when asked. Around 1951, Massey got a call from a young man named Bob Brueck, who had been in the same fraternity at Vanderbilt that Massey had been in at the University of Florida thirty years earlier. Massey spent about an hour with Brueck.

"He was very helpful, very cordial, and I suspect we talked for well over an hour," Brueck remembered. "I was very much impressed by the way he was willing to take time and talk to me." Massey explained to Brueck that there was a great future in the world of hospital administration, and it was somewhat because of this advice that Brueck took a job as a hospital administrator-in-training for Nashville's Baptist Hospital a few years later.

Unfortunately, Massey left few records that explain the steps under which he borrowed money and expanded his business in the 1940s. From all available evidence, no sooner would he start to pay back one loan than he would take out another.

"It always seemed like he was working on borrowed money," said Omega Sattler, who went to work as Massey's secretary in 1948.

Massey's daughter, Barbara Massey Rogers, remembered the time her mother found out that her father had borrowed a million dollars from the bank in the early 1950s. "My mother stayed up all night, she was so scared about that loan," Rogers said.

Another professional affiliation Jack Massey had in the late 1940s that changed his life was one with Nashville's Baptist Hospital. Because Massey did so many things, and because of his role in later starting Hospital Corporation of America and the for-profit health-care sector, it is tempting to overlook his involvement in the formation and operation of Baptist Hospital. Massey was not only a trustee of Baptist from 1948 to 1973, he was also one of its founders.

The Baptist Hospital experience taught Massey how to run a hospital, taught him what to look for in a hospital administrator, and taught him how to keep a hospital supplied and up to date. And it should be pointed out that of all the founders of HCA, Massey had the most experience in hospital administration.

"I had the opportunity to see that hospitals can succeed if run properly, and can finance their necessary expansion and modernization themselves," Massey later told a group at Harvard University, referring to his years at Baptist. "And I had the opportunity to learn how to manage a large hospital complex. That also came in handy in some later developments."

The (Tennessee) Baptist denomination's first attempt to own and operate a Nashville hospital occurred in 1924, when it took over a facility at the corner of Eighth and Union that was previously known as Women's Hospital. Many local Baptist ministers were excited about the prospects for Nashville's original Baptist Hospital, saying they wanted it to one day compare with a similarly named facility in Memphis. However, the Nashville hospital didn't last long; it probably filed for bankruptcy in the Great Depression.[5]

The Baptist Hospital that eventually survived is the successor of another medical institution called Nashville Protestant Hospital. Protestant Hospital was started in December 1918, a time when medical care was becoming a national priority because of the influenza epidemic earlier that year. Its organizers chose as it location the former site of the Nashville College for Young Women, a ten-acre plot of land with two mansions on it near the corner of Twenty-first Avenue and Church Street. The hospital opened in March 1919 and apparently chose its name to distinguish it from nearby Saint Thomas Hospital. (This was a period in which Americans drew sharp lines between Catholic and Protestant institutions.) Its original charter stated that no physician could ever be named to the institution's board of governors.

Protestant Hospital did not suffer from a lack of business. During its first year in existence the facility cared for 2,233 patients, 1,685 of whom had major surgery. "The hospital was so crowded that patients filled the sun parlors and virtually all other spaces," said a history of Baptist Hospital written seventy-five years later. "People had to be turned away, especially when a second influenza epidemic struck."

In an era before Medicare, Medicaid, and group life insurance, however, a steady patient load was no guarantee of solvency. Despite a talented and well-connected board of directors, Protestant Hospital declared bankruptcy at least three times: in 1921, 1932, and 1943. Then, in 1946, the institution fell on hard financial times yet again.

Meanwhile, there were conversations taking place elsewhere in Nashville that would eventually affect Protestant. In the years immediately following World War II, the pastor of Belmont Heights Baptist Church was James Sullivan and the pastor of Woodmont Baptist Church was G. Allen West. On their own initiative, Sullivan and West had several conversations about what they saw as the Tennessee Baptist Convention's need to establish institutions.

"We agreed that institutions are to a denomination what fortresses are to the military—they stabilize you and anchor you," said Sullivan, later the president of the Baptist Sunday School Board, from 1953 until 1975. "True, they are expensive and they are hard to operate. But you have to have them if you want to stabilize and grow and take advantage of your growth."

Sullivan and West decided the convention needed a college and a hospital, and with little direction or authorization from the state organization they began doing preliminary work on these two projects. Both located long-standing Nashville institutions which the denomination eventually took over: Ward-Belmont College (then an all-girls school with no connection to the Baptist Church) and Protestant Hospital. West took the school; Sullivan took the hospital.

"My background had made me almost fanatical in my support of our Baptist hospitals," Sullivan wrote. "Not only had I observed their influence in New Orleans, Memphis, and other cities, but I had served as chairman of the fundraising mission in Mississippi to expand the space and services of the Baptist Hospital there. I had emotional attachments to that Baptist Hospital because it was there that two of my children were born and both of my parents died."

Sullivan had already begun to research the state of affairs at Protestant Hospital when Jack Massey, a member of his congregation, came to him one night. "He came into my study, and I could tell that he was not doing well," Sullivan remembered. "He said to me, 'Brother Pastor, I have just learned that Protestant Hospital is going into bankruptcy tonight.' And I said, 'Well, thank the Lord!' And he said, 'Don't thank the Lord yet, until you get all the facts in hand, because it's going to throw me into bankruptcy! I just sold them forty thousand dollars worth of equipment, and I can't take a loss that big.'"[6]

Massey was one of Protestant Hospital's largest vendors. As the owner of one of Nashville's leading surgical supply businesses, he knew practically every doctor in town and had heard a lot of stories about Protestant Hospital. "As we were coming out of the depression . . . the hospitals were coming around," he later said. "If they were run properly, if they had the city or the county pay for the charity patients, the hospitals could collect most of their bills from the ordinary people. They could make ends meet if they were run right and accounting was right, if they priced their products right—which was something they didn't do for a long time."

But when it came to Protestant Hospital, "they didn't have management. They didn't take care of the doctors properly. They had pets that they'd save rooms for, and maybe they'd have twenty-five percent of the beds empty, waiting for certain doctors, rather than give them to other doctors to bring the income in. It was a bad situation."

Sullivan explained the situation to Massey, and the two men decided to clear the way for Baptist's takeover of the facility. It wasn't easy. Protestant Hospital's debt totaled about half a million dollars, and most of Nashville's business leaders, who were well aware of Protestant's financial record, wanted little to do with it.

Massey talked to several of his fellow vendors, asking them to give the hospital more time to reorganize. He met with many of the existing Protestant Hospital trustees to introduce to them the idea of selling the hospital to the Baptist denomination. He spoke with a lawyer to determine how the hospital could legally transfer its title to someone else's ownership and management. He also began picking prominent Baptists in the community who would want to serve on the board of directors, choosing, among others, Al Batts, Russell Brothers, and Albert Maloney.[7]

Sullivan, meanwhile, worked the problem from the denominational end, meeting with Baptist officials and convincing some of them to serve as trustees. Through this process, Sullivan decided Massey would be the best candidate for board president.

"I had no idea of managing it," Massey said years later. "[But] the committee decided it was not going to go through with the deal unless I'd be the president of the hospital board. I did not want to do this, since the hospital was a customer of mine and it appeared to be a conflict of interest. At the last minute, in desperation, I agreed to do it for a year to make the deal go through." In fact, Massey would remain president of the Baptist Hospital board for twelve years and would serve as a member of the board for twenty.

The transfer took place in April 1948, with Protestant Hospital officially renamed Mid-State Baptist Hospital at that time.

"Jack had discovered in his conversations with lawyers that the only way such a title could be transferred was by a rather prolonged and tedious process of accepting nineteen resignations and electing new trustees nineteen consecutive times," Sullivan later wrote. As each trustee of Protestant Hospital resigned from the board, he was replaced with a new Baptist Hospital trustee; as the old directors left, they thanked the new hospital directors for "taking so many headaches off their hands."

Massey thus became the president of the new Baptist Hospital board. "It was a little ninety-bed, a glorified boarding house that the convention asked me to help manage after they took it over," Massey said many years later. "I was elected president of the board because, I think, no one else would take the job. I was immediately swamped with problems but also the opportunities those problems produced."

Massey and his fellow trustees had a lot of work to do when they took over the hospital. They hired a new hospital administrator named Robert Murphy, who found that many immediate improvements could be made in the facility's operation.

"We discovered that the financial stress had been brought about largely by poor management," Sullivan later wrote. "For instance, there were dozens of items which had been bought new and delivered to the hospital that were still stored in bathtubs in the old buildings. They had never been used or even unwrapped."

Under Murphy's leadership, Baptist Hospital stopped losing money and even began to report surpluses. However, Murphy did not impress Massey much and as a result did not last long in his position. He was replaced by Gene Kidd in 1954.

There was plenty of work to be done on the fundraising side. To this end, hospital officials produced a twenty-two-page brochure that explained the hospital's purpose and need for funds. "Historically, care of the sick has been a major concern of Churches," the brochure began. "Today, it is more important than ever that the Churches should lead in bringing the benefits of medical knowledge within the reach of the people."

The brochure said Nashville was lagging in the area of hospital facilities for its residents, and that the new directors of the Mid-State Baptist Hospital were interested in not only serving the sick but also in building a modern institution. "There is hardly a family that has not experienced difficulty in obtaining a bed in a Nashville hospital, or does not know friends or acquaintances who have had such difficulty," it said. "A prominent businessman cites the case of his aged mother-in-law who had to occupy a bed in a corridor when an emergency gall-bladder operation was necessary. Another man recently underwent in his doctor's office an operation which should have been done in a hospital. These are typical examples."

The brochure cited a study by the Tennessee Department of Health that said that Middle Tennessee needed 4,057 hospital beds but had just 1,721. It also pointed out that the future of Hubbard Hospital (Nashville's predominant hospital for African-American patients) was in jeopardy, that Nashville's General Hospital had "plant deterioration," and that Vanderbilt Hospital would always be, at its core, a teaching facility.

The success of Baptist Hospital would be good for Nashville's economy, the brochure continued. "Medical science cannot thrive in a community which is backward in care of the sick," it said. And it cited a *Tennessean* editorial that admonished the city for its lack of support for hospitals. "Failure—bad, shameful, inexcusable—confronts the whole community," the *Tennessean* opined.

The brochure said that the Tennessee Baptist Convention had already pledged 3 percent of its annual cooperative program receipts to the hospital—an annual total of about thirty thousand dollars. But that wasn't nearly enough; in fact, it said that the hospital needed to raise a million dollars to pay its debts and expand its facilities.

The brochure said the money would fund a four-story, 100-bed expansion—including a new maternity department ($300,000), new medical and surgical floor ($250,000), pediatrics department ($175,000), dietary department ($105,000), x-ray department ($75,000), and laboratory department ($50,000).

It also made several Biblical references. "Next to His role as Redeemer and Teacher, Jesus is best known as 'the Great Physician,'" Charles Pope, executive secretary and treasurer of the Tennessee Baptist Convention, said in an article. "The sick, the lame, and the blind which thronged the streets and roads of Palestine touched his great heart and he healed them. We can best emulate his example of healing through well-equipped and efficiently administered hospitals."

About the time the brochure was printed, the trustees set up a mass meeting at the War Memorial Auditorium, next to the state Capitol, to kick off a fund drive for the hospital. Dr. Robert Lee, pastor of Memphis's Bellevue Baptist Church, was supposed to be the keynote speaker that day, but heavy fog prevented his plane from being able to take off. Sullivan made the speech instead.

"I did my best on short notice, speaking on the healing ministry of Jesus," Sullivan said. A soft-spoken man by Southern Baptist standards of the era, Sullivan must have made quite an impact on the two thousand attendees, for by the end of the second week, local Baptists had raised $750,000 for the new facility.

Baptist Hospital broke ground on a six-story addition in January 1951, completing the project in 1953. Other expansions followed. In 1955 came a new five-story building for the School of Nursing, replacing the facility that Protestant Hospital had used to train nurses.[8] In 1957, the facility added seventy-six beds and an auditorium. Next came a fourteen-story wing facing Twenty-first Avenue. Then a six-story professional building (later called the Mid-State Building) that was set up to be self-liquidating and provide a permanent endowment for the hospital.

Baptist Hospital, which had 120 beds in 1948, had 600 beds and a building for virtually every kind of specialist just ten years later. With each expansion, board President Jack Massey negotiated bond deals on behalf of the hospital, usually with Third National Bank.[9]

All this, of course, was not happening in a vacuum. Although it would be wrong to downplay the skill and energy that Massey and his fellow trustees devoted to the operation of Baptist Hospital, two factors contributed to the recovery of many American hospitals in the 1950s: group health insurance and the emergence of professional administrators. "Prior to World War Two, hospitals like Protestant were being run by nurses who were usually good nurses, but they didn't have any administrative background or ability," said Bob Brueck, who joined Baptist as an administrator-in-training in 1955.

By the mid-1950s the perpetually insolvent Protestant Hospital had been turned into the financially stable Baptist Hospital. Just about everyone officially connected to the institution credited Massey as being the most important person in this process.

"He was pretty much the boss," said Brueck. "I think that his influence and direction of Baptist Hospital, along with the hiring of administrators, had the major influence on the direction of the hospital. And certainly his financial abilities and talents and connections helped the hospital considerably when it came to finding financing for the expansion program."

R. Kelly White, president of Belmont College in the 1950s, wrote Massey a letter in 1955 praising him for his role in running Baptist. "One day we were riding by the old Protestant Hospital, we discussed its problems, and I told you that I had quite a dream in my heart that Baptists would take over this hospital and make it a good Christian institution," White wrote. "I knew only one man could swing it. That man was you."

Perhaps there is no better summary of just how much Massey and his fellow trustees succeeded at turning around the fortunes of Baptist Hospital than something Massey said to a U.S. Senate subcommittee in 1970. Called to Congress to defend his new for-profit hospital chain, Hospital Corporation of America, Massey said it was inappropriate to refer to taxpaying hospitals as for-profit and non-taxpaying hospitals as not-for-profit.

"I do not think we have any nonprofit hospitals in Nashville," Massey said. "I was president of one for twelve years and on the board for twenty. . . . It is a fine institution, and it never operated a day without making a profit."

Always the multitasker, Massey was engaged in other activities during this period that are worth mentioning. A member of Belmont Heights Baptist Church, Massey in the mid-1950s chaired the congregation's building committee. This was no small chore; it was, at the time, one of the largest building projects ever undertaken by a church in Nashville.

Much as he had done with the hospital, Massey went about things systematically, raising money at a dinner attended by more than six hundred people and through a house-to-house canvassing of the entire congregation. "We've got a job to do, and I know we can do it," Massey was quoted as saying in the *Tennessean.* "This will be one of the greatest churches when we finish it."

Through the project, the twenty-five-hundred-member congregation built a new auditorium, new sanctuary, and new office building.

Massey's involvement in Baptist church affairs naturally led to an interest in other things related to the denomination. From 1948 until 1954 he was a trustee for the Sunday School Board of the Southern Baptist Convention, a position of considerable stature in Baptist circles. As mentioned earlier, the Tennessee Baptist Convention purchased Ward-Belmont College in 1951.

For the first couple of years, Belmont College struggled to survive, and Massey made small donations to the school. He also spoke frequently to R. Kelly White, who had once been his minister at Belmont Heights and who was president of Belmont College from 1952 until 1959. In future years Massey's relationship with Belmont would become more important.

Finally, Massey made his first venture capital investment when he and two friends purchased a small manufacturing firm called Rigo Chemical Company. This episode is important, not because of how much Massey made through it but because it gave Massey his first experience as an investor/operator in a field outside the medical industry.

Little is known about Rigo, a private company with a low profile. L. G. "Lefty" Durr started Rigo in 1904 as an "old-time" patent medicine company. Its primary business was producing and selling an odd variety of products—castor oil, cough syrup, turpentine, and the like—to mom-and-pop grocery stores. Rigo even had an old-fashioned calliope, which Durr would take to county fairs all over the South.

After World War II, Durr told a friend, Nashville attorney Henry Goodpasture, about his intention to shut down Rigo. Goodpasture talked up the idea among his friends, including Massey. Sometime in the late 1940s Goodpasture, Massey, and William Bainbridge purchased Rigo.

When Massey got involved with Rigo, he may have thought it had a real future in pharmaceuticals. But this was an era in which drug companies were shutting down small operators. Rigo soon shifted its focus to the production and sale of insecticides, the primary line of which was known as Kill-Ko. In the winter months, when the demand for insecticide waned, the company produced and sold spices and cooking extracts.

By the mid-1950s the company had about forty employees in its plant and another two dozen or so traveling salesmen, all of whom operated solely on commission. "We would sell to anyone who would buy it," said Hunter Woods, who went to work for Rigo in 1952. "We would sell to a drugstore, to a filling station, to a country store, to anyone running up and down the side of the road peddling. Anyone with their door open who would buy the product and who would pay their bill was a potential customer."

Jack Massey was more than a passive investor in Rigo. Shortly after he and his two partners bought the company, Massey ran it for about a year as president. A series of short-lived managers followed, until in 1960 the three partners appointed Woods to be president, from which point onward the company turned a steady profit.

Woods never forgot the experience of working with Massey. "He was good," Woods said. "He was not the most well-educated man, of course, because he had left school so early, but he was the smartest man I've ever known when it came to business. He could just look at a financial statement and something would just jump out at him. He was just natively smart in that area. He was absolutely brilliant."

The three owners eventually sold Woods a share of the company, and Massey sold his one-third ownership to his partners in October 1961 for (according to Woods's memory) $250,000.

In 1969 an Indiana-based farm products company called Central Soya bought Rigo for $3 million. Thirty-five years after that transaction, Woods said that Massey's part-ownership of Rigo Chemical made a big difference in his life. "He changed my situation," Woods said. "He gave me a chance to own a piece of that business, and it is because of that that I was able to retire at the age of fifty-five."

Had Jack Massey held onto his surgical supply business for several more years, he certainly would not have had the chance to take a company to the New York Stock Exchange, let alone three. Because of this, it's tempting to assume that Massey intended all along to sell the surgical supply business and venture into other sectors. But that's apparently not the case.

In 1959 Chicago-based Brunswick Corporation was primarily known as a manufacturer of bowling balls and pool tables. It decided to diversify into several other things, including boating, fishing equipment, and surgical supplies. Brunswick's first acquisition in the surgical supply sector was St. Louis-based A. S. Aloe Company, which operated mainly in the Midwest. Massey Surgical, which operated in a six-state area based in Tennessee, made a natural follow-up acquisition.

Massey said his age had a lot to do with why he listened to Brunswick's offer. "When they came to see me I was almost fifty-five years old," he said later. "I had worked hard ever since I was a youngster of seventeen. My children were adults. My wife, Elizabeth, kept saying I had earned retirement. I knew a number of retired men who insisted they were having a wonderful time in Florida. I had actually bought a house in Fort Lauderdale for vacation purposes. Suddenly the idea of devoting my days to fun—golf, swimming, lying in the sun, all the rest of it—seemed to be the real reward for the years I had spent working. So I listened to the Brunswick people."

Brunswick initially offered to buy Massey Surgical Supply only if Massey would manage the company for the next five years. Massey declined that offer, insisting that he didn't want to work for anyone else and that he had two people (Ray Goff and George Gray) qualified to take over. Talks broke off for several months. Then Massey went to Brunswick's Aloe office and brought up the subject again, pointing out that he had starting turning over the operation to Goff and Gray, and that they were doing a splendid job without him.

At a November 1960 meeting at Nashville's Andrew Jackson Hotel, Brunswick agreed to buy the company without

Massey's agreement to stay with it. "I sold them everything except my exclusive deal with the Picker x-ray company," he said. "Leasing x-ray equipment had become highly profitable. I insisted on retaining that, and the Brunswick people made the concession. So we shook hands."

Under the deal, inked on February 16, 1961, Brunswick acquired Massey Surgical Supply for 16,754 shares—about $1.6 million. Massey said later that his decision to accept stock instead of cash was wise.

*J*ack Massey always carried a blank check in his pocket so that if he ever ran across a hot deal, he could close it on the spot. At least one time that habit paid off.

In 1963 John Y. Brown Jr. introduced Massey to Harland Sanders, the founder and sole owner of Kentucky Fried Chicken. Massey had a goal at that first meeting.

Whenever Sanders made a deal with someone to sell Kentucky Fried Chicken, the franchisee needed to buy a few things, such as pressure cookers, ovens, and signs. Up to that time General Electric had been loaning the necessary capital to franchisees, with Sanders backing the loans. But at that first meeting Massey suggested to Sanders that he stop using GE and start doing business with his company, Commercial Investment Company.

Sanders wasn't too keen on the idea at first, saying that Massey's small company wasn't big enough to handle his business. "Sometimes the little ones can give you better service than the big ones," Massey told him.

The Nashville businessman then asked Sanders how long it typically took for GE to approve a loan to a new franchisee. Sanders said two or three weeks. Massey asked Sanders if he had any franchisees whose applications were currently at GE. Sanders said there were three. Massey asked Sanders if he could see their applications. Sanders pulled them out, and after looking them over, Massey wrote Sanders a check for the amounts requested in the loan applications. He then promised Sanders that from then on, his company would respond to any credit applications within twenty-four hours.

Sanders was baffled. "I don't understand how you can be that smart," he reportedly said to Massey.

"We're not smart," Massey said. "We're just going to look after our business, and we're going to look after yours, our principal customer."

Massey thus stole one of GE's clients and in doing so began doing business with Colonel Sanders.

4

THE COLONEL'S
HOROSCOPE

J ACK MASSEY SAID THAT WHEN he sold his surgical supply
business to Brunswick, he tried to retire. However, it should
be noted that after he sold Massey Surgical Supply, Massey
still owned at least three other firms: Rigo Chemical Company,
X-ray & Nuclear, and Commercial Investment Company. Rigo
Chemical was a privately held insecticide company. X-Ray &
Nuclear was the regional franchisee for Picker, the nation's top
manufacturer of x-ray machines. Commercial Investment was
an equipment leasing business that largely catered to health-
care clients prior to the sale of the surgical supply business but
which shifted its focus to restaurants after that time.

If Massey did flirt with the concept of retirement, he
didn't do it for long. "I found out pretty quick that there are
days of the week when you can't get up a golf game, that gin
rummy every day becomes monotonous, and that for a person

whose entire life has been work-oriented, not working is not fun," he later said. He decided to go back to work.

After looking into the idea of becoming an executive with the Howard Johnson hotel chain, Massey decided he would rather buy his own company. In 1961 he began searching for a new business to buy, eventually looking at sixteen enterprises. Massey never listed the firms he examined, although he later said one of them was a trucking company.

Massey's search eventually led him to two men. The first was John Y. Brown Jr., a Kentucky lawyer whose father had been a U.S. Senator and trial lawyer. After selling encyclopedias for five years and practicing law for two, Brown realized that the only reason he had become a lawyer was because his father was one. He decided that he wanted to be an entrepreneur, and he began looking into the idea of starting his own small business.

The second man who would soon change Massey's life was Harland Sanders. Sanders had once operated a single restaurant in Corbin, Kentucky. But in the early 1950s, after Interstate 75 bypassed his café by seven miles, he began trying to franchise his fried chicken recipe to mom-and-pop diners across the country. By the time Brown was thinking about starting a business, Sanders was widely known in Kentucky (but in few other areas). With his white suit and trademark goatee, Sanders almost looked like an anachronism from Reconstruction. It is no wonder the Kentucky Legislature named him an honorary Colonel.

Sanders, a friend of Brown's father, sent some of his company's legal work Brown's way. At some point Brown expressed an interest in Sanders's business, and Sanders told the attorney that he wanted him to start a new barbecue restaurant for him.

"I didn't know anything about barbecue, but I was interested in the promotional aspects of the business," Brown later said. "I wanted to be involved in the franchising. So I told him

I'd raise the money and put up the barbecue place and we'd be partners, and he agreed."[10]

Brown found a place for his restaurant and started fixing it up, but he needed about sixteen thousand dollars in financing. Through friend Jim Cavanaugh, whose father was a partner in the Nashville real estate business Kimbro Cavanaugh, Brown found out about Massey's business that loaned money to restaurants. Massey invited him to Nashville. The two men met and argued for three hours over whether the loan would be at 6 or 6.5 percent interest.

"All this over a sixteen-thousand-dollar loan," Brown said. "We went back and forth, and at one point he stood up and said, 'Well, it doesn't look like we are going to make a deal.' And I said, 'Now, Mr. Massey, you sit down there; we are going to do a deal.' And that is how our relationship got started. I think he was impressed with my tenacity. And in the end he wrote me a check for sixteen thousand dollars, which paid for my equipment."[11]

After making the loan, Massey kept in touch with Brown and asked him questions about how the restaurant, called the Porky Pig House, was faring. As it turns out, the Colonel's venture into barbecue didn't do well; the top-selling item on the menu was Kentucky Fried Chicken. "We were selling about eighty percent fried chicken and about twenty percent barbecue," Brown said. "I was in the wrong end of the right business."

Massey was interested in loaning money to Kentucky Fried Chicken's franchisees, so Brown introduced him to Sanders. One day in the summer of 1963 the three men got together at a restaurant in Shelbyville, Kentucky.

It turned out to be a meeting Brown would never forget. "We go to lunch, and right off the bat the Colonel says, 'I just want you to know that no slick Southern so-and-so is going to come in here and buy my company,'" Brown said. "It just came out of nowhere. That was something Jack and I hadn't even talked about."

It was by no means out of character for Sanders to have made such a bizarre impression on Brown, because the Colonel had a tendency to make a strange impression on just about everyone he met. Harland Sanders had led a hard life and had made his living doing everything from working on a railroad to selling insurance door to door. Years earlier, he had begun wearing a white suit and a string tie and carrying a cane, and he had long used the image of himself to symbolize his business.

The general public loved his grandfatherly image, but most people were unaware of just what a cantankerous man Colonel Sanders actually was. He could be a foul-mouthed, hot-tempered perfectionist, and one never knew what would set him off. One time, Brown later recounted, Sanders got so angry at a locked door at corporate headquarters that he got a loaded handgun and shot off the lock. Another time, when a lawyer had the audacity to light up a cigarette in his presence. Sanders reached out, grabbed the cigarette, and put it out on the wall.

Perhaps the most bizarre Colonel Sanders story of all time took place when he and his wife, Claudia, stopped at a restaurant in Illinois to eat breakfast in 1961. The Colonel didn't care much for the scrambled eggs that were brought to his table that morning, and he told the waitress to take them back and tell the cook to scramble them right. When they came back unimproved, Sanders stormed into the kitchen, called the cook a son of a bitch, and threw the eggs in the man's face. The cook grabbed a knife, Sanders grabbed a stool, and the two took their fight into the dining room.

What Brown and Massey didn't know during their first meeting, but they soon learned, was that the Colonel had admitted to himself that his business was too big for him to run anymore.

Sanders operated his company on a basic agreement under which franchisees paid him five cents for every chicken sold.

(Sanders did this by charging a nickel for a spice packet large enough to season a chicken.) Every person who learned how to cook Kentucky Fried Chicken learned the process directly from the Colonel. Sanders didn't have many employees, and many of the key ones were his relatives, such as his nephew Lee Cummings. The company left business decisions such as advertising and store design up to the individual franchisee.

Despite the Colonel's unexpected comment about not wanting to sell his business, the first meeting with Massey went well. As a result of it, Sanders began using Commercial Investment Company to finance loans to his franchisees. And, according to several interviews that Massey gave later in his life, a few weeks after that first meeting Sanders showed up at Massey's office in Nashville and made an unexpected offer.

"He wanted me to run his company," Massey said. "He offered me a hundred thousand dollars a year and half the profits—a great deal. But I turned it down. He couldn't understand it, but I told him, 'Colonel, I can't work for you. We'd never get along. You'd fire me the first month because I'd do things differently than the way you do them.'"[12]

What Massey suggested instead was that he help Sanders set a value for KFC, with the idea of brokering its sale to another company. In an interview years later, this is how Massey described his offer to Sanders: "I'd like to come up and spend two or three days, and you give me your people in accounting and give me all the franchises and all the contracts you have, and everything you're doing, and let me study it, and I'll tell you what I'll sell it for. And if you don't like it, you don't have to take it."

Sanders took Massey up on his offer, and it didn't take Massey long to realize that he had stumbled across a virtual gold mine. "When I got through with it, I saw that there was a great, great opportunity," he later recalled.

The man who had first put Sanders and Massey together remained very much a part of this process. In fact, Brown later claimed that the very idea that he and Massey would buy Kentucky Fried Chicken was originally his.

After Massey studied the company, he sat down with Sanders and admitted to him that he was now seriously considering buying the company in partnership with Brown. Rather than haggle, Massey suggested that he and Sanders each write down a proposed figure on a napkin and then turn the napkins over at the same time to reveal how much each person thought the company was worth. Sanders went along with the idea, and both men jotted down the figure $2 million. This would have amused some men—but not the Colonel.

"His face got red and he couldn't believe it," Massey said. "So we took a couple hours of talking before he would go any further. Finally, he opened his desk drawer, read something, closed the desk drawer, and said, 'It's a deal.' I later found out from his secretary that it was his horoscope, and his horoscope said, 'Today something good is going to happen to you.'"

Nevertheless, the Colonel had by no means made up his mind. During the next few weeks, as he pondered what to do, Brown did his best to influence him. Brown told the seventy-four-year-old Sanders that he had built a wonderful company but that he needed people skilled in management to take it to the next level. He told him that Massey was offering him a lot of money and that he was entitled to it, and that if Sanders didn't find a suitable buyer for the company, the franchisees might squabble with his family after his death.

"There is no reason on earth why you should be wasting your time bothering with cookers and ovens and that sort of thing; anyone can do that," Brown said, according to an interview years later. "You are one of the greatest salesmen in the world, one of the great promoters. You belong in front of the public. I'll put you there, where you belong, and make you a rich man to boot."

Some accounts later claimed that KFC was "ailing" at the time the Colonel sold it. This is not true; in fact, Sanders had several hundred franchisees and was making a six-figure salary. But at that time, KFC wasn't a company as much as it was an extension of its founder. The Colonel had made unsuccessful attempts to turn over the business to his relatives, and by this time Sanders had to admit that there was no telling what would happen to his business when he died.

He would not, however, sell the business to Massey and Brown without the permission of his best franchisees—the most successful being Pete Harman of Salt Lake City, Utah.

Sanders had a special relationship with Harman. The two men had met a dozen years earlier and seemed to have a lot in common because neither of the men drank alcohol (Harman was Mormon). Sanders later stopped by to see Harman while on the way to a religious conference in Australia, a trip that the Colonel hoped would cure him of his foul mouth.

Sanders fixed Harman and his staff a fried chicken dinner that night, and when the Colonel came back through Salt Lake City a few weeks later, Harman was so excited about selling the stuff that he had already printed a sign advertising "Kentucky Fried Chicken" (prior to that time the Colonel's chicken had no name). The two men worked out a franchise deal that would ultimately be duplicated by every other franchisee while Sanders owned the company. Harman was quite an innovator in his own right; he would eventually be credited with developing the carryout bucket.

On Friday, January 3, 1964, Massey, Brown, and Sanders flew to Utah to meet with Harman. Massey reportedly did most of the talking at that meeting, explaining that he and his partner wanted to buy Kentucky Fried Chicken, expand it, increase its sales, and give existing franchisees a part of the action. Massey also offered to sell Harman twenty-five thousand shares of stock in the new Kentucky Fried Chicken for a dollar a share, for a total of 5 percent of the company. To the Colonel's surprise, Harman agreed. That was enough for Sanders to finally make up his mind.

"Let's get this damn thing settled and over with," he reportedly said. "I'm going to bed. You fellows draw up a contract. I'll sign it in the morning."

Massey and Brown knew how apt the Colonel was to change his mind, so this was a rather critical moment—made all the more urgent by the fact that it was late and that their flight left at 7:30 the next morning. Incredibly, the two men had not yet written up a proposed contract, and it was at this juncture that Massey asked his junior partner if he could write one. "I'm a trial lawyer," Brown said. "Never drew up a contract in my life."

Massey shut himself up in his room at the Covered Wagon Motel in Salt Lake City at about one o'clock in the morning, found a pen and a yellow legal pad, and started writing. Neither a lawyer nor a writer, this wasn't easy for Massey. He didn't go to sleep until he had finished a five-page document that was full of lines that were crossed out and corrections that were filled in on the margins.

At about 5 a.m. Sanders banged his cane against Massey's hotel door. "Is that contract ready?" he demanded. Massey said he had written one down but said that he would rather get it typed first. Sanders said he didn't care if it was typed or not, and the two men sat down and went over one of the messiest contracts ever written. "So I read it to him word for word," Massey later said.

Under the agreement Massey and Brown would pay $2 million for the company, which basically consisted of the Colonel's method and recipe for cooking chicken, the existing franchise agreements, and the right to sell new franchises in most of the United States. They would pay $500,000 cash, with the balance to be paid in regular installments, plus 3 percent interest, over the next five years. The Colonel would also be paid $40,000 a year and remain an employee of Kentucky Fried Chicken for life, mainly as a public relations representative.

Massey and Brown offered to sell Sanders stock for a dollar a share, which was the same price for which they had sold it to Harman. However, in a move that he would regret for the rest of his life, Sanders turned down the offer.

"It was hard for him to accept the possibility that the company could possibly be better off without him running it," Brown later said. "And so he said, 'I don't want any of your stock. It's not going to be worth toilet paper.'"

Interestingly enough, it was only after the Colonel signed this agreement that Brown and Massey worked out an agreement between each other. Years later Brown remembered the meeting at which he and Massey worked that out.

"Finally, I asked him if we could talk about our deal, and he said sure. I said, 'What do you think is fair?' And he said, 'What do *you* think is fair?' And I said, 'I think sixty-forty would be fair.' And he said, 'Fine,' and he stuck out his hand and we had a deal. And this entire time I had been promoting it and trying to put it together, and I didn't know until the last minute what the deal was."

The next several weeks were nervous ones for Brown and Massey, as they lived in perpetual fear that the Colonel would change his mind.

"It seemed like every day we were hearing something different, that the Colonel had told someone that he wasn't going to sell us the company, or that the Colonel was saying that they don't know how to run it because they don't know anything about chicken," Brown said. "Finally I had an idea, and I went down and talked to the publisher of the [Louisville] *Courier-Journal* and gave him the story. The next day it ran in the paper with a picture of me and the Colonel looking over a white picket fence, and a couple of days after that, it ran all over the country. After that he sort of accepted it."

A few weeks after signing the deal, Sanders had lunch in Nashville with Massey and some other Third National Bank directors, among them, Sam Fleming and Webb Johnston. It was then that Sanders signed a more official contract—written by a commercial lawyer, typed, and copied.[13] The Liberty National Bank & Trust of Louisville loaned Brown money to invest in his share of KFC stock (a loan that Massey backed with one thousand shares of Third National Bank stock).

In the end, Massey invested $265,000, Brown $160,000, and franchisee Pete Harman and company officials Lee Cummings and Harlan Adams—both of whom were related to the Colonel—pitched in $25,000 each. A second franchisee, Kenny King of Cleveland, Ohio, was originally supposed to invest $25,000 as well. However, King's lawyer advised against it.

"The lawyer said he was foolish. Said, 'I wouldn't put a dollar in that thing. Not a single dollar,'" Massey later recounted.[14]

Because Massey sold his surgical supply business three years before he bought controlling interest in Kentucky Fried Chicken, people generally assumed that he used the money from the surgical supply sale to buy KFC. In fact, the $240,000 that Massey actually pulled out of his pocket to buy KFC is almost the exact same amount of money that he had made a few months earlier when he sold his one-third interest in Rigo Chemical Company.

In his own mind, Massey might have viewed the KFC purchase as something on which he was spending money he had made in a side venture. He wasn't risking the family nest egg.

*J*ack Massey had to deal with setbacks, detractors, and failures just like any other person. But he did not dwell on his failures. And he generally did not let bad things, bad experiences, or bad days get to him.

Virtually everyone interviewed for this book was asked whether Jack Massey frequently showed anger. Just about everyone seemed surprised by the question and, after thinking about it, had to admit that they had never seen him lose his temper.

"He wasn't the kind of person to react that way," said John Neff, who partnered with Massey in many business ventures during the 1960s and 1970s. "I remember the time that First American pulled out of the loan package at HCA. That was a huge setback for us. He did get angry at the bank, but he didn't really show it. He was the kind of person who would just say, 'Let's get the thing done, and to hell with those guys.'"

Lonnie Stout, who would later work for Massey at Volunteer Capital, said Massey one time gave him some advice about anger. "One time we had a meeting and it was with someone I didn't care for, and during the meeting I guess he thought I might have showed a little anger," Stout said. "When the meeting was over, he called me in his office and said, 'Lonnie, you don't ever want to show any public anger. If you don't approve of someone or don't like someone or don't like the direction in which a deal is going, don't do it, just say no thank you. But never show any emotions.'"

Clarence Edmonds, an accountant who may have spent more time with Massey during the last two decades of his life than any other person, was once asked whether he ever saw his boss get angry. "He yelled at me twice," Edmonds said. "Both times were because I was inhaling my cigar smoke, and he didn't think much of that. We were sitting at a table together, me across from him, and all of a sudden he yells over at me, 'Stop that!'

"Scared me pretty good."

5

CHICKEN STOCK

T HE FIRST TIME MASSEY AND Brown walked into the Shelbyville, Kentucky, headquarters as the new owners of Kentucky Fried Chicken Corporation, they were greeted by the
news that the company warehouse had flooded, inundating all
the pressure cookers, cardboard buckets, publicity pictures of
the Colonel, and just about everything else needed for the day-
to-day operation of Kentucky Fried Chicken.

"We got a boat and went in to look at it; everything we
had was covered in water," Massey said. "We went back to the
office and sat all the rest of the day, and the phone didn't ring.
All day long the phone didn't ring, and we thought that we must
have bought a mess, because it was just a terrible situation." A
few weeks later the new Kentucky Fried Chicken board of
directors met at the Executive Inn Motor Hotel in Louisville.[15]

Franchisees were told not to build any new KFC locations for several months while Massey and Brown came up with a strategy. Meanwhile, Massey quickly came to the realization that was going to take more of his time than he had originally thought. He ordered the company headquarters moved to Nashville, into a nondescript building in a largely industrial area south of downtown. It was the first of many moves by the company that Colonel Sanders didn't appreciate. "This ain't no goddamned Tennessee Fried Chicken!" Sanders reportedly said when he heard that the company was moving.

After about a year of looking over the books and studying the industry, Massey and Brown came to several conclusions. One was that Kentucky Fried needed standardization. At the time most KFC franchisees were full-service restaurants that offered the Colonel's recipe as a menu item. Other franchisees were in strip-mall locations or stand-alone buildings. The stand-alone operations clearly made the most money.

Since the long-term plan was to build Kentucky Fried Chicken into a national chain, it made sense to come up with a building that had proven to be the most appealing to the public. The company ended up with a variation of a red-and-white-striped building with a cupola roof, very similar to the one used by Atlanta franchisee Ted Davis. With the new stand-alone design, Massey and Brown decided they would phase in arrangements with sit-down restaurants, while allowing franchisees to develop only stand-alone locations in the future.

Kentucky Fried Chicken also needed to get the word out. Since the company had left advertising up to each individual franchisee, there were no Kentucky Fried Chicken advertisements on television. For the most part, the only people who knew about Kentucky Fried Chicken were the people who had stumbled across a location or heard about it by word of mouth.

Another necessary change concerned the financial arrangement between the company and franchisees. A nickel per bird may have made sense when the Colonel and Pete Harman worked out their deal in 1952, but it didn't make sense over a decade later for a nationally franchised restaurant company dominated by stand-alone locations. Accountants preferred a verifiable system where franchisees paid a percentage of revenues.

It would be easy to work all these new concepts into contracts with new franchisees, but that left the issue of the existing contracts. To get existing franchisees on board, Massey and Brown used both the carrot and the stick. Under the proposed new program, existing franchisees had to agree to build standardized buildings, contribute twenty-five dollars per month per location to a national advertising campaign, and pay 3 percent of revenues to the company if they wanted to build new outlets. If franchisees refused to play this game, they ran the risk of losing their businesses (under the deal that they had with the Colonel, franchisees didn't have protected territory). The new management also came up with a program of stock options that allowed franchisees to buy into Kentucky Fried Chicken as new locations were opened.

This new arrangement at first caused a rift between the company and its franchisees. "Massey and Brown had an adversarial relationship with the franchisees throughout the whole course of the situation, even though there were a lot of people who were doing extremely well," said Nashville franchisee Marvin Hopper. "It was totally different from what the franchisees had been accustomed to under the Colonel."

Franchisees who stayed with the company, signed new contracts, built new outlets, and acquired stock options would eventually have cause to be happy about the new program. "According to my memory, for each store you opened, you would sign a contract that would give you stock options for three years," Hopper said. "I think my options cost me about four thousand dollars, and when I executed them they were worth about eighty-four thousand."

Hopper stuck with the program but was one of many franchisees who did not get along with the new regime. "We were at loggerheads the whole time, and I think the fact that I owned the franchise for [Massey's] hometown made it all the worse," said Hopper. "For example, when the Colonel owned the business, my restaurants were called Marvin Hopper's Featuring Kentucky Fried Chicken. Well, Massey insisted that I take my name off there, and I didn't want to. And I remember that they wanted me to put little wet-naps in the meals so people would have them to wash their hands with after they ate, and I didn't want to incur the expense. Things like that."

Massey later recounted an episode involving a franchisee, possibly Hopper: "He [Sanders] found this man making a different kind of slaw, and he asked him why he wasn't making his. The franchisee said that he liked his own better. . . . Colonel Sanders came back and told me about it. So I told the man, 'Either you make the slaw right or you don't get any more stores, and the minute we can possibly do it, we're going to cancel your franchise.' So, with a great deal of reluctance, he changed back to the other slaw. His sales picked up, and he sold a lot more slaw than he ever had sold before, because what he liked wasn't what the public liked."

One of the curious things about Kentucky Fried Chicken under Sanders's ownership was the way its stores were interspersed. There were, for instance, plenty of places to buy the Colonel's chicken in Salt Lake City, but, oddly, no franchisee in Louisville, Kentucky. One of the first orders of business was to fill in those obvious gaps, and the two new owners drew on personal contacts to do this. In late 1964 Massey called Shoney's Big Boy franchisee Ray Danner and talked him into being the KFC franchisee for Louisville.

"He [Massey] calls me and says that they had just had a meeting, and that he knew I was from Louisville and knew I knew it well, and I had just been awarded the franchise for Louisville," Danner said. "I said, 'Jack, I don't want to do that!' He said, 'Ray, it has been decided. Now get up there and open some stores.'"

About the same time, Brown called former law school classmate George Baker and offered him the franchise for Norfolk, Virginia. No sooner had Baker accepted that offer than he was offered the franchise for Dallas. Baker moved there and within three years opened fourteen locations.

"I went down to Texas in August, and by February of the next year we were making money at a rapid clip and expanding," Baker later said. "It was like a dream. I'd like to tell you that it was real, real hard, but it wasn't."

How the firm handled the production and distribution of its secret recipe added to the mystique of Kentucky Fried Chicken. To minimize the number of people who knew the entire formula, half of the spices were blended in one place and half in another before they were mixed together by a third group of employees. The spice packages were then shipped to franchisees, who combined them with twenty-five bags of flour and five cups of salt.

Kentucky Fried Chicken did so well that there would inevitably be differences of opinion about who came up with each innovation. In a 1982 biography of Colonel Sanders, author John Ed Pearce gave most of the credit for the rise of Kentucky Fried Chicken after 1964 to Brown, naming him as the person who came up with everything from the advertising campaigns to the idea for freestanding locations. In fact, Pearce used Brown's name and the company's name interchangeably, as if Massey didn't even exist.

Had Pearce spent time with Massey, he would have heard an alternative version of the KFC story. Interviewed in 1978, Massey made it sound as if his original intention was for Brown to actually run the company. "When I bought it, I had planned for John Y. Brown Jr. [to run it], but he couldn't even read a balance sheet, and he just couldn't run the company," Massey said. Massey also said that, in the early years of his ownership, he did "everything there was to do" related to running the company.

Massey said, for instance, that he had the idea of emphasizing freestanding locations when he, Brown, and Sanders
first visited the Utah franchisee. "Pete Harman had a window,
and people could park in the parking lot and come up to the
window and buy chicken to take home," Massey said. "Well,
the idea hit me right there. Why not have drive-ins? Why not
have freestanding buildings? . . . I didn't say a word about it
because I didn't want anybody to know that I had the idea.

"But when we got home, I told John that the secret to the
success of this thing is to have freestanding buildings, so let's
build some right now. So we built a couple of them in
Louisville, and they were the hottest thing in town. And we
went out to other places and we built freestanding buildings.
And they were all successful; man, they were just going to
town."

Massey also said he played the key role in getting franchisees to think big in terms of getting the best locations. "I
convinced a lot of people who were operating in strip centers
to sell and go to a higher-priced piece of real estate," he said.
Massey said one time he asked a franchisee to move his store
from a place that cost $150 a month to a location that was
going to cost $1,000 a month. After the franchisee hesitated,
Massey told him that if he built a restaurant at the new location, he would guarantee its success by buying it back in six
months if it wasn't successful.

"Well, he built it," Massey said. "And he was making so
much money off that store, he wanted to open two more."

There is also some evidence in Massey's own appointment books that he controlled Kentucky Fried Chicken's decision-making process. Within a few days of Sanders's decision
to sell the company, Massey began making notes to himself
that often reflect changes made months later. On Thursday,
January 16, 1964, Massey wrote down the names "King, Harman, Harlan, Lee, Brown, Sanders, and Massey"—obviously
an early draft of a board of directors.

Three days later, using handwriting that is difficult to decipher, Massey wrote the following passage: "Let up future franchises as franchise fee of $3,000 for 10 years or $300 per year payable in advance."

During the next few weeks Massey met numerous franchisees (including Dave Thomas), talked to the Colonial Bakery in Nashville about the idea of making bread for KFC, and met with numerous accountants, lawyers, and bankers to set up the deal. He made himself a note to research McDonald's and to produce a "placemat showing KFC locations." Always mindful of the need to be political, Massey even sent Colonel Sanders's wife a crate of oranges on February 23.

Nevertheless, Brown said that when he worked for Kentucky Fried Chicken, he did far more traveling around the country and put in more hours working for the company than his older partner. Brown even claimed that Massey only came to work about one day per week, a claim that is disputed by several other people associated with KFC at that time. But Brown did agree that the decision-making process was a team effort.

"Jack and I talked six or eight times a day and agreed with just about everything before we put it into place," Brown said. "And let's face it: I could never had done it without Jack. He is the one who gave me my opportunity. I always thought that we were a wonderful complement to each other. He gave me the experience and the input and the judgment and wisdom that I didn't have as a young fella. And I think I put in the energy and I was a good people person. He gave me maturity and credibility, and I think I gave him performance."

There are people who say that Massey ran the company and those who say Brown did. Hal Kennedy, who spent large amounts of time at the corporate office doing public relations for KFC, downplayed Brown's role. "He was a big, attractive guy and fairly articulate, but I never saw him do anything as far as running the company was concerned," Kennedy said.

Lou Karibo, head of training for KFC from about 1966 onward, said just the opposite. "From what I knew of the operations of KFC, John Brown ran the company," Karibo said. "Jack Massey was a wonderful guy, but I don't even know if he came to the office every day."

Perhaps the truth is somewhere in between. Perhaps the roles carried out by each man changed over the years. Or perhaps each man gave the people he worked with the impression that he—and not his partner—was running the company.

It should also be pointed out that, in the history of business, innovations are rarely credited to the person who actually "invented" them, only to the person who introduced them to the largest number of people. Under Massey and Brown's ownership, Kentucky Fried Chicken was credited with inventing the drive-thru window. However, when the duo first bought the company, Nashville franchisee Marvin Hopper already had a drive-thru window at his Gallatin Road location, and he was building one at a location then under construction in the Green Hills area.

"And if memory serves, I wasn't the first," Hopper said years later. "There was a fellow in Memphis named Jack Pirtle, and he had drive-thrus at several locations, and I think I got the idea from him."

Interestingly, when they first took over the company, Massey and Brown ordered the drive-thru windows removed because of a belief that people would spend more money if they were forced to get out of their cars.

However, there is one other area in which Brown undoubtedly played a critical role: he often kept peace between Massey and Colonel Sanders.

"The friction between the Colonel and Mr. Massey developed mostly over Nashville, but they just rubbed each other the wrong way," said Maureen McGuire, the Colonel's long-time secretary. "Mr. Massey was a successful man. He had made a lot of money, and he knew how he wanted things done.

And when he wanted something done and the Colonel didn't, Mr. Massey just went ahead and did it, and that made the Colonel mad. Mr. Brown was more diplomatic, talked the Colonel into things, tried never to hurt his feelings."[16]

Many years later, Brown described ways in which he would do this. "I just had ways of calming him down," he said. "He would start fussing about something, and I'd say, 'Colonel, what kind of light is that over there?' or 'Colonel, who gave you that over there?' or whatever, and the next thing you know, he had forgotten what he was mad about." Massey had less patience with Sanders and his temper tantrums.

It's too bad that Sanders and Massey got along so poorly. The two men actually had a lot in common. Both came from poor backgrounds, both worked all the time, both were utterly opposed the idea of retiring.

"I'm against retiring," Sanders once told a U.S. House of Representatives subcommittee on aging, expressing a sentiment with which Massey was in complete agreement. "The thing that keeps a man alive is having something to do. Sitting in a rocker never appealed to me. Golf or fishing isn't as much fun as working."[17]

However, Sanders always seemed to find a reason to be angry at Massey. One time, while reading the company prospectus before the company's initial public offering, Sanders was furious to discover that Massey was paying himself a hundred thousand dollars a year. Upon his return to Nashville, Sanders stomped into Massey's office and demanded that he get a raise. Massey raised the Colonel's pay to seventy-five thousand dollars on the spot. But Sanders was still upset about it.

"He was jealous of us, jealous of the fact that we were successful, and [he] did a lot of things to make us unsuccessful," Massey said years later, when asked about Sanders. "If he'd had any stock in the company, he probably would have enjoined us every time we did anything that he didn't like. We would have been in court with him all the time, never would have been able to be successful. I realized in the beginning that he was a difficult man to work with. He loved you today and hated you tomorrow. And when he loved you, he really loved you; and when he hated you, he really hated you. He was a man who could turn it on and turn it off—in minutes."

Massey, however, said there were some things he really admired about Sanders. "He loved little children," Massey said. "The Colonel always carried balloons in his hip pocket. And when he'd see little children—he could be talking to you and fussing at you and cursing you for everything in the world—a little child would walk up, and he'd turn around and turn on his beautiful personality and his smile and pull out a balloon and blow it up."

One of the many children Sanders showed kindness to was Massey's grandson, whose name is also Jack Massey. Many years later, the younger Jack Massey treasured a photograph of Colonel Sanders giving him a kiss the day of his grandmother's funeral.

Eventually, Sanders at least learned to appreciate Massey's business acumen and integrity. In August 1970, after Massey had stopped playing an active role in the operation of the company, Sanders wrote Massey a nice letter thanking him for purchasing a table at a Muscular Dystrophy fundraiser he had organized. "You could lend some new direction to the company that I feel would be very beneficial," Sanders said. "I have never met or knew anyone that has the business acumen and the ability that I have observed in you."

In early 1966, KFC got back to the business of selling franchises. Under the new arrangement, new franchise holders had to pay a three-thousand-dollar fee, buy or lease sixteen thousand dollars' worth of cooking equipment, and build or lease a store that cost about forty thousand dollars. They were also required to attend a company-owned school in Louisville where the cooking methods of Professor Harland Sanders were the required curriculum.

The new arrangement between company and franchisees would eventually put Kentucky Fried Chicken commercials on national television. But during the first couple of years after Massey and Brown bought the company, the advertising program hadn't started to jell, leaving KFC to make do with whatever free press it could muster. In this area, Massey and Brown were truly fortunate, because they had on board a one-man publicity machine named Harland Sanders.

Years later, when the effect that free television publicity had on a brand became better understood, it would be quite difficult to get the front man for a fried chicken outfit on national television free of charge. But network television shows were easier to crack in the 1960s, and Colonel Sanders was a novelty.

Shortly after Sanders sold the company, Brown hired New York public relations consultant Stan Lewis. Lewis did a great job, and within a few weeks the Colonel had appeared on the game show *What's My Line* (where, by the way, none of the professional occupation-guessers could identify him). Shortly thereafter, Sanders appeared on *The Tonight Show*, where he walked on stage with $2 million in cash in a transparent case.

Massey and Brown also encouraged the cult of Harland Sanders by wearing—and requiring all other KFC executives and franchisees to wear—string ties at work.

With the company now based in Tennessee, Massey had a preference for Nashville-based vendors. In 1965 the company hired Noble-Dury, an ad agency started in the 1950s, to run the advertising program for Kentucky Fried Chicken. Noble-Dury's first series of commercials was loosely based on the recently released British movie *Tom Jones*. In the ads, costumed men and women devoured chickens by candlelight while gazing lustily at each other. "I remember when they hit the air, because they just blew the roof off of our business," Marvin Hopper said.

Successful as they were, however, the *Tom Jones* commercials were short-lived. The next year, KFC began producing commercials featuring the Colonel himself. Soon a majority of Americans recognized Sanders and had heard the company's two catch phrases: "Finger-lickin' good" and "Secret recipe of eleven herbs and spices." In 1968 alone Kentucky Fried Chicken spent over nine million dollars in advertising.

When Sanders sold his company, the only thing he agreed to do was serve as a public relations spokesman and symbol. However, he wasn't about to let KFC's food quality suffer. Sanders became a one-man quality-control team that no one at KFC could—or wanted to—reign in.

"He was a stickler for having quality," Massey said. "He would go out and inspect stores for us or by himself, and he would be very adamant about going in and seeing that the chicken was the right size, that the chicken was fresh, that it was stored properly, and that it was cooked properly. He had a cooking process that was absolutely essential to the chicken being good. Of the few little side items that he made, like slaw and potato salad and gravy, it just had to be exact or he would get upset."

In 1970 the *New Yorker* published a profile of Sanders that described the Colonel's quality-control methods in detail. "During his travels on company business, he will occasionally pay an unexpected visit to a KFC outlet in order to inspect the kitchen and sample the gravy," the story said. "If the gravy meets his low expectations, he delivers one of his withering gravy critiques, sometimes emphasizing his points by banging his cane on whatever furniture is handy. Months or even years after these ordeals, franchisees winced at the memory of such gravy judgments from the Colonel as 'How do you serve this goddamned slop? With a straw?'"[18]

In spite of such media reports, Sanders usually voiced his criticisms behind closed doors. "He would generally raise all of this hell in the kitchen and wouldn't let it bleed over into the customer area," said Lou Karibo, head of training for KFC during most of the Massey/Brown years.

As for the franchisees, they grew to appreciate the Colonel because he gave them helpful advice behind management's back. Dave Wachtel III, who worked for Louisville franchisee Ray Danner in the 1960s, remembered the time Sanders tasted his chicken and said there was something wrong with it. "The Colonel came in and said, 'The ginger's wrong; they're using domestic ginger. They're not using imported Jamaican ginger,'" Wachtel recalled. "So from then on, we added four ounces of Jamaican ginger to our spice pack. And the next thing you know, our sales went up."

Nashville franchisee Marvin Hopper said he had a great relationship with Sanders. "He was just like your grandfather," Hopper said. "He could go from one extreme to the other. He and I had a wonderful relationship because he had taught me how to make the gravy and I made it his way." Dallas franchisee George Baker gave a similar description. "One time he got real upset in one of my stores, and the next day he baby-sat for my children," he said. "The kids still remember it. They thought Santa Claus was there."

Although Sanders frequently complained about the company making alterations to his chicken and gravy recipes, most people affiliated with KFC said the company devoted considerable attention to the food. "They were extremely meticulous about the quality of the chicken that came out of every store," said Ben Betty, owner of a Nashville machine shop that designed and produced cooking equipment for KFC in the late 1960s.

The Colonel could, however, make a scene, and the most dramatic occurred at a franchisee convention in 1967. With all the KFC restaurant owners and their spouses present, Sanders was expected to make a few pleasant remarks. Everyone knew something was wrong when he showed up at the head table wearing a black suit instead of the white one he usually wore.

Many years later Brown said he did not remember what had made Sanders so angry that night. (One written account maintained that the Colonel had discovered something about the company's pension fund that bothered him.) But Brown remembered the gist of what he said.

"He got up in front of a thousand people and proceeded to just chew us out unmercifully," Brown said. "He said that we didn't know anything about the chicken business; that we were only there to steal their money. He said that we didn't know anything about this and that we were going to change the recipe. It was really mean-spirited. . . . Everyone didn't know what was going to happen. And here we had just given the Colonel a Christmas tree with all these checks worth about thirty-five thousand dollars on it toward his Easter Seals campaign.

"You could hear a pin drop. I remember looking over at Jack, and he was trying to sort of half-laugh, and he said to me, 'Can't I just fire him?'"

Brown then stood up and made what was one of the most important speeches of his life. Instead of blasting Sanders, he praised him. "I said that the Colonel was an artist, and like all artists, he is a perfectionist," Brown remembered. "I said that what the Colonel has done is create a dream for all of us. And I said it was our responsibility to go out and reach and try as hard as we can to meet up with the Colonel's perfection."

Brown then asked the crowd of KFC franchisees if any one of them had made a deal with the company in the previous two years that the company hadn't honored. No one raised his hand.

Kentucky Fried Chicken went public on March 18, 1966, with 425,000 shares of stock hitting the market at fifteen dollars per share. For the next three years the company's sales, franchises, and stock growth were unparalleled in the history of restaurants.

"Our numbers were going up so fast that, for a while, instead of announcing earnings quarterly, we'd announce them monthly," said Hal Kennedy, who started doing corporate public relations for Kentucky Fried Chicken as an employee of the Noble-Dury advertising and public relations firm in March 1966. "We'd try to do this without anyone necessarily noticing that we were doing it. If we'd go to an analysts meeting, we'd say something about last month's earnings while we were up there."

Asked about the KFC experience decades later, Kennedy said his proudest achievement was the time he made, in his words, "twelve million dollars for Mr. Massey in four days." In June 1967 Kennedy talked *Business Week* reporter Reuben Smith into writing a story about the company.

"The new owners have converted Kentucky Fried Chicken from the loosely knit, one-man show that it was under Sanders . . . into a smoothly run corporation with all the trappings of modern management," said the article, illustrated with a photo of Jack Massey eating a drumstick. "The only elements of the business that have not changed are the product itself and the image of the Colonel. These remain as the most important ingredients in KFC's recipe for success."[19]

During the week following the story's release, the stock rose from about fifty-eight dollars to seventy dollars a share—at a time when Massey owned about a million shares of it.

Kennedy also said that Colonel Sanders, despite his fiery temper tantrums in private, always came through for the company when it mattered in public. At one point Kennedy arranged for Massey and Brown to make a speech before a group of stock analysts in New York. After the two executives had made a serious presentation, a man in the back of the room (planted by the company) stood up and asked the speakers whether the Colonel really existed. At that moment Sanders came walking down the aisle wearing his white suit and carrying his trademark cane, receiving a standing ovation from what was normally a reserved audience.

In 1966 and 1967 the company opened about three hundred new outlets. In 1968 it opened about six hundred. In 1969 the number reached nearly nine hundred. Soon the red-and-white-striped chicken stores were more plentiful than the McDonald's arches.

Revenue per unit soared because the stand-alone locations, which were largely set up for takeout sales, made much more money than did the old system of selling chicken as a menu item at a sit-down restaurant. "The takeout arrangement worked wonderfully, because it turns out that chicken is an eat-at-home food anyway," Brown said.

As KFC was going public, Massey frequently told people he knew in Nashville to get in on the stock. Few took his advice. "He offered me some early stock, and I didn't take it because I couldn't believe he would make it go," said Hunter Woods, who was president of Rigo Chemical. "I should have known better."

Another person who ignored Massey's advice to buy KFC stock was Kirk Todd, a plastic surgeon who had been one of Massey Surgical Supply's most reliable customers. "He came around to a bunch of us and told us that he wanted us to buy some stock," Todd remembered years later. "I told him I didn't have any money and couldn't buy any. A few weeks later we went out and played golf. He said, 'You know that stock I told you to buy? You know it's doubled.' I said, 'I know that, Jack.' He said, 'Well, now is still a good time to buy it.' But I still didn't buy it.

"The next time we played golf he said the stock had doubled again. I said, 'Jack, I know it did!' He said, 'Now is a good time to buy it.' I said, "Jack, it can't possibly go up again.' He said, 'Well, you just wait. It will.' And it went up again! So the next time I saw him he said, 'Now it is a good time to buy it,' and I said, 'Jack, you are beginning to get to me.' So I finally bought some and I made a profit, but I can't remember how much." A couple of years later, when Massey started Hospital Corporation of America, physicians such as Todd were more likely to pay attention.

Many KFC franchisees were smarter. One of the hardest-working was Dave Thomas, who owned Kentucky Fried Chicken stores in Indiana. Massey became close to Thomas, and right before the stock went public, Massey told Thomas to buy a thousand shares. "Jack, I don't have ten thousand dollars," Thomas told Massey. "That's not a problem," Massey replied. "Pay me when you get it." A couple of months later, when the value of those shares had risen from $10,000 to $500,000, Thomas made good on the loan.

Not only did Massey advise many people to buy the stock, he gave some away to friends and friends' children. In 1966 he gave ten shares of KFC stock to each of Dr. Thomas Frist's five kids.

"I remember those ten shares of Kentucky Fried Chicken stock he put in my name just after KFC went public," one of those children, Bill Frist, wrote many years later. "I always kept those shares and never sold them." It was the first lesson in finance for a man who later became a surgeon, then a U.S. Senator, and then Senate Majority Leader.

During Massey and Brown's first two years running the company, they devoted their attention to standardizing stores, selling franchises, and advertising. But after the initial public offering, they came up with another way of building the company's profitability, and that was to buy up the more successful franchises. "Since the restaurants themselves were very profitable businesses, it made a lot of sense to buy them and make a fifteen percent royalty, rather than a two percent royalty," Brown said.

Between 1968 and 1970, KFC bought out more than fifty of its franchisees and acquired more than five hundred restaurants, exchanging stock in the company for an amount equal to five to six times the franchise's earnings. Many franchisees, such as Dave Thomas and George Baker, cashed out again, and it was through this process that nearly twenty of them became millionaires.[20]

In 1965 Kentucky Fried Chicken earned $800,000 on a gross of $8.5 million. Four years later it earned $12.1 million on a gross of $430 million. The Nashville venture capitalist and the young Louisville lawyer—neither of whom had taken a business course in his life—had revolutionized the restaurant business.

"I had a big time!" Massey said a few years later, when asked about the KFC experience. "I had a ball! Had a lot of fun and learned how to take the company public, how to do subsequent offerings, and raise equity. It was a thing that taught me a great deal."

Harland Sanders regretted his decision not to take KFC stock as a part of its sale. But the former train engineer got his two million dollars and at least had the satisfaction of knowing that he had many of his friends rich. He also had the satisfaction of being warmly received in that most inhospitable of places, the New York Stock Exchange. In January 1969, when KFC was listed on the Big Board, floor traders mobbed Colonel Sanders while KFC employees handed out free pieces of fried chicken.

By that time, however, KFC was no longer the pride of Nashville. In October 1968—a few weeks after Massey allowed Brown to replace him as chief executive officer—the company announced it was moving its corporate headquarters to Louisville. There are conflicting stories related to the cause of this move.

Brown, interviewed in 1997, said he and Massey had decided back in 1964 that the company would only stay in Nashville for a short time, but that Massey effectively reneged on this agreement. "When Jack and I bought the business, we made a deal that we would only be based in Nashville for two years, but things got so hectic that that turned into four years," he said. "That was the only big thing that Jack and I disagreed on, and it strained our relationship and I regret that. But I felt almost patriotic about Kentucky Fried Chicken being in Kentucky. I grew up hating Tennessee and hating the [University of Tennessee] Big Orange, mainly because of football."

In fact, Massey never assented to the company's move back to Kentucky. In a sequence of events kept hush-hush at the time, Brown secretly lobbied members of the KFC board to get the headquarters moved back to the Bluegrass State. "I thought that our legitimacy and credibility was at stake, and so I went to the board to get the board's support, and I ended up winning," Brown said. Massey was not amused, saying in later years that Brown had started the equivalent of a "palace revolt" against him.

By 1969 the franchise industry that KFC had helped create had gotten a bad name, mainly because many ill-fated franchise companies had come and gone and hurt a lot of investors in the process. Two ventures started by KFC—a chain of fish-and-chips restaurants and a chain of roast beef eateries—failed. And Wall Street had become so used to enormous earnings growth that Kentucky Fried Chicken's stock price was being damaged by the fact that its growth was coming down to earth.

"I remember going down to Wall Street and telling them that we were only going to grow fifty percent a year for the next five years," Brown said. "Our stock fell eight points the next day."

After KFC moved its offices to Louisville, Massey continued to make six or eight trips a year to the company headquarters. But by this time he had become more involved in other enterprises, such as Hospital Corporation of America and Massey

Investment Company. In March 1970, Massey resigned as KFC chairman. About that time he began to consider selling his KFC stock.

The details under which Massey sold KFC remained hidden in the years immediately following the transaction. But according to an interview Massey gave a few years later, he made a deal to sell the company without Brown's knowledge, then set it up so that Brown would think that it had been his idea all along.

After Massey resigned as KFC chairman, the company began to struggle and its stock performance declined. Part of this was due to KFC initiatives that failed, but much of the trouble had to do with the performance of franchise stocks in general. By August 1970 even Colonel Harland Sanders asked Massey to come back.

"Wouldn't it be a good thing for you to keep your eye on Kentucky Fried Chicken stock, and when you think it has reached the lowest point it is likely to go, yourself and some of your associates, together with banks and mutual funds you could influence, buy up control and come settle down in our new headquarters building here in Kentucky?" Sanders asked Massey in an August 25, 1970 letter.

Massey was also irritated by the fact that Brown didn't want to bring in new executives to help him run the company. "I had left that company saying that John would have to bring a president and an operating officer in. He had committed to do that in front of the board; I asked the board to make it a matter of record that it be done. But John remained as president. He wanted to sign as chairman, president, and chief executive officer."

Massey was so convinced that KFC needed a new president to assist and, to a certain degree, counteract Brown, that he even talked about it to Rockwell International President Bob Anderson, a friend of Massey's brother Harry, who lived in Pittsburgh, Pennsylvania.

"He asked me if I'd become president of KFC," Anderson said many years later. "It didn't interest me too much. I told him that there were a lot of things that I wanted to do in my life, but as someone who had built some glamorous cars and who was working on the space program, I just couldn't tell my friends that I had left to become president of Kentucky Fried Chicken."

About this time Massey's friend John Hill and Heublein Chief Executive Officer Stewart Watson, who had known each other for years, had a theoretical discussion about the possibility of Heublein buying KFC.[21] Those discussions led to talks between Watson and Massey. However, Massey was nervous about how Brown would react if he found out about the secret merger discussions. So after working out an agreed price for KFC, Massey asked Watson to approach Brown about the idea as if Massey had nothing to do with it. Watson did so.

A few weeks later Brown called Massey to tell him that Heublein wanted to buy KFC. Massey played dumb and arranged it so that he and Watson would pretend that they had never met when they were introduced in Brown's presence. Massey and Watson even prearranged a bit of haggling back and forth so that Brown would be under the impression that the negotiations were real.

"When we got up to New York they made an offer a little bit less than the agreed price," Massey said. "This was part of the way we were going to do the deal. John just said absolutely no. And I said, 'John, I have to agree with you. You can't do that. It's just not enough.' So they stood by their figures and then raised them a little bit, and finally that's it, and John said, 'Let's you and I go in the other room and talk.' So for an hour we talked."

Shut up in a room together, Massey convinced Brown to take the offer. He never admitted to Brown that he had planned the whole thing.

Under the deal that was worked out, Heublein purchased KFC for $239 million, about $70 million of which went to

Massey. A year later Brown resigned from KFC to run for governor of Kentucky.

Now in his early sixties, and with KFC's early challenges as a national company behind it, the idea of an extremely enjoyable retirement must have at least occurred to Jack Massey. However, 1967 and 1968 were years in which Massey did just about everything except retire. He formed an investment firm that eventually evolved into Nashville's first modern-day venture capital company. He put together a group of investors which bought a small Nashville-based bank. He began focusing his charitable efforts on a small, financially strapped Baptist college called Belmont, and he announced his intention to help build a traditional business training program there.

But the most important thing he did was start a for-profit hospital chain.

*J*ack Massey's entrepreneurial tendencies were contagious, sometimes too much so. In the late 1940s Vanderbilt medical student Jeff Pennington noticed that the school bookstore was selling microscopes for considerably more than Massey Surgical Supply. Pennington worked out a deal with Massey whereby he bought twenty microscopes at wholesale prices from the surgical supply company and sold them to his classmates.

Everything seemed to be working out fine until the bookstore found out about it and complained to the dean. "Would you like to get kicked out of school?" the dean asked Pennington when he found out about his side venture.

Massey felt bad about the whole episode, and years later he offered his friend the chance to buy insider stock in Kentucky Fried Chicken. Unfortunately, Pennington turned down that offer. "He had utmost confidence in the chicken business from the start," Pennington said. "He didn't have any doubts about it. I did, but he didn't. Unfortunately, I did."

6

THE STUPID SEVEN

HOSPITAL CORPORATION OF AMERICAN IS arguably the most important company in Nashville history. That being the case, it is not surprising that there are many versions of how it came about and who was responsible for starting it.

One thing that is clear, however, is that several relationships were key to the formation of HCA. The most important of those was between Massey and Nashville cardiologist Dr. Thomas Frist Sr.

Frist's life paralleled Massey's in many ways. Born in Meridian, Mississippi, Frist's father died when he was eight years old, and his mother had to support him and his siblings by converting the family home into a boarding house. One of those tenants was a doctor who owned his own small hospital. He became Frist's father figure (a role akin to Massey's uncle Alex) and gave the fourteen-year-old Frist a job.

"I worked in the hospital assisting the nurses and order-lies," Frist later said. "I became an expert orderly, cleaning bed pans and helping people in their rooms and pushing wheel-chairs, taking the people to and from the operating room and the emergency room. I did a great deal to help run the hospital, so I got to know all about hospitals."

Frist graduated from the Vanderbilt Medical School in 1933 and set up a practice in Nashville along with an older doctor named Will Cate. Like most physicians of that era, Frist didn't make much money. He had to supplement his income by doing physicals for the Interstate Life Insurance Company (for one dollar a head) and by treating patients at the Tennessee State Prison. Frist's involvement at the prison led to one of the first times he made a major purchase from Massey Surgical Supply.

"I put on a program of tuberculosis detection, and I found a hundred inmates out of two thousand had TB, so I started a TB hospital there," Frist later told an interviewer. "I dealt with Mr. Massey a great deal in ordering supplies for the penitentiary. That was in 1936, and I came to know Mr. Massey very well at that time."

During the 1930s Frist's office was in the Doctor's Build-ing at 710 Church Street, while Massey Drugs was located in the Bennie Dillon Building next door. After World War II, when Massey moved his surgical supply business to 2110 West End, Massey convinced Frist to follow him there and sold him a house just three doors down.

The two men developed a friendship that involved their families; Frist became the family physician for the Massey fam-ily, and he and Massey began playing gin rummy together (a habit that would last for the rest of their lives). By the late 1950s Frist had developed a large referral practice from all over Middle Tennessee, southern Kentucky, and northern Alabama.

Another piece of the HCA puzzle was Henry Hooker, who was a generation younger than Frist Sr. He got to know

Frist through his father, legendary Nashville trial lawyer John Jay Hooker Sr. After Henry graduated from Tulane Law School and returned to Nashville, Frist tried to help him by sending business his way.

"Sometimes Dr. Frist would pick me up and take me with him when he was going out to see a patient at some rural hospital," said Henry Hooker. "He would take me with him, and we would ride in the car and talk about various things."

The first time Hooker did legal work for Frist, it involved Park Manor, a high-rise residential project for elderly tenants that got into financial trouble during its construction. A few months later, in the summer of 1960, Hooker and Frist were still working together when Frist became one of seven Nashville physicians (the others being Robert McClellan, John Tudor, Tom Nesbitt, Addison Scoville, Douglas Riddell, and James Calloway) who organized a medical institution called Park View. This facility—the Park View Convalescent Hospital and Nursing Home—would eventually become the flagship hospital of a new Massey-related venture called Hospital Corporation of America.

Architect Donald Cowan later said he could remember the exact conversation that started Park View. In 1957 Cowan designed a Dickson, Tennessee, facility called Goodlark Hospital. Frist was a consulting physician for Goodlark, and Frist often took Cowan on house calls or medical rounds with him (in much the same way, Frist took Henry Hooker around with him). According to Cowan, Frist first suggested the idea of a physician-owned hospital in Nashville on a drive back from Dickson.

"He started talking about the idea that if these country doctors [L. C., William, and Jimmy Jackson] could run a successful hospital, then why can't some real doctors in Nashville do the same thing?" Cowan said. "The next day he came by my office and started thumbing through the phone book, looking at doctors' names. And by the time he was finished, he had picked a handful of doctors he wanted us to ask to invest."

According to Cowan, the group held a meeting at John Tudor's house a few weeks later, which is when it hired Cowan to design Park View. Cowan also said that part of his job was to organize the investors and to line up financing.

Meanwhile, McClellan was also doing a lot of legwork—so much, in fact, that some of the original seven investors later described him, not Frist, as their leader. "He [McClellan] was a visionary; he had energy; he could turn his ideas into reality," Tudor said.

McClellan wanted to build a nursing home because Nashville had few good nursing homes at the time. According to Tudor and Nesbitt, it was McClellan who got the investors together and arranged financing. McClellan also picked the real estate—an acre-and-a-half lot adjacent to Centennial Park that the group purchased from the Knights of Columbus.

As Jack Massey had experienced when he first began telling people he was buying Kentucky Fried Chicken, the seven Park View investors had to live with the fact that many of their colleagues thought the physician-driven venture was a bad idea.

"There were colleagues and others who thought it was a crazy idea," Tudor said. "I can't remember names, but we were known at the moment as the 'Stupid Seven.'" By the time Park View broke ground in February 1961 it had evolved into part hospital, part nursing home. The number of investors, all of whom put in either six thousand or eleven thousand dollars, had grown to twenty-five.

Most of the new investors were physicians who would theoretically be referring patients to the facility, such as Ben Alper, a physician who had founded Vanderbilt's arthritis clinic a few years earlier. "More than fifty percent of my practice was out of state, and when they would come down [for] extensive workups in those days, I needed a place to put them in the hospital," he said. "At that time in Nashville there was a shortage of beds for just about every kind of patient, unless they were critically ill."

Another "second-wave" investor was Dr. Kirk Todd, a plastic surgeon who started his Nashville practice in 1946. Todd said it wasn't difficult to get physician-investors as the project gained momentum, because so many doctors wanted to practice medicine out of the reach of Nashville's existing hospitals.

"Doctors are just like everyone in that they are anxious to have a place where they can practice and where no one can tell them what to do," Todd said. "At many other hospitals, if the hospital administrator comes around and tells you that you need to do such and such, you have to do it. So there is someone who is indirectly in charge of you. But if we own our own hospital, we can tell them to go fly a kite."

At least four of the twenty-five investors were not physicians: Henry Hooker and his brother John Jay Hooker Jr. (also a lawyer), General Hospital Administrator Bill Crosley (hired to be administrator of the new facility), and *Nashville Banner* sportswriter Fred Russell. It was Frist's idea to bring Russell on board because the two men had known each other for so long. In fact, back when he was in medical school, Frist had even dabbled in sportswriting for extra cash.

"Everyone knew Freddy Russell, and he added sort of another dimension of respectability to our group," Tudor said. "Freddy was an icon in the community, and he added an aura of prestige."

Park View is an interesting business story in itself because its owners were able to reshape their plans to make the venture profitable. Within a few months of the new facility's opening its owners realized that their business plan needed to be changed. The demand for hospital beds was much greater than the demand for nursing home beds, and the nursing home and hospital concept did not mix well.

"People came out of the hospital into the nursing home and they would expect the same type of care that they had in the hospital, and for much, much reduced cost," Frist later explained. "It was not very practical."

A bigger problem was that Blue Cross, the dominant health insurance company for the area, did not recognize Park View as a hospital, because under Blue Cross's definition, a health-care facility wasn't a hospital until an operation had been performed there. Nesbitt took care of that shortcoming.

"We found an unused storage room in the basement that was barely large enough to accommodate the necessary operating table, anesthesia machine, portable lighting machines, and sufficient sterilization equipment to perform what would be considered a major operative procedure," Nesbitt wrote several years later. "On the door was placed a big sign that said 'Operating Room.' About a week later I performed a right ureterolithotomy (removal of a ureteral calculus), under a general anesthetic, from a readily accessible mid-third position in a young, thin, healthy male, without incident."

Park View thus told Blue Cross that it was now a "full-service" hospital. But knowing that such an arrangement would not do for long, the hospital immediately got to work on a surgical wing and fifty-bed expansion, growth that required the recruitment of more physician-investors. With the opening of the new surgical wing in October 1965, Park View completely phased out its function as a nursing home.

About this time the Park View team had lost one of its original members. Architect Donald Cowan designed the original Park View building, and in doing so added some touches to it (such as blue brick) which architect Batey Gresham would later copy when he designed many of Hospital Corporation of America's hospitals. In 1964 Park View's physician-investors hired Cowan to design the surgical wing and told him that it should cost about $500,000. But as Cowan got to work on the wing, the project grew.

"We had many meetings, and doctors would come to the office and they kept adding and adding and adding to the project, like a woman building a house," Cowan said many years later. The bids came in at nearly twice the original estimate, and Cowan told the physician-owners that since the overall coast of the project was going up, his fee would have to go up as well. "This infuriated Frist," Cowan said. "I remember he came to my office and hit the drawing board so hard that a picture came off the wall in the next room.

"That night, all the doctors and I had a meeting in what we called the 'war room' in the Park View basement. And at that meeting, right in front of everyone, Frist stood up and said to me, 'Donald, you are either stupid or crooked.' And so I got up and said, 'Tommy, you choose your weapon,' and walked out."

By 1966 Park View had 194 beds, a full-service operating room, a clinical laboratory, and a pharmacy. It also had quite a few owners—sixty-five, to be exact. And running the facility was getting more complicated. Hospitals constantly need upgrades, and every time Park View needed a new piece of equipment the company had to take out a loan or find new investors. Many of the investors were concerned about long-term estate planning, and would have preferred to transfer their ownership stakes into something more liquid. Meanwhile, the physician-owners had begun to notice something about Park View: it turned a profit.

"We weren't businessmen, and we didn't know what to do with it," Dr. Morse Kochtitzky said. "It was making money and that was not our purpose, and we wanted to get someone who knew what the hell they were doing to run the hospital."

In this context, Atlanta attorney Eli Freedman, a cousin of Park View physician-owner Ben Alper, suggested selling the hospital to the city in exchange for tax-free municipal bonds. Henry Hooker investigated the idea, and he and Dr. Thomas Frist Sr. met with Nashville Mayor Beverly Briley about the possibility. Briley went along with the suggestion and recommended that the Metropolitan Council of Davidson County acquire the hospital for $5.25 million in bonds.

Had it all gone according to plan, Park View would have become Nashville's second public hospital. The plan for the city to buy Park View passed its first two council readings. However, on August 21, 1967, the *Nashville Tennessean* contained a very stern editorial about the transaction.

"It is a tax dodge, legal under federal law, to benefit the current hospital owners," the paper claimed. The editorial, which grudgingly endorsed the proposal, raised so many questions about it that the council rejected the proposal on its third reading. The owners of Park View Hospital thus went back to the drawing board.

A few weeks later Henry Hooker met with Frist and discussed an alternative plan for the hospital—turning it into the flagship facility for a chain of proprietary hospitals that would be franchised around the country. Frist said he liked the idea but said that there was no way that they could pull it off without his friend Jack Massey.

"He was the main man with the business know-how; he was obviously the only experienced business person in the crowd, and the only person with money in the crowd," Frist said. "Mr. Massey always thought big in everything he did."

So where did the idea of building a chain of for-profit hospitals come from? This question would be debated often during the succeeding decades in Nashville.

When HCA was founded, franchising was the big trend on Wall Street and an obsession in Nashville. Of course, some of the most important franchised companies, such as McDonald's and Holiday Inn, had been turning a profit for years. But thanks largely to the success of Kentucky Fried Chicken, companies with franchising as the cornerstone of their business plan were soaring on Wall Street in 1968. It seemed like everyone in Nashville was trying to cash in on the trend, starting short-lived franchise companies such as Tex Ritter's Chuckwagon, Al Hirt's Sandwich Salons, and Eddy Arnold's Tennessee Fried Chicken.

The most interesting of all the KFC wannabes was Minnie Pearl's Fried Chicken, a short-lived company that is oddly linked to HCA's early history. Minnie Pearl's was the brainchild of Henry Hooker and his brother John Jay, a colorful, energetic, and outspoken attorney who had narrowly lost the Democratic nomination for governor in 1966.

As KFC grew and its franchisees and shareholders became wealthy, the Hooker brothers became convinced that there was room for a second fried chicken chain. Thanks to their salesmanship and the help of Nashville's two newspapers (both of which shamelessly promoted the company), they sold stock in the new venture for fifty cents a share to some of Nashville's elite. Several people from various corners of the South, most of whom had no experience running restaurants, agreed to sign on as franchisees.

The idea caught fire, and by February 1968 the company had sold the rights to almost three hundred franchised stores (only five of which were actually in operation). The company went public on May 2, 1968, and its stock rose from $20 to $40.50 that first day.

The Hookers did a great job selling the company, but within the next few months they would fall victim to hype, as Minnie Pearl's stock—by this time traded under the name Performance Systems Inc.—rose to over fifty-five dollars before crashing to less than a dollar.

"It could have been a great company," Massey later said, when asked about Minnie Pearl's. "But they didn't have the product, the service, nor the supervision that they had to have to have a good company."

Nevertheless, when the fate of Park View was being debated, Minnie Pearl's was flying high. In fact, among the many Nashvillians who made sizeable profits from Minnie Pearl stock were Park View physician-owners Thomas Frist Sr. and Morse Kochtitzky.

It was in this context, according to Henry Hooker, that he and Dr. Thomas Frist Sr. first discussed the idea of a proprietary hospital chain. As for the idea's origin, Henry said that it actually came from his brother John Jay.

"My brother and I were walking in a parking lot, and we were discussing the whole Park View thing," Henry Hooker said. "I told him that running a hospital was kind of like running a hotel, except that instead of getting X dollars a night you are getting Y dollars a night. And he said to me, 'Well, why don't you go around the country and franchise them?' And I told him that was a pretty interesting idea. I'd like to claim credit for it, but the truth is, that is the way it happened."

A different explanation of how the idea got started came from Dr. Thomas Frist Jr., who was also a member of the group. Many years earlier Massey had given Thomas Frist Sr.'s children shares of stock in Kentucky Fried Chicken as Christmas presents. That stock did so well that Tommy Jr. began dabbling in the market. When he was serving in the Air Force from 1965 to 1968 he was constantly buying and selling shares of companies, sometimes based on Massey's tips.

"I know that on at least one occasion when I came home from the military, I went out to the Kentucky Fried Chicken headquarters on Sidco Drive to wait outside his door just to thank him for giving me that stock and for all the other things that he had done for me," Frist Jr. said. "And while I was up here, he told me about other things he knew about."

During this time Massey asked Frist Jr. if he had any interest in working for Kentucky Fried Chicken when he got out of the air force. Massey even sent Tommy a letter in which he suggested the idea that he help operate KFC's roast beef division.

Stock profiteering turned Frist Jr. into someone who was always on the lookout for entrepreneurial ideas. And one of the companies that Tommy Frist was interested in during this period was Medi-Centers of America, a Memphis-based nursing home chain started by Holiday Inn co-founders Wallace Johnson and Kemmons Wilson, who was the father of one of Frist's college friends. Interviewed many years after the formation of HCA, Tommy Frist Jr. said that when his father and the other physician-investors were trying to decide what to do with Park View, he suggested that they try to sell the hospital to Medi-Centers.

"Some of them even went down there," Frist Jr. said, "but Wilson and Johnson said no." He added that after Medi-Center turned them down, he began trying to convince his father to start a chain of hospitals.

The other thing that should be pointed out about the group discussing the formation of a hospital chain is that one of its members was already part-owner of several hospitals. Dr. Thomas Frist Sr. didn't necessarily give the impression that he had a mind for business. But those who knew him well knew that behind that gentle bedside manner beat the heart of a calculating entrepreneur and accomplished physician.

Frist Sr. was associate professor of clinical medicine at Vanderbilt and had also once been chairman of the board of Metropolitan General Hospital in Nashville. A cardiologist who made house calls as far away as northern Alabama, he had a way of befriending just about everyone he met.

After participating in the formation of Park View, Frist was frequently called by doctors throughout the South for advice on how to start similar institutions. He was always willing to help because it never occurred to him to do otherwise. And along the way Frist had learned a lot about hospital development.

One example of this phenomenon was in Lewisburg, Tennessee, where a general practitioner named William Taylor wanted to form a hospital. Unable to get any local physicians to take part, Taylor approached Frist. No longer on good terms with Park View architect Donald Cowan, Frist asked a Nashville firm called Howard Neilson Line Batey & O'Brien to come up with the design for a tiny, forty-bed facility.

The firm gave the job to young architect Tom Batey, and he never forgot the experience. "I remember that Dr. Taylor said that if we are not successful as a hospital, we need to build it in such a manner so it could be converted to a motel if need be," Batey said.

Batey also remembered that Frist was very interested in the architecture of the hospital. "When I was designing it, he was very busy with his practice, but he still wanted to talk with me about it," Batey said. "So I would sit in his office during the day and in between his appointments with patients he would come in and talk to me about the plans. Then we'd go to his house for dinner, and we would sit at his dinner table with his wife and talk about the plans. We would even go out together on house calls and talk about the plans."

When Taylor Hospital finally broke ground, it had five investors: Taylor, Frist, Taylor's two sisters, and Lewisburg attorney John Wallace. After it opened, its first administrator was Dr. Taylor's wife, Polly, who had no experience in hospital administration but apparently didn't need any. "She ran a tight ship," Batey said.

Frist was also asked by two doctors in Erin, Tennessee, for advice on how to build a hospital there, and by a group of about twenty doctors in the Nashville suburb of Donelson for advice on how to build one there. Whenever Frist would start to talk to these doctors he would do so with attorney Henry

Hooker and architect Tom Batey. It is no wonder that the idea for a hospital company came about.

Unlike some of his fellow founders, Jack Massey didn't claim to have come up with the idea for HCA. Nevertheless, Massey is unique in the group in that he is probably the only member whose role was absolutely critical. In other words, if Hooker, Frist Sr., or Frist Jr. were removed from the picture, the company might still have gotten off the ground. But if Massey were removed from the list, it's hard to imagine how HCA could have grown, acquired hospitals, or borrowed money during its first two years.

In September 1969 Massey made a speech to the Nashville Security Dealers Association on the subject of HCA. He said that in the spring of 1968 he and Frist Sr. believed that the health-care industry was growing fast.

"The need for facilities is becoming almost impossible to fund, despite the billions of dollars that have been dumped into new hospital construction by the federal government," he said. "Why, we thought, cannot the efficiencies of business management, the techniques proven in industry, be applied successfully to the operation of hospitals, toward a solution of many of the problems of the health-care field?"

Regardless of whose idea it was, there were a lot of important details to be worked out between conception and execution. Several meetings between founders, or people who were thinking about becoming founders, took place between February and April of 1968 (one was at the Master's golf tournament in Augusta, Georgia). It wasn't an easy time for Massey, for it was in the middle of this process that Elizabeth, his wife of thirty-eight years, died of an aneurysm.

Discussed at some length in these meetings was which made more sense: building a chain of hospitals owned and operated by the company, or building a chain of hospitals franchised by the company and owned and operated by someone else. Massey, knowing that running a hospital was far more complicated and delicate than running a restaurant, made it clear that he wanted nothing to do with the project unless the company owned all the hospitals.

Another question was whether the company would just buy existing hospitals or also build new ones. The decision was made to do both. With the concept of new hospitals in mind, the group invited architect Tom Batey to the meetings.

The company came up with a financial strategy that required the least amount of actual cash. In the end, the founders started with an initial investment of $5.25 million, plus $9 million in short-term construction loans. But most of the early acquisitions of existing hospitals would be made by issuing stock.

"This is the reason we couldn't have done this without Mr. Massey," Tommy Frist Jr. said. "I mean, during the first eleven months of our existence we managed to acquire about a dozen hospitals prior to going public, and we didn't do it with cash but by issuing what I call 'Chinese Money.' That took a lot of blind faith on the part of these doctors who were selling us their hospitals. And we could not have convinced them to do this had it not been for Mr. Massey."

There continued to be uncertainty as to who would take part in this rather unusual venture. Massey was somewhat reluctant to get involved at first, but he finally decided to plunge ahead after other members of the group assured him that he wouldn't have to do very much work—a promise that didn't turn out to be accurate. Many years later Massey's daughter said that he agreed to be a founder of the company at a meeting at his house in February 1968. "It was right after my mother died," Barbara Massey Rogers said.

For a while, Frist Sr. said he might drop out, concerned that he wouldn't be able to balance his medical practice with helping to run the company. "I had such mixed emotions I couldn't enthusiastically condone the idea," he later said. But after some reflection he changed his mind.

Thomas Frist Jr. was always certain that he wanted to be a part of the new company, although his excitement was tempered by the fact that his father wanted him to devote his full attention to being a doctor rather than a businessman. "Dr. Frist [Sr.] was very anxious for Tommy to go ahead and be a physician, a doctor, and a surgeon," Massey said in 1978. "But Tommy wanted to be a businessman, there's no question about it. . . . Tommy was persistent enough to say that he would make his choice to come with the company."

John Jay Hooker Jr., who attended many of the early meetings, did not become a founder or director, in part because he and Massey were the principal operators of rival fried chicken chains.

Gene Kidd, a Baptist Hospital executive whom Massey had brought into the group, changed his mind and decided that he would stay with Baptist Hospital.

Job security and a desire to spend as much time at home as possible were probably the main reasons Kidd decided to stay at Baptist. But, interviewed many years later, Batey said he had another theory as to why Gene Kidd changed his mind.

"I was very much under the impression that Gene was going to be working for HCA," Batey said. "Well, one day we all flew out to Erin, Tennessee, with Tommy [Frist Jr.] flying his Apache [airplane]. There is a little grass runway on the edge of town where Tommy landed. We got ready to leave that night, and it was dark and there were no lights on the runway. So one of the doctors parked his car on the end of the runway and turned his lights on, and that is what enabled us to take off. Gene Kidd was not in any more meetings after that."

By the time the group approached Park View's physicians, it consisted of Massey, Henry and John Jay Hooker, Frist Sr., and Frist Jr. and it had come up with the name Hospital

Corporation of America. The company was first capitalized with $5.25 million, with each of the four original investors contributing one-fourth of that amount. It is believed that all four of the original investors—even Massey—borrowed most of the money from Third National Bank or Capital City Bank.

Hospital Corporation of America never would have gotten off the ground, however, without Park View. After preliminary meetings with people who represented the hospital's physician-owners, the presentation to all of them took place on May 6, 1968, at the Woodmont Country Club.

At that meeting, Massey and Frist Sr. explained that the group was proposing that Park View's physician-owners sell their hospital to HCA for a combination of cash ($1.3 million) and stock, with one share of Park View to be traded for 34,000 shares of stock in HCA. HCA planned to acquire existing hospitals and build others. Massey and Frist said the company intended to run the facilities in a manner that would ensure their profitability, much as the group had already run Park View Hospital.

Hal Kennedy, who had handled public relations for Kentucky Fried Chicken and Massey for the two previous years, had been asked by Massey to attend the meeting. Interviewed many years later, Kennedy said that there were two things that he remembered. One was that Massey showed Park View's physician-investors a chart that depicted what might theoretically happen to their stock value if they agreed to be acquired by the new company. The other is that one of the physicians present (probably McClellan) stood up at one point and wanted to know who Kennedy was.

"He said that we are not going any further until they figure out who this guy is in the back of the room," Kennedy said. "I guess he thought I was a reporter or something."

The Park View physicians were no doubt impressed by the group's credibility. The Hooker brothers were riding high with Minnie Pearl's Chicken, while Frist Sr. was a physician, friend, and fellow investor whom they knew and trusted. But of course Massey had the most impressive resume. He was effectively the founder of Baptist Hospital, the man whose surgical supply business they had known for years, the capitalist who had just made a mint from selling drumsticks. And by the time the meeting took place, Massey was convinced that this was an incredible business opportunity.

"I made the statement . . . that we would have one hundred hospitals in ten years, and that gives you some idea of what I thought about it," Massey said in 1978. "I knew the possibility was there . . . there was never a worry in my mind that we wouldn't be successful."

In an interview that took place the same year, Frist said that, in his opinion, the reason the doctors decided to go ahead with the plan was Massey. "I think they went with us because of Mr. Massey's reputation, his success with Kentucky Fried Chicken, and with everything he had done," Frist acknowledged. "The timing of the idea was right because the doctors saw all the franchised companies starting. They saw the opportunity for making a great deal of money."

The vote to go along with the proposal was 64–1. The only dissenter was Dr. Sumpter Anderson, an anesthesiologist who later admitted that he had never voted for anything in his life.

About two weeks later the *Tennessean* published its first-ever story about Hospital Corporation of America. "The founders of the corporation believe that private enterprise can build and operate hospitals with an efficiency which will help combat the spiraling costs of hospitalization," Frist Sr. was quoted as saying. The article went on to say that HCA planned to put together a large central hospital with smaller satellite hospitals within a radius of 100 miles. "This will provide a cost reduction in contract services, warehouses, technical equipment, maintenance, computers, microfilming services, purchasing of commissary supplies and pharmaceuticals," he added.

By this time HCA's board consisted of Massey, Henry Hooker, Frist Sr., Frist Jr., Bob Brueck, John Neff, Robert McClellan, Richard Ottarson (Frist's CPA), and Omega Sattler (Massey's administrative assistant).

Jack Massey, the pharmacist from Georgia, was the chairman of an organization of which few Americans could even conceive: a hospital company.

*J*ack Massey dressed impeccably. He not only wore a coat and tie every day of his working life, he wore a stylish, pressed coat and tie that fit him perfectly. One of his close friends remembered that Massey frequently wore French-cuff shirts. When Colonel Harland Sanders first laid eyes on the man, he immediately described Massey as "slick."

Massey not only thought his own appearance was important, he did not tolerate poor dress habits by people who worked for him or with him. One on occasion he advised a Kentucky Fried Chicken franchisee to stop wearing white socks with his suits; that franchisee (Dave Thomas) took the advice and later credited Massey with helping him to improve his appearance.

Another time, Massey noticed that Tommy Frist Jr. was wearing black socks that were so short that when he crossed his legs, they exposed parts of his calves. The next day when he arrived at work, Frist found a brand-new pair of long black socks sitting on his desk.

Vic Campbell, who spent many, many hours with Massey after the HCA co-founder came back to the company as its president in 1975, said Massey had subtle ways of giving him tips on how to dress.

"During a trip to New York with Mr. Massey in the early seventies, we were in a men's store looking at shirts and ties," Campbell recalled. "Mr. Massey picked up two ties and asked me which one I liked best. Being a twenty-seven- or twenty-eight-year-old, I obviously picked the brighter and wilder of the two ties. Of course, Mr. Massey said nothing and replaced the ties.

"Late that evening, he told me he had a small gift for me. It was the more conservative of the two ties."

7

CHINESE MONEY

THERE WERE TWO REASONS THAT Nashville, Tennessee, in 1968 was a great place and time to start a chain of for-profit hospitals.

Historically, the great American medical institutions were in the Northeast, funded by prestigious universities, strong local governments, and an influential Catholic Church. When the South began to develop industrially, many parts of it did not have hospitals. Population centers such as Nashville and Atlanta eventually built them, although more often than not with the help of Northern foundations such as the Rockefeller-funded General Education Board. But smaller communities could not afford to do so.

Because of this, many Southern hospitals, like Park View, were financed by physicians. Even though doctor-owned hospitals were not as respected as some other hospitals, they served the needs of many people who did not live near big cities. But they had a long-term problem: as the cost of medical technology rose in the 1950s and 1960s, physician-owners had to take out more loans to get their hospitals updated. Eventually, they began to wonder if they would ever reap any money from their investments.

The second reason was Medicare. In 1965 the federal government started the Medicare system to provide guaranteed health care for elderly Americans. Within two years of Medicare's implementation the amount of time older people spent in the hospital more than doubled, filling beds and creating a demand for new facilities.

In its early years Medicare's system of reimbursement— known as "cost-plus"—was simple and rather generous. When a patient went to the hospital, a doctor diagnosed his condition and treated him. The hospital sent the government the bill for its cost plus a fee, and the government reimbursed the hospital. Few questions were asked.

"The government came in and basically said that they would pay hospitals reasonable and standard fees," said Bob Brueck, HCA's first chief operating officer. "So whatever we were charging, that's what they were paying." It is not surprising that health-care costs rose at twice the rate of inflation during the first four years in which Medicare existed.

When HCA was first being discussed, the idea behind it seemed rather simple. At a time when equipment was becoming more expensive and medical-care billing more complicated, it made sense for hospitals to combine their operations. Not only could merged hospitals save money by sharing expensive equipment, they could also save by buying supplies and pharmaceuticals in bulk. If those merged hospitals had a shrewd negotiator such as Jack Massey on their side, so much the better.

The people who founded HCA also said their company would do well because privately owned operations were simply better run than those owned by the government. "The main purpose was to take the politics out of medicine that exist so strongly in all government-run hospitals, such as city hospitals and university hospitals," Thomas Frist Sr. said a few years later.

Many of these arguments sounded logical, but when it came to acquisitions, it hardly seemed as though HCA had a coherent strategy during its first year. Rather than focusing on one geographic area, one facility size, or one type of market, the company basically bought just about any hospital whose owners would sell to them.

One of the first was Taylor Hospital in Lewisburg, the forty-bed facility in which Frist had been an investor and Batey had been the architect. Others included Epperson Hospital in Athens, Tennessee (where Dr. Robert McClellan had a relative interested in developing a hospital); Smith County Hospital in Carthage, Tennessee; Selma Baptist Hospital in Selma, Alabama; and the Miller Medical Clinic in Nashville.

Word spread quickly about HCA in the health-care world. In Roanoke, Virginia, the physician-owners of an inner-city institution called Lewis-Gale Hospital were trying to finance a new suburban building for their hospital. Hospital Administrator David Williamson suggested he visit HCA and talk to its principals about whether the new company might be willing to take over the hospital and build the new building. In August 1968 Lewis-Gale became the sixth existing hospital acquired by HCA.

HCA also broke ground on a handful of hospitals—some tiny, some medium-sized—in markets where the company could put together enough physicians willing to refer their patients to them. Four of these were forty-bed facilities in Erin, Smithville, and McMinnville, Tennessee, and Morganfield, Kentucky (where, incidentally, HCA used the same architectural plans that Tom Batey had come up with for the Taylor Hospital in Lewisburg a few years earlier).

But the big projects HCA broke ground on during its first year were 200-bed hospitals in Macon and Albany, Georgia, and in Chattanooga, Tennessee. "We bet the ship on those three new hospitals," Tommy Frist Jr. said years later.

All the original HCA team members brought something to the table. In Frist Jr.'s case, his ability to pilot a plane was quite critical in the company's early years.

"If we hadn't had that airplane, we would not be as big as we are today," Massey said in 1978. "Tommy practically lived in that airplane for the first few years, going out talking to people about buying hospitals." Frist wasn't the only pilot on HCA's early team; Chief Operating Officer Bob Brueck had been an air force pilot, and he and Frist often took turns at the controls.

Meanwhile HCA ran its headquarters out of what was probably the most unimpressive commercial building of any growing company in America, a small, run-down house next to Park View Hospital.

"I came down here in 1972 to interview, and they were still there at that time," Vic Campbell said several years later. "I jumped in a cab at the airport and told the cab driver that I wanted to go to the headquarters of Hospital Corporation of America. So he drives me across town and stops at this little house. And I said to him, 'No, you don't understand. I want to go to the headquarters of HCA.' And he pointed at it and said, 'Boy, that is it!' Now, the only place I had ever worked at before was DuPont, at a massive headquarters building in downtown Wilmington, Delaware. And so my first thought when I saw this place was what a waste of time this job interview was going to be." Thirty-two years later Campbell still worked for HCA.

In late 1968 HCA made its most impressive purchase up until that time, acquiring the Johnston-Willis hospital in Richmond, Virginia. Not only was Johnston-Willis, with three hundred beds, the largest facility in the small chain, it was also one of the few with a long history, having been founded in 1909 as the Johnston-Willis Sanitarium.

The meeting at which Johnston-Willis's trustees voted to sell the hospital was a memorable one. The doctors had elected physician Tommy Johns to be their spokesman, but they had also hired a financial consultant to negotiate for them. After an extensive meeting, Johns wanted to sell the hospital to HCA, but the financial consultant, who happened to be blind, was trying to hold out for a higher price than Massey was willing to offer.

"Mr. Wheat [the financial consultant] was trying to drive a bargain that was just unreal," Massey recalled years later. "He would not be realistic about it. He worked on commission, and the bigger the deal, the bigger the commission he'd get, so that had something to do with it."

As they stood up to leave, Massey said he wanted to say goodbye to Johns. Wheat told him not to. "Well, he's blind, totally blind," Massey said. "So we went by there anyway."

When he and HCA's other representatives got there, Massey told Johns that he was making a terrible mistake to let Wheat squelch the transaction. "We made you a fair price," Massey said. "If you want your stock to be worth something, then you've got to deal on a fair price." Massey and Johns worked out an agreement.

It was Massey's recommendation that HCA hire Brueck, former assistant to Gene Kidd at Baptist Hospital, to be its first chief operating officer. "Bob had worked with me, and I knew him very well," Massey said. "He was an operating man, and a good one. That we had to have."

Other than Brueck's hiring, Massey focused on the financial side of HCA and did not get heavily involved in the hiring of administrators, the construction of hospitals, or the manner in which the hospitals were being run. He didn't play a major role in hiring other people at HCA, and he certainly didn't throw his weight around when it came to hiring vendors.

It might seem logical, for instance, that as HCA got into the business of building hospitals, it would have used the same architect (Hart-Freeland-Roberts) and the same general contractor (J. A. Jones) that Baptist Hospital had used when Massey was the president of its board from 1948 until 1960. But HCA didn't let either of those vendors bid on any of its new projects. Instead, the new hospital company became the best thing that ever happened to a young architect and a young general contractor who both happened to be at the right place at the right time.

The first of these two men was Batey Gresham. Gresham, who happened to be the first cousin of Tom Batey, was only a couple of years out of architecture school at Auburn University when he first met Frist Sr.. After his blood pressure registered high on a physical exam he took for the military, Gresham went to go see Frist as a patient. Frist remained friends with Batey Gresham and his wife, Ann, for the next several years. "I think one time Dr. Frist prescribed my wife some medicine on the phone, and she baked him a pound cake," Gresham said.

Then came the phone conversation that changed his life. In 1967 Gresham and his new partner, Fleming Smith, successfully bid on a housing project in Decatur, Georgia. Gresham was so excited that he wanted to tell someone. Unable to find any close friends to tell, he called Dr. Frist on a whim and told him the good news.

"He was very happy for us," Gresham remembered years later. "And then he told me that he and Tommy were thinking about an idea and that they wanted to talk to me about it."

Weeks later Gresham and Smith met with Frist and heard about his plans for the hospital chain. They gladly agreed to come up with a prototype for the three planned HCA hospitals in Chattanooga, Macon, and Albany—which, it had already been decided, would have identical floor plans to save money. Frist had several good ideas that he wanted his young architect friends to incorporate into the design.

"He took us out to Park View, gave us the tour, and showed us what architectural features he liked," Gresham said. "He liked windows at the end of the corridor—windows with low window sills so patients could see the ground outside from their bed. He liked colorful rooms that didn't look like the old hospital grays and greens. And he liked carpeted floors."

Gresham came up with three plans before he found one Frist liked. "On the third attempt we finally figured out what the key was," Gresham said. "It was the blue-glazed brick under the windows, just like Park View. So we went with the blue brick, and that blue brick hung around for a long time and it showed up on every prototype we did for the first five years or so. Dr. Frist [Sr.] loved it and everyone else hated it." Frist apparently never told Gresham that the blue brick had originally been the idea of Park View architect Donald Cowan.

Gresham and Smith went on to design every new hospital HCA built during its first ten years. By 1980 their architectural firm had nearly a hundred employees, most of whom worked on HCA business.

Nashville general contractor Joe Rodgers had similar good fortune. Rodgers came to Nashville in 1966 and started a construction company with $250 of his own money and six investors who each put up $125. About two years later Rodgers was invited to attend the Master's golf tournament in Augusta, Georgia, and to stay in a house in which several other people, including Thomas Frist Sr., were staying. During that weekend Rodgers heard about Frist's plans to build a hospital chain. When the elderly Frist asked the young Rodgers if he would like to build a small hospital for them in Erin, Tennessee, Rodgers said he would be delighted to do so.

For the next decade Rodgers Construction could hardly keep up with HCA and all the hospitals it wanted to build. The contracting firm, which did $1.2 million in business in 1967, did $10 million its third year of operation because of all of its HCA work, enabling Rodgers to pay back those who had originally invested in his business.

"I paid them eighty thousand dollars each for the stock that had cost them a hundred and twenty-five dollars only a couple of years earlier," Rodgers said. "Obviously, neither my investors nor I had any idea that HCA was going to appear out of nowhere and hire us."

From that point on, Rodgers Construction grew until its revenue hit $180 million its tenth year. "For many years I did almost nothing else other than build hospitals for HCA," Rodgers said.

A third Nashville business dramatically affected by HCA was the law firm Waller Lansden Dortch & Davis. When Massey, Frist, and others began talking about organizing a chain of proprietary hospitals, they knew that they needed an experienced securities lawyer, an area in which attorney Henry Hooker had limited background.

At this time Massey was using Nashville attorney Clarence Evans to do most of his legal work, but he decided to use a different attorney to do something as specialized as this. Frist met with a friend, attorney Dick Lansden, and Lansden put HCA's organizers together with his younger partners William "Billy" Waller Jr. and Bob McCullough. HCA remained one of Waller Lansden Dortch & Davis's largest clients for at least the next thirty-five years.

The experience of being a part of a company that was building and acquiring several hospitals while it was still hiring people to do all of this was something no one involved would ever forget. Years later the people who were a part of HCA in the early years emphasized how hard they worked and how much fun they had.

"My first official day with the company was January 2, 1969, although I had been working for the company as a 'consultant' of sorts for several months already," said Batey, head of construction in HCA's early years. "Sometime that morning Tommy [Frist Jr.] told me that we were going to be flying to Detroit to look at a hospital or do something. He said that we were meeting out at the airport at one o'clock. So I go out to the airport and get ready to board the plane, and he comes out and says that we aren't going to Detroit anymore, we are going to Chicago. So we go to Chicago, and I think I got home at about two o'clock in the morning."

Everyone was so caught up in the moment that the most basic questions sometimes went unanswered until someone had the courage to speak up.

"One time we were about to break ground on that hospital in Erin," Batey recalled, "and on the way back from Erin we stopped at Montgomery Bell State Park to have dinner. Now this is back when Joe Rodgers still smoked, and Dr. Frist was all over him about it, so he didn't do it in front of Frist. And so Joe was fuming and fidgeting because he wanted a cigarette, and finally he said, 'Dr. Frist, how do y'all plan on paying for this hospital?' And Dr. Frist said, 'Well, Joe, we've got a couple million dollars in the bank, so we thought we'd just pay cash for it.' So someone had put some money in the bank; I always figured it was Mr. Massey."

For the Albany hospital, HCA hired an administrator named Clayton McWhorter, a pharmacist who had previously been head of a not-for-profit hospital in that city. "We opened Albany one weekend, and the next weekend we opened Macon, and the third weekend we opened Chattanooga," McWhorter remembered. "That was a major undertaking for a young company, and a lot of what we had to do we did by the seat of our pants. And it was a heck of a learning process.

"I remember hiring an entirely new staff from scratch. I remember going to furniture stores in Albany to pick out furniture for the waiting areas at the last minute. And I also remember that, since the company didn't have procedure manuals yet, the administrators for the hospitals in Chattanooga and Macon and I decided to split that work into thirds, and we shared what each of us did."

HCA's young executives said that Massey, with his business acumen, and Frist Sr., with his ability to motivate, made quite a pair. "Doctor Frist was great at building physician relationships," McWhorter remembered. "But more importantly, he had that Midas touch of being able to pick you up. I don't know how many times he put his hand on my shoulder and said, 'Son, I don't know what we'd do without you; you are a real asset to this company.' Well, let me tell you, I could go through that wall after the old man did that."

Frist also had a way of motivating people by using the carrot rather than the stick. Fred Callahan, who later started a stroke research institute funded by Massey and Frist, said Frist would often come into a hospital and look for things to compliment.

"He might go visit a hospital, and if he saw a room that was really dirty, he'd frown and say that he wanted to be shown a room that was really clean," said Callahan. "And then, when they'd take him into the clean room, he'd say, 'I want to meet the person who cleans this room.' And then when he did, he'd tell them that it was the cleanest hospital room he'd ever been in, great work.

"Then he'd go down and eat in the cafeteria. And he'd try this and try that, and when he found something he liked—let's say it was green beans—he'd say, 'I want to meet the person who cooked the green beans.' They'd take him back and introduce him to the chef, and he'd say, 'Greatest green beans I ever ate in my life; great green beans.' He'd find the good and build up the person responsible for the good."

A few years later Frist Sr. told a reporter how to run a good hospital. "When a patient comes into a hospital he judges it on how nice people are, how nice the telephone operator is, how courteous the people are, how kind and thoughtful the person is who takes him to his room," he said. "Patients are always frightened coming into a hospital, and a little warmth and compassion means so much to them. They will notice how kind and efficient the nurses are and that the hospital does not smell like antiseptic. They notice what kind of food they have, whether the food is not only nutritious but tasty, with a little sprig of flower or some greenery on the plate."

Jack Massey's job wasn't to think about the greenery on the plate; it was to find money to build and acquire all these hospitals. In the summer of 1968 Massey and John Neff, former financial vice president of American General Life Insurance Company, started a money management business called John Neff & Associates and a corporate consultant firm called Capital Investment Services. As the hospital-company idea evolved, Massey asked Neff to shift gears and become HCA's first chief financial officer.

In spite of Jack Massey's stature, and in spite of how excited everyone was about the business plan, they had, in Neff's words, "a hell of a time." In the late 1960s the very idea that a company could raise money to build a hospital and then run it profitably was an alien concept to many bankers and insurance company executives. Some of the biggest doubters were in Nashville.

After Neff became HCA's CFO, it didn't take him long to realize that the company had a problem: it was building about $15 million worth of hospitals but had just a $9 million line of credit to pay for them. That $9 million line of credit consisted of $3 million each from First American, Third National, and Commerce Union banks, all based in Nashville.

"These were effectively short-term loans that could be called in at any time, like construction loans," Neff said. "We had to get something better."

Massey called his friend Sam Fleming, Third National Bank's chairman, and the two went to visit some New York financial institutions. The first two banks turned down their request. Then they called on Third National's correspondent bank in New York, The First National City Bank of New York (later Citibank). Many years later, a banker named Bill McKnight remembered the visit well.

Massey and Frist came up on a rainy day. "They arrived about noon, and I was just about the only person who wasn't at lunch," McKnight said. Since everyone was late coming back from lunch because of the weather, a secretary asked the twenty-seven-year-old McKnight if he would entertain the two gentlemen from Nashville. A few minutes later Ed Palmer, head of the bank's corporate banking division, walked in and greeted the visitors. Seeing that they had already made a new friend, Palmer asked McKnight, whose area of coverage was supposed to have been Pennsylvania, Delaware, and West Virginia, to join them.

Fleming did most of the talking on this introductory visit. He said that Hospital Corporation of America had a promising business plan, but that it had outgrown its local financial resources. He talked about Park View; listed the other hospitals the company wanted to build and acquire; outlined how the company believed it could provide quality care while turning a profit; and bragged about the expertise Frist and Massey were bringing to the table. Fleming explained that the company was, in the short term, looking to find a group of banks to extend construction loans.

Massey's fame from Kentucky Fried Chicken preceded him on this visit, and after Fleming had stated his case, the pharmacist from Sandersville, Georgia, said a few things as well. "'You don't have any relationship with anyone in the hospital field or in the medical field,'" Massey later said he told the bankers. "'Don't you want to be the first one in? Don't you want to lead out and get the business of this company as it grows and the others that'll start?' Well, they thought about it and they said, 'Well, you might be right.'"

Palmer told the visitors he was intrigued by the idea. He then gave McKnight the job of going down to Nashville to investigate HCA further. "This really surprised me because this wasn't even my area of responsibility," McKnight said. "But of course I did what I was told, and the next thing I knew I was on a plane to Nashville."

Massey handled McKnight's visit. Rather than let the young man stay at a hotel, Massey put him up in his home. Massey took McKnight to lunch at the posh Belle Meade Country Club. He arranged a cocktail party in McKnight's honor and invited many of his friends and some the city's most powerful business people to come.

All of this made quite a heady impression on McKnight, who regarded himself as "a poor banker from New York." But of all the things about this trip, nothing struck him as forcefully as one curious anecdote. As the cocktail party was winding down, Massey asked McKnight if he ever played backgammon. McKnight said he had, and Massey asked the young visitor if he would teach him the game, because he had recently obtained a backgammon table but didn't know how to play. The two men sat down in the library, and McKnight taught him the rules and some basic strategy.

After a couple of practice rounds Massey felt pretty confident. "Let's play for money," he suggested. McKnight, a little nervous at this point, suggested that they play for a dollar a game. "Let's make it five dollars," Massey said, "because if you play for more than you think you want to lose, then you really focus on the game." McKnight reluctantly agreed—and proceeded to whip his host, collect his five dollars, and head off to bed.

The next morning McKnight was awakened at six o'clock by a family servant who said that Massey would like to meet with his visitor before breakfast. McKnight walked into the library a few minutes later to find his host sitting at the backgammon table, asking if the two men could play some more. This time Massey won and got his money back.

"You should have seen how happy and elated that made him," McKnight said. "He just didn't like to lose. Now that he had learned the sport, he was determined to be the best backgammon player ever."

That day McKnight visited the HCA headquarters building (which wasn't much to speak of) and got a detailed briefing from Massey and Neff on the company's financing plan. He flew back to New York, and, based on his report to Palmer, the bank decided it would back $15 million of the needed $25 million loan package, leaving Nashville's three local banks to divide the other $10 million in loans.

All seemed well. But a few days later First American executive Bill Greenwood called John Neff to tell him that his bank was not going to take part in the loan package.

"I nearly dropped the phone," Neff remembered. "I said, 'What do you mean you are going to drop out? What are you talking about?' And he said, 'Well, there are a number of people on the board who don't see eye to eye with Mr. Massey.'"

Three and a half decades later, no one in Nashville who knew the background of Massey's problems with First American's board was willing to talk about it.[22] Of course, the fact that Massey had been a director of Third National for decades might have had something to do with it, but there was certainly more to it than just bank affiliations.

The only person on First American's board whose inability to see eye to eye with Massey was commonly known was Parkes Armistead, First American's president in the 1940s. If this personal relationship was in fact the source of Massey's problem, then this would be ironic. The widow of Parkes Armistead's nephew Bill Armistead would later become Jack Massey's second wife.

With the news that First American's involvement had

been called off, Massey reacted in a calm but deliberate manner, which he often did, according to people he worked with during his life. "He wasn't the kind of person to have a temper tantrum or anything, but he was mad at the bank, I can assure you," Neff said. "He also wasn't the kind of person to call the bank and confront them over the phone. He was the kind of person who would say, 'Let's get this thing fixed and to hell with those guys.'"

Personal grudges aside, this was a real crisis for Nashville's new hospital company. First, Neff had to call the New York bank and break the news to them that Nashville's largest bank had decided not to get involved. "What worried me was not so much their [First American's] three million, but I was worried that City Bank would want to know what it was that First American apparently knew, and that their reaction might be that they would rethink it," Neff said. "It was grim."

Neff called McKnight and told him the news, asking him not to panic. He then called Sam Fleming. Fleming said that his bank could be counted on to raise its loan offer by one million dollars (thus reaching its statutory limit), and then he gave Neff the name of two banks in Virginia—the First National Exchange Bank and the Bank of Virginia—that he thought could be counted on for another two million. "Sam Fleming saved the day," Neff said.

Thanks to Fleming's connections, HCA got the $25 million loan. But the company did not forgive First American. "That is why HCA never did any more business with First American until long after we were gone," said Neff.

The $25 million bank loan wasn't permanent; it only ensured that HCA could finish its construction projects in Albany and Macon, Georgia, and Chattanooga, Tennessee. The company still needed long-term financing before it could go public, and to do this, Neff knew he had to turn to the insurance industry. He made arrangements for representatives of several national insurance companies to meet at HCA in the spring of 1969.

Bill Weaver, an executive with National Life & Accident Insurance Company parent NLT, helped HCA arrange the meeting. As it neared, several insurers said they would come, including Mutual Life of New York, Connecticut General, and several others. The day of the meeting, Neff was surprised and dumfounded when Weaver called at the last minute to say that NLT wasn't going to attend because it, too, had decided that HCA wasn't a good investment.

"I thought we were snakebit," Neff said. "You talk about a bucket of cold water. Here we were asking all these insurance companies to take a chance on us, and the big guru of the Nashville insurance business was a no-show."

The meeting did not go well. Connecticut General said it might be interested in loaning a lot of money to HCA, but only in return for warrants on about 40 percent of the company's stock. Massey said that there was no way that the company would consider that. Most of the rest of the potential lenders sat there stone-faced. Finally, the meeting ended.

As it turned out, the two executives from Mutual of New York had a problem. They had to get down to the Atlanta airport to catch a plane to New York, but they had no way of getting there. Tommy Frist Jr. overheard them talking. Frist said he would be glad to fly them down to Atlanta, so long as they didn't mind stopping at the hospital groundbreaking in Macon, Georgia, which was taking place that same day. The Mutual of New York executives agreed.[23]

The groundbreaking turned out to be a gala affair, attended by doctors, citizens, and the mayor of Macon—all of whom talked about just how glad they were to have HCA building a hospital in their community. This apparently made quite an impression on the visitors from New York, because a few weeks later Neff received a call from Jay Jackson at

Mutual of New York. "He said that they really liked what they had seen in Macon," Neff said.

Eventually, Mutual of New York agreed to back the company with $7.5 million; Jefferson Standard agreed to do likewise, making up the bulk of a loan that enabled HCA to finally break away from temporary lines of credit. Thirty-five years later, Neff still believed that the stopover in Macon made the difference. "It just saved our fanny," he said.

The group loan package turned out to be one of the company's first great achievements. In 1969 and 1970 HCA was not the nation's only proprietary hospital chain; among the others were Philadelphia-based American Medicorp and Louisville-based Humana. What set HCA apart from the others was its ability to secure permanent financing from groups of insurance companies.

"That was what made HCA the Cadillac of the industry," Neff said. "None of the other companies could do this, and it drove them crazy that we could. And I think that Mr. Massey, with all his credentials, and me, with my experience in the insurance business, were the keys to making this work."

In January 1970 Neff and HCA secured another line of permanent financing from a group of six insurance companies. This time the amount was thirty million dollars, and this time the group included NLT.

As if its run-in with First American National Bank and NLT weren't enough to give HCA a sense of "us versus them," the founders of the company also had a local rival to worry about. In February 1970 the U.S. Senate's subcommittee on antitrust and monopoly held hearings on the increasing cost of health care. The emerging world of for-profit health care was among the topics of discussion, and Jack Massey, Dr. Thomas Frist Sr., and Bob Brueck were called to testify. The hearings provided an early glimpse of the hard feelings between for-profit and not-for-profit hospitals—feelings that remained very much alive in Nashville through the rest of the century.

Massey began with a prepared statement (which is included in its entirety as an appendix at the end of this book). He said companies like HCA were providing a tremendous service to the public because there was such an unmet demand for hospital beds. He boasted about HCA's early achievements, pointing out that the company already operated twenty-three hospitals and had twenty more either under construction or in the planning stage. He then described some of the situations in which HCA had built hospitals, pointing out that prior to the company's construction of a hospital in Erin, Tennessee, the community had two doctors and no hospital serving its twelve thousand residents.

"The doctors and the community had attempted to build a hospital but failed in their efforts to raise the necessary money," Massey said. "One doctor announced that he would leave the community because he had no facility in which to care for his patients. The second doctor said that if the other one left, he would go too, because he didn't want twelve thousand people knocking on his door at night. We built a hospital for Erin."

Massey did not use the phrases "for-profit" and "not-for- profit" in his statement. "You notice I prefer to use 'non-taxpaying,' rather than 'nonprofit,' because I think they all have to make a profit to be able to stay in business," he said.

Later in the morning Massey took another shot at the concept of for-profit and not-for-profit hospitals. "I do not think we have any nonprofit hospitals in Nashville, or in the area that I know, that are tax-free—they do not pay taxes, but they are not nonprofit. I was president of one [Baptist Hospital] for twelve years and on the board for twenty. . . . It is a fine institution, and it never operated a day without making a profit."

Without being prompted, Massey addressed the main issue for which for-profit hospitals were already being criticized: their treatment of poor people. His comments in this regard were very frank.

"It is important to emphasize that in cities where we are the only hospital, we treat everyone who needs care, regardless," Massey said. "Certainly, we do not encourage the so-called indigent patients to come to HCA hospitals if other, more appropriate facilities are available. We pay large amounts of taxes to the federal government and to the states and counties and cities in which we operate. These taxes help to support the tax-supported hospitals, which are in business to care for the non-paying patient and were established for this purpose. We think that this is where they should go. But we never turn down a patient."

Later in his statement Massey made a more impassioned defense of the company. "We do not see anything wrong with taxpaying hospitals earning a fair return on investment," he said. "Other companies make profits on building automobiles and bombs that kill. Doctors and laboratories and clinics make profits on treating the sick. We are not ashamed to be profit-oriented. In the great American tradition of free enterprise, we feel that investors are entitled to a fair return on their capital."

Several members of the subcommittee questioned Massey, Frist, and Brueck. A primary area of focus during the questioning was the degree to which physicians were participating in the company as investors. The HCA representatives said that the main reason the company had so many physician-investors at that time—about five hundred out of a total of more than four thousand stockholders—was that the company had acquired several existing hospitals from physician-owners, many of whom still owned stock as a result.

However, Massey acknowledged that even he was wary about the idea of a hospital company dominated by physician-owners. "The question—we hope—of doctor ownership would gradually breed itself out, and with a little profit, maybe a lot of them will sell," he said.

HCA wasn't the only Nashville-based health-care organization whose representatives testified that day. Joe Greathouse, director of Vanderbilt University Hospital, addressed the same committee. Greathouse made it clear at the beginning of his statement that the views he expressed were his own and did not represent those of his employer.

He made a long public statement in which he argued that the nation's health-care system was "overloaded" and that it did not have the "facilities, the skilled personnel, or the system efficiency" to handle the crisis. Greathouse then shifted to the development of proprietary chain hospitals. He made it clear that organizations such as Vanderbilt felt financially threatened by organizations such as Hospital Corporation of America.

"Many of the institutions owned by such corporations seek to gain their profit margin through the exclusion, by one technique or another, of patients who cannot pay the full cost of their hospital care; by using methods of patient selectivity to insure that the institution does not care for more complex types of medical and surgical conditions; through the exclusion of such services as obstetrics, emergency services, pediatrics, or other services which have traditionally been money losers for hospitals; through the exclusion of educational programs; or through a combination of all of the above factors," Great house said.

Later, after listing some of the bigger challenges facing community-owned hospitals across the country, Greathouse said proprietary chains were making the problems worse.

Greathouse never mentioned HCA, Massey, or Frist by name. It should also be mentioned that, later that day, another representative of a not-for-profit hospital was far more critical of proprietary chains than Greathouse had been. That man, John Gadd of Lee Memorial Hospital in Fort Myers, Florida,

Above: Jack Massey's childhood home in Sandersville, Georgia.
Left: Young Jack Massey.
Below: Massey, third from left, with his high school basketball team.

Photos courtesy of Barbara Massey Rogers except where noted.

Above: Massey behind the counter at one of his drugstores in the 1930s.
Below: Massey opens a new drugstore on Twenty-first Avenue in
Nashville, near Vanderbilt University. His wife, Elizabeth, is standing
to his right.

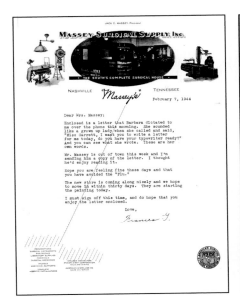

Above left: Correspondence showing the Massey Surgical Supply letterhead. Above right: Jack Massey in his office at Massey Surgical Supply. Below: An annual dinner meeting for the employees and sales staff of Massey Surgical. Massey is standing in the middle of the group in the back; to his right is his longtime secretary, Omega Sattler.

Above: The Massey family circa 1940. From left are Jack, son Don, wife Elizabeth, and daughter Barbara. Below: Massey and the rest of the board of Nashville's Baptist Hospital in the 1950s.

Above: The Masseys clown around with friends at a costume party. Below: Massey with daughter Barbara and Colonel Sanders. Right: Massey, Colonel Harland Sanders, and John Y. Brown Jr.

Above: HCA's early board, from left, David Williamson, Dr. Robert McClellan, Dr. Robert Fowler, Dr. Cleo Miller, Massey, Dr. Thomas Frist Sr., Dr. Thomas Frist Jr., Henry Hooker, and Dr. William Taylor. Right: Early photo of Park View Hospital, which later became the first HCA hospital.

Above: Jack Massey with John Hill, left, on the day Hospital Corporation of America made it to the New York Stock Exchange.

COURTESY OF HCA

Above: HCA's executives at the 1980 groundbreaking for an addition to the company's Nashville headquarters. From left are John Hill, Dr. Thomas Frist Jr., Massey, Dr. Thomas Frist Sr., and Donald McNaughton. Below: Former Tennessee Governor (and now U.S. Senator) Lamar Alexander says hello to Massey during an event at Belmont University.

COURTESY OF MASSEY SCHOOL OF BUSINESS AT BELMONT UNIVERSITY.

Above: Massey is honored by actor Yul Bryner and Nashville Mayor Richard Fulton, left, for his contribution to the Tennessee Performing Arts Center (TPAC). Right: Jack Massey during his induction into the National Business Hall of Fame in 1987. Below: Greeting U.S. Senator Howard Baker and President Ronald Reagan.

described for-profit hospitals as "fast-buck hospitals," described for-profit hospital companies as "corporations masquerading as benevolent competitors," and said that their executives were "get-rich-quick hospital operators." Gadd was especially upset that HCA was in the process of building a hospital that would compete with his, saying it would result in a "crisis" for the Fort Myers community.

Gadd's accusations aside, Greathouse's testimony irritated Massey and added to resentment he apparently already felt toward Vanderbilt from his surgical supply days. "Vanderbilt spent many dollars to try to get us out of business," Massey later told a reporter.

The rivalry between HCA and Vanderbilt lasted for several years. In 1988, when surgeon and Vanderbilt staff member Jeff Pennington told Vanderbilt Medical Center Director Roscoe Robinson that he was going to work for HCA, Robinson told Pennington he couldn't believe it. "He told me he was extremely disappointed," Pennington said. "I could almost see tears welling up. He felt that I was doing the wrong thing and an immoral sort of thing. . . . He had a real concern that Vanderbilt doctors who practiced at both institutions would send the charity [cases] to Vanderbilt and the paying patients to HCA."

Nashville wasn't the only city in which doctors and administrators were made aware of the rivalry between for-profit and not-for-profit hospitals. When Clayton McWhorter first announced that he was leaving a La Grange, Georgia, not-for-profit hospital to work for HCA, the chairman of the hospital called him into his office.

"He basically said that he couldn't believe I was leaving, because he thought the very idea of for-profit health care was wrong," McWhorter said. "But I said, 'Well, even at this hospital, if I didn't have more coming in than going out, then we wouldn't be able to survive.' But I could tell from the look in his eyes that he didn't much buy my argument."

Nineteen sixty-eight was an exciting first year for HCA, but things got even more interesting as the next year started. With nearly a dozen hospitals in its portfolio, many of the company's shareholders were quite ready to cash in their "Chinese Money," as Thomas Frist Jr. called the stock, for cash, or, at the very least, to see the public market put a price on the stock.

"The entire business plan was dependent upon the idea of going public, because we had to have the capital to support all the money that we were borrowing to build all those hospitals," said John Neff. "Meanwhile, the world was just full of companies going public at that time, and the market was being very receptive."

Some people in Nashville were so anxious to get in on the deal that quite a bit of HCA stock was sold in that city prior to the initial public offering. Some buyers were paying as much as fifty dollars a share for HCA's "Chinese Money."

HCA became publicly traded on the NASDAQ on March 11, 1969, and it is hard to imagine the initial public offering going better. Four hundred thousand shares of HCA stock, which had been issued to most of the physician-investors from whom the company purchased hospitals at the equivalent price of ten dollars a share, went public that day at eighteen dollars. By the end of the day the stock was selling at about forty dollars.

An original share of Park View Hospital, for which Nashville physicians had paid $11,000, was now worth nearly $1.4 million. The five investors in little Taylor Hospital in Lewisburg, each of whom had invested $15,000 five years earlier, could now sell their HCA stock for more than $5 million.

Able to breathe easier, HCA's executives went on to announce more acquisitions and construction projects that year: buying a large hospital in Houston, Texas; announcing plans to build a $4 million hospital in Bowling Green, Kentucky; and announcing expansion plans for Park View Hospital.

However, about halfway through the year the company lost one of its founders because of another stock market ride. By the middle of 1969, Minnie Pearl's Fried Chicken, doing business under the name Performance Systems, was failing operationally, and its stock price began to reflect this. Performance Systems and a related company called Whale Industries thus fell on hard times, forcing Henry and John Jay Hooker to sell their two hundred thousand shares of HCA stock and leading Henry to resign from the HCA board in November 1969.

HCA became listed on the New York Stock Exchange on November 21, 1970, only a year and a half after Kentucky Fried Chicken had made the Big Board. By 1972 HCA was on solid ground, praised on Wall Street, accepted in Washington, D.C., and entering a growing number of cities across the country.

The company also had an experienced president in John Hill, a former executive with the Aetna Life Insurance Company; a new controller named Sam Brooks, who had previously been with Ernst and Ernst; and in-house legal counsel Don Fish. Thanks largely to Massey's connections, the company had recruited some rather impressive outside directors, one of whom was Rockwell International President Bob Anderson.

"I was living in Pittsburgh at the time, and one of our directors was Harry Massey, Jack's brother, who ran the Buick dealership in Pittsburgh," Anderson explained many years later. "Harry told me that his brother was looking for people to go on his little hospital company board, so I talked to Jack and he talked me into it.

"I will never forget it. I flew down to Nashville and we had our first board meeting at a little motel—I think it was a Howard Johnson's out near the airport. There couldn't have been more than a half a dozen of us, and I kind of wondered what I had gotten myself into."

The board wouldn't have to meet at a motel much longer. In 1973 HCA completed a real headquarters structure, a long, four-story building located across the street from Park View. Massey scaled back his direct involvement and began focusing on other ventures.

Granted, he didn't like to bet large amounts of money. But Jack Massey loved to gamble. He would make bets on everything—sporting events, gin rummy games, golf tournaments.

According to nephew Joe Massey, "Uncle Jack was always competing with himself and everyone else on everything. When he played golf, for instance, he always had to bet. This is one of the reasons I tried to avoid playing golf with him. If I played golf I didn't want to be distracted by worrying about whether I won or lost. But he wasn't like that."

"If you played golf with Jack Massey," friend Sydney Keeble remembered, "betting was something you had to expect. If you were winning on the last hole, you knew that he would go double or nothing on you. And if you won then, you'd know that he'd want to keep playing."

"I remember what it was like to watch a football game with him," said stepson Bill Armistead. "In the middle of the game, one team would be lining up to kick a field goal, and he'd suddenly say, 'I'll bet you five dollars he'll miss it.'"

"Never will I forget my winning a ten-dollar bet from him on the flavor of a piece of pie, said HCA executive Helen Cummings. "I bet peanut butter and he bet toasted coconut. What difference did it make? None. He simply loved to compete on a small thing like the flavor of a piece of pie."

Friend Bill Tyne recalls, "When I had my first child in 1974, we had a ten-dollar bet as to what it was going to be. I won, and he opened a savings account for my daughter at the Nashville City Bank as a result of this, which was made all the more ironic by the fact that I worked at Commerce Union Bank at the time. Then we bet on my next child and I lost, and so I had to send a ten-dollar check to his favorite charity."

"At the very end of his life," said secretary Jackie Gorman, "when he needed help walking from his car to the office, part of my job was to be there waiting when his car got there every day. There was a temperature gauge in his car, and if I could guess close to what it said, he'd give me a dollar. And if I was off, he would make me give him a dollar."

8

INVESTMENTS
GALORE

J ACK MASSEY WAS NOT A happy bachelor. After his first wife, Elizabeth, died in 1968, he found that he was lonely and unaccustomed to having to do all the things single men have to do.

"He really wasn't himself," said longtime employee Clarence Edmonds. "Instead of showing up at the office first thing in the morning, as he had always done before, he'd call in at nine thirty or ten o'clock and ask me to come out to the house for lunch. I'd go out there, and he'd still be in his pajamas and hadn't shaved, and we'd play gin for a couple of hours. He really was depressed."

In the summer of 1969 the sixty-four-year-old Massey started "dating" again, and in the fall of that year he went to Europe with a handful of Nashville friends. Then, in the winter of 1969-70, friends Sheila and Sydney Keeble introduced Massey to Alyne Queener Armistead.

Armistead was the daughter of a prominent attorney from Columbia, Tennessee. Her late husband, Bill Armistead, had been the editor of the *Franklin Review Appeal*, and his uncle Parkes Armistead was the former president of First American National Bank and a longtime rival of Massey. Alyne was headstrong and loquacious and had once worked as a social writer for the *Nashville Banner*. She had two teenage sons, Bob and Bill, and lived in a small house in downtown Franklin. At the time she met Massey, she was working at Commerce Union Bank.

Massey became fond of Alyne, who was about three decades younger than he. The two began dating and, as wealthy widowed men often do, Massey began showering his new girlfriend with gifts. A few months into their relationship, Jack took Alyne to Cat Cay, a remote island off the coast of Florida which he often visited with his brother Harry Massey. The couple wed in May 1971.

Most wealthy older men are content to invest their money in a combination of government bonds, real estate, and stocks of companies run by someone else. But Jack Massey was not like most wealthy older men. Driven by his love of the "deal," Massey in 1968 founded a firm that eventually blossomed into one of the largest venture capital companies in the South. It, in turn, played a major role in the founding or growth of dozens of other companies, such as Shoney's, Wendy's, Spectronics, Intermedics, Corrections Corporation of America, Mr. Transmission, Club Car, CompuCare, Norrell, and Surgical Care Affiliates.

This venture capital business not only spread the legend of Jack Massey to other parts of America, it started an entrepreneurial tradition in Nashville that outlived Massey himself. The whole thing started through Massey's relationship with John Neff.

In the early 1960s Neff had been vice president of investments for the Nashville-based Life & Casualty Insurance Company when the firm loaned Massey money to purchase a hotel near the Nashville airport. In 1968, after Houston-based American General took over operational control of L&C, Neff reluctantly moved to American General's corporate headquarters in Texas. At about this time Massey was looking for someone to manage his assets full time. He offered Neff the job, and after Neff discussed the matter with Sam Fleming, Neff accepted the offer and moved back to Nashville.

Many years later Neff remembered what Fleming said to him. "He told me this could be a really good deal for me, and that this was a real entrepreneurial opportunity and a chance to make some real money instead of drawing a salary and working for a big institution," Neff said. "But I also remember that he told me to start off on the right foot with Mr. Massey. He told me that I had to be even with Mr. Massey and be on the same level he was on. He told me that I can't be working *for* Massey, that it would never work if I were working *for* Massey. I had to start out equal with him and be partner with him."

It was in large part because of Fleming's advice that Massey and Neff structured their new venture, called Capital Investment Services, as a partnership. And as fate would have it, the *Nashville Banner* story announcing the creation of Capital Investment Services appeared the same afternoon a young man named Lucius Burch III moved to Nashville.

Burch was no stranger to Nashville or to Massey. His grandfather had once been dean of the Vanderbilt Medical School, and his father's doctor's office was literally next door to the Massey Surgical Supply office on West End Avenue. After graduating from the University of North Carolina, Burch had worked five years for various New York financial firms, and he was moving back to Nashville to take a job with Third National Bank.

When Burch read about Capital Investment Services, he decided it sounded more interesting than working for a bank. He called Massey, but the Kentucky Fried Chicken chairman sounded skeptical at first. "He said to me that I could apply, but he said that he had a hundred applications for the job," Burch said. "He sort of said to me, 'Son, you don't really have a chance of getting this job, because I've got so many applications from people who want to come work for me.' So I just kind of gave up and didn't do anything.

"Well, about a week later he called me on Sunday night from New York, where he was on Kentucky Fried Chicken business. And he said that he wanted me to talk to him and to John Neff."

Burch got the job. Since Massey was still running KFC and Neff was still living in Houston, Burch did much of the legwork to get Capital Investment Services going, such as buying furniture and hiring secretaries. Within a few months the company was operating and had hired two other people with investment responsibility: Earl Beasley and Louis Hibbetts.[24]

For its first few months, Neff, Beasley, and Hibbetts basically bought and traded stocks that were held in Massey's portfolio. As Burch remember it thirty-five years later, this at first largely consisted of his Kentucky Fried Chicken stock and about twenty million dollars in various stocks and bonds. "There were a lot of franchise stocks in there—companies like McDonald's, Lums, IHOP, a lot of the early franchise companies," Burch said. "He made a fortune on those things."

As the months went by, Massey and Neff became more tied up with Hospital Corporation of America, leaving Burch and Beasley with more responsibility. Capital Investment Services began to take a more active role in the formation, expansion, and management of companies rather than just the speculative buying of securities. "We started doing venture capital even though we didn't really call it that," Burch said.

One of Capital Investment Services' first successes was Shoney's restaurants. Shoney's started as the Nashville franchisee for a California-based drive-thru chain called Big Boy. Its owner, Ray Danner, worked tirelessly and ran better restaurants than his competitors. After a couple of years Danner purchased the Big Boy franchise for the entire Southeast from Alex Schoenbaum of Charleston, West Virginia, who called his locations Shoney's. Danner continually expanded his business, and by 1968 Danner Foods Inc. had nearly a hundred Big Boy locations throughout the Southeast and annual revenue of more than four million dollars.

Danner wanted to go public, but he needed advice on how to do it. He approached Massey, whom he knew because Danner Foods was also the Louisville, Kentucky, franchisee of Kentucky Fried Chicken. Massey advised Danner Foods throughout the process of going public and bought a large chunk of the restaurant chain's stock at its initial public offering in April 1969.

"That was how I met Ray Danner," said James C. "Jimmy" Bradford, whose company handled Danner Foods' initial public offering. "Massey and Neff introduced me to Danner when they were advising him on how to go public."

Once Massey got into the business of investing money in other people's companies, he began to get requests from all over. Eventually, the people who worked for him at Massey Investment Company and Massey-Burch Capital Corporation (Massey's venture capital company after 1980) said they only invested in a tiny percentage of the deals that came their way. "The other day I heard from a guy in Colorado who said gold mines are coming back," Massey told a reporter. "He wanted me to put up one million dollars for forty percent of his production. That's as far as we got."[25]

There were successes, there were failures, and there were lessons learned along the way. Volunteer Capital would prove to be all three. And it would evolve into the third company that Jack Massey would take to the New York Stock Exchange.

In 1969 a small Nashville brokerage house called Tennessee Securities ran a publicly traded mutual fund called the Volunteer Capital Fund. Volunteer Capital was doing poorly because it had invested in several boom-and-bust franchise-related businesses. The fund had originally been capitalized at $2.5 million, but by 1969 it was only worth about $1.5 million.

One day Beasley and Neff were discussing what could be done with Volunteer Capital. Knowing Massey was turning a profit in the equipment leasing business (through Commercial Investment Company), Beasley suggested the idea of taking control of the mutual fund, liquidating its assets, and changing it into a much larger equipment leasing company. By doing it this way, Beasley reasoned, you could have a publicly traded leasing company that could make use of the capital markets like any other publicly traded company.

Neff thought it was a great idea, and the two men took it to Massey, who also liked it. By the time the idea matured, Massey decided that he and a group of investors would also put one million dollars into the venture, giving the new equipment leasing company about $2.5 million in initial capital. Beasley, meanwhile, would become president of Volunteer Capital.

With the help of lawyer Brad Reed of Bass, Berry & Sims (who had done some legal work for KFC), the creation of Volunteer Capital Corporation came off as planned and the company did, in fact, go into the equipment leasing business. It turned out to be marginally profitable. The company leased all sorts of personal property, from dentist's chairs to restaurant equipment. But no sooner had it carved out its niche in the leveraged leasing business than banks began to get into the same business.

Another business opportunity soon came along by way of one of Massey's old connections. One of the most successful Kentucky Fried Chicken franchisees, and one of many who became a millionaire because of Massey's ownership of KFC, was Indiana franchisee Dave Thomas. Thomas and Massey got along wonderfully. "Jack gave me confidence in myself to do things I never knew I could do," Thomas said.[26]

In 1969 Thomas started a new hamburger restaurant in Columbus, Ohio, that focused on producing a better-tasting and more expensive burger than McDonald's. Unlike so many of the failed restaurants of that era, Thomas spent a year perfecting the concept with one location before he tried to build it into a chain. When Thomas began signing up franchisees, he relied mainly on people he had met through KFC. He sold the franchise for North and South Carolina to former KFC franchise Don Greer. Greer turned to Volunteer Capital for equipment leasing help.

After looking into Wendy's, Beasley and Massey got so excited about the company that they decided Volunteer Capital should do more than lease equipment to Greer; it should become a franchisee. Since most of the markets east of the Mississippi were already sold, Volunteer Capital at first had to be satisfied with Shreveport and Baton Rouge, Louisiana.

Eventually, the company bought Greer's franchise and ended up with large parts of California and Massachusetts as well. By the time Wendy's went public in September 1976, Volunteer Capital was the largest franchisee in the chain (which meant that Dave Thomas, head of Wendy's, and Jack Massey, who controlled its largest franchisee, had actually swapped roles from their KFC days).

Since he and Thomas were friends, former KFC colleagues, and now partners with Wendy's, Massey couldn't resist playing an active role when the company went public. The first time the restaurant chain was written up in the national business press was in a profile of Massey.

"Massey is currently arranging to take public yet another fast-food franchise, Wendy's International of Columbus, Ohio," *Forbes* reported. "Wendy's hopes to be to McDonald's as Neiman Marcus is to Woolworth's. It uses only fresh, not frozen, meat, sells its hamburgers for as much as a dollar sixty-nine, and offers a drive-up window for takeout service."[27]

Massey also took Thomas to New York and helped him negotiate with investment banks and take the company public. "He introduced me to an investment banker and helped me get the first big offer on Wall Street," Thomas told a reporter many years later. "He was a guy who was a great salesman. The best."[28]

Massey Investment Company, i.e., Jack Massey, got involved in businesses of all sorts. It made a substantial seed investment in Spectronics, an early semiconductor company based in Dallas that was eventually purchased by Honeywell. It was part-owner of Cummings Sign Company, a business operated by Massey's friend Tom Cummings. It took over Mr. Transmission, an automobile services chain that originally came out of the wreckage of Minnie Pearl's Fried Chicken. It bought and operated Club Car, an Augusta, Georgia-based company that manufactured golf carts.

Massey's involvement in these firms was usually low key. But then there was Black Diamond Enterprises, the venture that Jack Massey later described as the "biggest mistake of my life." Around 1969 a partnership consisting of Massey, Neff, Cummings, and Nashville businessmen Fred Wright and Stirton Oman Jr. purchased Kingsport, Tennessee-based Black Diamond, which was primarily in the business of manufacturing and selling tractor-trailers. Black Diamond looked like a good investment and a vehicle under which the investors could build a "conglomerate" of sorts.

Within a couple of years Black Diamond had diversified with the purchase of an Oregon-based motor home company called Cabana Coach. Cabana Coach seemed like a great idea at the time, as Americans were becoming more enthusiastic about off-road camping. But Black Diamond's investment in it was rendered practically worthless when the energy crisis of 1974 destroyed motor home sales. "If I remember correctly, Cabana Coach went a couple of quarters with revenues of zero when they were rationing gasoline," recalled Brad Reed, who did legal work for the company.

Black Diamond got into the coal business in 1976 with the purchase of the Wolford Enterprise Coal Corporation, whose main asset was a mine in Mingo County, West Virginia. That investment didn't work out either, because the mine wasn't nearly as valuable as the investors had been led to believe.

A few years later the man who had sold the mining business to Black Diamond bought it back, in part with a $750,000 loan from Barclays Bank International of London. He later defaulted on that loan, which resulted in Barclays filing a $4.1 million lawsuit against Wolford, Black Diamond, and the five principal owners of the company, one of whom, of course, was Jack Massey.

The lawsuit was later dismissed, and all the parties affiliated with Black Diamond were cleared of any wrongdoing. Still, Black Diamond was more than just a bad investment. It left a bitter taste because of the lawsuit and a rather large story in the *New York Times* about the situation. "Barclays lost money in the hills of Appalachia," the *Times* said. "Now the courts may tell them how it happened."[29]

Tom Cummings later took over management of the coal business, then operating in bankruptcy. "We mined and mined and mined, but we just could not get enough coal out of there," Cummings said a few years later. After a couple of years of mining unsuccessfully and dealing with organized labor with mixed success, Cummings managed to sell the mine to another coal company operating in the area.

Ultimately, Black Diamond also fell into bankruptcy. "It was very interesting from a lawyer's standpoint," Brad Reed said. "But from an investors' standpoint it was a disaster."

Other than Kentucky Fried Chicken and Hospital Corporation of America, Jack Massey's greatest investment from a percentage gain standpoint might have been Intermedics. In the late 1960s Texas resident Albert Beutel was a salesman for Minneapolis-based Medtronic, the national leader in the cardiac pacemaker industry. At some point Beutel recognized there would be a shift in the industry from mercury-zinc batteries to lithium batteries because lithium batteries lasted longer and were smaller, lighter, and more reliable.

Using a new pacemaker invented by two professors at Pennsylvania State University, Beutel started a company called Intermedics and set up a manufacturing plant in Texas. He also robbed Medtronic of some of its best salesmen.

"As I remember it, Medtronic gave an award every year to the top salesmen in the country," Burch recalled. "Well, Albert went out and hired every single one of them and gave them a franchise, told them that they would have a protected territory. He gave one guy Michigan and one guy Georgia and Tennessee, this sort of thing. And those people became the exclusive distributors of Intermedics pacemakers in those areas."

Massey heard about Intermedics while attending an American Heart Association convention, and he told Burch to look into it. "His marketing system was selling more pacemakers than could be produced, and the banks would not loan him money to expand his manufacturing plants," Massey later said.

Burch called Buck Lyon, a businessman Massey knew in Dallas, and Lyon did some quick research on the company. "As it turns out, the very night that Lucius called me I went to a school picnic for one of my kids, and the man sitting next to me turned out to be an employee of Intermedics," Lyon said. "So I was able to gather an enormous amount of information on the company in short time."

Beutel was looking for an investor, and Massey Investment Company bought 10 percent of the company for $2 million. Massey also arranged for a $10 million bank loan so Intermedics could increase the size of its manufacturing plant.

"Jack didn't spend six months reading our financial statements," Beutel told *Forbes* a few years later. "He flew down here, talked to me and my father and made up his mind."[30] Massey's innate intuition struck again.

Intermedics was expanding before Massey got involved, but its growth after Massey invested was startling. "The year that we invested in the company Intermedics did two million dollars in business," Burch said. "The next year they did nine million, the next year twenty-nine million, the next year forty-nine million, then eighty-nine million dollars, and it went up and up."

The future of Intermedics came into serious doubt in March 1979, when Beutel died in a helicopter crash. Beutel was replaced by one of his franchisees, Russell Chambers, and the company continued to grow through the 1980s, eventually taking over about a third of the worldwide pacemaker industry. In June 1988 Intermedics was acquired by Sulzer Brothers of Switzerland for $800 million. Massey's $2 million investment was thus worth about forty times that amount.

As if this weren't enough, Massey had multiple side ventures completely unrelated to HCA, Kentucky Fried Chicken, and

Capital Investment Services. One was his role at Thomas Nelson Inc.

In 1961 Lebanese immigrant Sam Moore started a religious book publisher in Johnson City, Tennessee. By 1967 Royal Publishers had moved its headquarters to Nashville, largely because of investments made in it by Massey, Fred Wright, Stirton Oman, Jack Clay, and John Jay Hooker Jr.

According to Moore, Massey was by far the most important of these. He bought twenty thousand shares of the company in 1967 for seven dollars a share and sat on the company's board of directors for the rest of his life. "The first time I approached Mr. Massey about investing, he told me to come down and catch him after a board meeting of the Baptist Hospital," Moore said many years later.

In 1969 Moore's success attracted the attention of a British company called Thomas Nelson and Sons. As the original publisher of John Bunyan's *Pilgrim's Progress*, Nelson had a history dating back to 1798. It was also the world's largest publisher of Bibles. But by this time Nelson had fallen on hard times because of its failure to defend its exclusive right to the Bible's Revised Standard Version. Nelson originally contacted Moore because the company wanted him to be its new president. But before he went to New York to meet with the owners of the company, Moore talked to his board chairman, Jack Massey.

"I told Mr. Massey that I thought they might be willing to sell the company," Moore recalled years later. "He says to me, 'Well, Sambo [Massey's nickname for Moore], this is an old, established company.' I said, 'Yessir.' He said, 'It's been in business since 1798. If you can buy it, and you need the money, then don't worry about it, because we will come up with it.'"

Moore's meeting with the owners of Thomas Nelson went well, and Royal Publishers purchased Thomas Nelson for $2.64 million through a secondary stock offering. Moore then moved its headquarters to Nashville, thus bringing Bible publishing to Nashville for the first time in generations. Thomas

Nelson became one of Nashville's most important publicly traded companies during the last quarter of the twentieth century. Among its more impressive products were the *Giant Print Bible, The New Clarified Reference Bible, The New King James Version of the Holy Bible,* and *The Open Bible.* According to Moore, Jack Massey's interest and involvement in the company was consistent.

"I used to go to his office and bring my problems and my numbers and my plans and lay them on that table," Moore said. "I would tell him that this is what I want to do, and he would say what he would do. He and I basically ran the company. He was my main board member. Whenever Massey would agree with me, it was a like a fait accompli. He was that influential."

Another Nashville-based public company with which Massey became involved during the 1970s was primarily known for making shoes. Genesco rose from obscurity after World War II to become one of the world's largest apparel companies by the mid-1960s. But the company struggled when apparel production shifted overseas and as Americans began buying fewer dress shoes.

In January 1977 the Genesco board fired CEO Franklin Jarman—whose father, Maxey Jarman, had effectively built the company—and began looking for a full-time replacement. Genesco director Sam Fleming approached Massey, and the two men together purchased 6 percent of Genesco's common stock. At the time Massey said he thought Genesco would be successfully run by its new CEO, Jack Hannigan, whom Massey had met years earlier when he sold his surgical supply business to Brunswick, Hannigan's former employer.

Hannigan's tenure, however, was unsuccessful, even painful. During his three years as the head of Genesco he sold off so many divisions and laid off so many people that he earned the nickname "Hatchet Jack." He was also unable make Genesco profitable.

It is unclear when Massey sold his Genesco stock, but it is very likely that he did so at a loss. And although Massey was no doubt frustrated by his inability to turn around one of Nashville's oldest and most important companies, he wasn't the only person who tried and failed to fix Genesco in the latter quarter of the twentieth century.

This was also about the time Massey co-founded American Retirement Corporation. ARC, as it became known, was largely the brainchild of Dr. Thomas Frist Sr., who had been interested in the concept of building housing for the elderly ever since he had served on a national commission on aging in the late 1950s.

Sometime around 1976, HCA told one its hospital administrators to study the idea of starting a division that would build and operate assisted living centers and nursing homes. That administrator, Jack Bovender, who later became CEO of the hospital chain, concluded that the idea made sense, but the board of directors decided not to move ahead with it.

Frist and Massey thought it was a good idea, though, and they began looking for young partners with whom to start such a firm. ARC's other founders included Nashville architect Earl Swensson, lawyer Lee Barfield (Frist's son-in-law), HCA Treasurer Sam Brooks, and Wilford Fuqua, whom Massey and Frist picked to be ARC's first president.

"There were six founders and seven shares," Fuqua said. "Mr. Massey bought two shares and everyone else bought one."

ARC's initial strategy was to build and operate retirement centers. But with interest rates high in the late 1970s, the company focused on operating existing developments. It didn't take long for its founders to learn that there were big differences between the retirement business and the hospital business.

"In the retirement business, revenue per square foot is basically the same as it is for residential living, with a few services thrown in, such as housekeeping, food services, and activities," Fuqua said. "Your dollar per square foot can't be nearly as high as it can be for a health-care facility, and there is no third-party reimbursement for retirement living. Since there is more money that flows through a health-care facility, more of it sticks to your hands."

American Retirement made a big statement with the design, construction, and operation of a large retirement community in Williamsburg, Virginia. But, contrary to Massey's original hopes, the firm grew slowly.

Jack Massey also decided he was no longer content to merely sit on the board of someone else's bank. Back in 1960 a group of Nashville businessmen led by general contractor Nile Yearwood started Capital City Bank, Nashville's first new financial institution since before the Great Depression. In its early years Capital City Bank was tiny, with total assets of $7 million during its second year of operation. In April 1968 Massey purchased working control of the bank by buying shares from Yearwood and on the open market.

"I think that the development of another bank here is simply good business, and I consider Capital City a good little bank, with a marvelous opportunity for growth along with Nashville," Massey said at the time. Before long the bank board was dominated by Massey and several people with whom he had multiple business relationships, including Fleet Transport President Calvin Houghland, Fred Wright, Tom Cummings, Stirton Oman, Ray Danner, and John Neff.

Capital City Bank would within a few months merge with a larger bank, and the account of this transaction requires a bit of background. In the 1940s and 1950s one of Nashville's oldest financial institutions was the Nashville Bank & Trust Company. This organization was owned by grocery chain owner H. G. Hill Jr., who ran the bank conservatively and had a reputation of being someone who would never sell.

Around 1963, however, word hit the street that Hill was looking to sell Nashville Bank & Trust. He entertained several offers and finally accepted one from a group of thirty-six investors led by National Life & Accident executive Bill Weaver.

A few months later, Weaver made the surprising move of selling the trust company to Third National Bank. "Hill passed it to Weaver, who then lateraled it right over to [Third National Bank President Sam] Fleming," said Ed Nelson, a Nashville banker who had tried unsuccessfully to convince Hill to sell Nashville Bank & Trust to a group led by Bronson Ingram and himself.

Third National bought Nashville Bank & Trust with apparent confidence that federal regulators would approve the takeover. But a few weeks after the merger was announced, the U.S. Justice Department filed an antitrust suit to block the merger. That case dragged on for four years. Finally, in 1968, the U.S. Supreme Court sided with the Justice Department and ordered the bank to spin off the trust company, reasoning that it was unhealthy for Nashville to lose another financial institution.

After a long series of negotiations the federal government agreed to let Third National keep Nashville Bank & Trust's trust business but still required that it sell its banking operation. The divestiture was a complicated and awkward one, described by many who were familiar with it as "unscrambling eggs." In the end, Nashville Bank & Trust became an independent financial institution once again, though now under public ownership.

In August 1969 Nashville Bank & Trust merged with Capital City Bank, mixing one of Nashville's oldest financial institutions with its newest. The tiny bank that Massey had acquired working control of was now a notable bank with more than $50 million in deposits. When asked about the series of events leading to the merger, bank director Tom Cummings said that the eventual combination of the two banks was what Massey had in mind all along.

"Sam Fleming and Jack [Massey] knew that as soon as Third National acquired the bank, the regulatory authorities would resist it and make Sam spin off a thirty-million-dollar bank," Cummings said. "That was OK with Sam, of course, because it wasn't the banking business of the Nashville Bank & Trust that he was interested in; it was the trust business. Well, Jack knew all this was going to happen. And he decided that when they got ready to spin off that bank, we would need to have something ready to pick it up."

The merged institution became known as the Nashville City Bank. Within a couple of years its board hired former Third National Bank executive Jimmy Webb to be its new president. "I decided that I had enjoyed my career most when Third National had been a much smaller bank, and I thought it would be fun to go to a little bank and see what could happen," Webb said.

Asked what it was like to run a bank in the 1970s with Massey as his chairman, Webb said it was wonderful. "We were a very small bank and a very personal bank, and we were very much run by our board instead of by investment bankers because over half of the bank stock was owned by board members," Webb said.

"The finance committee met weekly, and Mr. Massey came to every one of those meetings and based on the things that he would say at those meetings, I can tell you that he had a brilliant mind, a creative mind, and a shrewd mind. There are some people who thought small. He thought big."

Then there were the real estate ventures.

First on the list was Maryland Farms, the business venture that took the most legal work to settle after Massey's death in 1990. In the 1950s and 1960s it might have seemed unusual for Life & Casualty Insurance Company executive Truman Ward to commute all the way from downtown

Nashville to his horse farm just south of the Davidson County line. But after Interstate 65 opened, real estate agents began to view Ward's property—named Maryland after his wife, Mary—as a prime site for future development.

Ward only had one child, son Jimmy, and most of his estate consisted of the family farm. He wanted to come up with a way to leave the farm to his son without his son having to sell a large chunk of it to pay taxes. Eventually Truman Ward, developer Al Johnson, and attorney Frank Berry Jr. came up with a plan.

In 1970 Ward signed an option to sell his property to an entity called Maryland Farms Development Corporation, which had the legal right to buy the land for ten thousand dollars an acre and develop it piecemeal. The development corporation was owned 50 percent by Jimmy Ward and $16^2/3$ percent each by Massey, Neff, and Johnson. It was formed to come up with a long-term master plan for the property and to develop it as the market would demand.

"Mr. Ward loved it because it did everything that he wanted it to do," Neff said. (Editor's Note: More on the Maryland Farms development and how it came out in Chapter 12.)

Second on the list of real estate investments was property in Texas. About 1971 Buck Lyon, who had been involved in helping Massey with Spectronics, called Massey and told him about a 5,600-acre tract of land for sale near Dallas.

"It was in southwest Dallas County, which has historically been the cheapest real estate in the county, but this land was for sale for fifteen hundred dollars an acre, which was incredibly cheap even for that area," Lyon said. "Being about thirty years old and not knowing any better, I picked up the phone and called Jack Massey and told him that I thought he should buy it."

Massey bought the land sight unseen and held it for about a decade, then later sold it to the Army Corps of Engineers for about three times what he paid for it. "When you consider that he only put fifteen percent of the money down, the profit he actually made from the investment was off the scale," Lyon said. Most of the land eventually became the site of a body of water known as Joe Pool Lake.

Next on the list was Stuart, Florida. In 1971 Nashville developer Fred Webber was vacationing in Delray Beach, Florida, and decided to research the price of land in the Sunshine State. Webber became convinced that property in Stuart, Florida, about forty-five minutes north of Palm Beach, was a bargain. He found about eight thousand acres—some oceanfront, some inland—under the same ownership. Webber convinced Massey to buy it for $8 million under the business name M&W Developers.

At the time, Massey had every intention of developing the property, and Webber was making plans to eventually move there to spend his career doing so. But Massey eventually changed his mind and sold the land for $13 million about five years later.

"We never developed the first thing. I have to admit that this was very disappointing to me at the time," said Webber, who later went on to start numerous upscale residential communities in Nashville. "But I think [Massey] just had too much on his plate and that he was getting up in years and this would take too long to develop." Webber's disappointment was, of course, tempered by the commission he made from handling the two transactions.

Stuart, Florida, wasn't the only place where Massey didn't follow through with a real estate development involving Fred Webber. Back in 1914, the Louisville & Nashville Railroad dammed up a creek south of Nashville to create a water supply for a nearby train yard called Radnor Yards. Several residents of the area were opposed to this effort and even sued to block the railroad's plan, but that litigation was dismissed by the Tennessee Supreme Court. The body of water eventually became known as Radnor Lake. After the L&N stopped using the reservoir, the land immediately around it became a private hunting club.

In 1972 Webber obtained an option to purchase the body of water and the seven hundred acres surrounding it from Oman Construction Company for $3.5 million. Webber then approached Massey about the idea of building an upscale residential subdivision on the property. Massey signed off on the idea but told Webber not to use his name in connection with the plan (which is why accountant Clarence Edmonds was always listed as Webber's co-developer).

The problem was, many of the residents of the area were opposed to the plan, as was Vanderbilt University, which was afraid that a development on the site would hurt visibility at its nearby observatory. A movement to "Save Radnor Lake" gained momentum during the first few months of 1972, and it eventually found sympathetic ears with U.S. Representative Richard Fulton and Governor Winfield Dunn.

A few months after announcing the plans, Webber and Edmonds backed away from their option to buy the property and allowed the state to purchase it from Oman for the same price they had agreed to pay. The federal and state governments—but, curiously, not the local government of Nashville—came up with sizeable sums to buy the property to preserve it. When a fund drive to raise half a million dollars for the project failed, Webber, Edmonds, and Massey pitched in forty thousand dollars to put it over the top.

"In the end, our attempt to develop the area cost us money," Edmonds said.

Radnor Lake thus became a state park and by the end of the century was being described as "Nashville's Walden."

When buying, Jack Massey always tried to get a price as low as possible. But he had a very curious strategy whenever he sold stock in his own companies on Wall Street. He didn't necessarily try to get the highest price. In fact, whenever Massey took something of his to the public marketplace, he always tried to price it a bit below its actual value, to ensure that people and institutions who bought his stock made money and would therefore buy his stock in the future.

"Mr. Massey used to always say that he wanted the initial public offering price to be the lowest price at which the stock ever sells," said Lucius Burch III.

When he took Kentucky Fried Chicken public in 1966, the first brokerage firm Massey approached told him to price the initial public offering at twenty dollars a share. Massey insisted that the million shares be sold for three-fourths of that price.

"If you price them at twenty dollars," he reportedly said, "they'll drop to seventeen, and every purchaser will take a loss and be unhappy. We could have trouble selling Kentucky Fried Chicken shares in the future. But issue it at fifteen dollars, and it will go up two points. That will make every investor happy, and it will be good for our company."

The firm said it would do it for twenty dollars a share, not fifteen, and Massey stood up and walked out, to the shock of Third National Bank President Sam Fleming, who was present at the meeting. Massey found another brokerage house that agreed to sell the stock at fifteen dollars a share.

"Massey stuck by his instincts, won his point, and Kentucky Fried Chicken got the finances it needed," Fleming said.

9

PROPERTY AFFIXED TO THE HOUSE

A BIOGRAPHY OF JACK MASSEY would be incomplete without a chapter devoted to his whims, his preferences, and the things that were surprising about him. There was plenty that made Massey an extraordinary person in the eyes of just about everyone he ever met.

First of all, there was his dry sense of humor. Massey, especially late in life, used humor to communicate—sometimes in a way that was almost hard to understand.

Vic Campbell, who went to work as Massey's administrative assistant in 1975, was startled the first time he became aware of this. But he eventually got used to it. One time, the two men were riding a taxi in New York City when Massey decided to tell young Campbell it was time for a haircut. "Mr. Massey leaned over with his hand and flicked the back of my hair, saying—without a smile—how he liked how my hair flipped over the collar of my coat," Campbell said. "He went on to ask if I thought his wife would like it if he let his hair grow like mine. He quickly changed the subject, again without a smile.

"Guess who got a haircut when he returned to Nashville?"

Campbell, who spent countless hours in Massey's office during his tenure, said he never ceased to be surprised by the man. "He wasn't pretentious, and he didn't tolerate other people who were," Campbell said. "He had a real hangup about PhDs, for instance.

"We had one PhD at HCA who referred to himself as Doctor, and one time Massey got a memo from this person that was signed 'Doctor.' So Massey turns to me and says, 'What kind of doctor is this guy?' And I told him he had his PhD. So Massey picks up the telephone and calls him and tells him not to call himself a doctor in this building or send Massey a memo that says 'Doctor' on it until he had a medical degree."

Next on the list of things that surprised people about Massey is the fact that he could be thrifty to the point of being annoying. Just about everyone who spent time with Jack Massey came away with an anecdote about how he would impulsively try to bargain over the price of anything, from a pair of shoes to an expensive painting.

"I used to often say that it would be easy to steal a million dollars from Mr. Massey, but by God you couldn't get a dime from him," Lucius Burch III said. Massey also had a tendency to give his first wife, Elizabeth, nice things, such as jewelry, that didn't necessarily come from expensive stores. One year, Massey asked Elizabeth what she wanted for Christmas. "I don't care what you get me," she reportedly said, "so long as you pay full retail."

Here is more evidence of Massey's penny-pinching tendencies: the man kept a small black appointment book, and a handful of these books remained in the attic of his widow Alyne's house long after his death. However, it is harder to read the appointment books today than it might seem. The month and year in which Massey used them often doesn't match the month and year stamped on the cover; he actually used the book meant to be used in September 1963 during the month of February 1964. From available evidence, it would appear that Jack Massey was too frugal to buy new appointment books; he probably grabbed a handful of free ones at Third National Bank in 1963 and used every one in the stack.

Once, Massey had to seek treatment at Nashville's Saint Thomas Hospital. When he checked out he was annoyed to learn that he was being charged two dollars for aspirin. Massey paid the bill minus the two dollars, then drove across the street to Moon Drugs, an establishment he partially owned. He took a bottle of aspirin off the shelf and hand-delivered it to Saint Thomas.

A few years later Commerce Union Bank President Ed Nelson bought a house Massey had previously owned. Massey was so excited about this that he came over and gave Nelson a tour of the house, complete with special instructions about how things worked—"Sometimes you have to jiggle the toilet flusher to make it work right"—and the stories behind additions he had made. While on the tour Massey noticed a fire extinguisher that had been in the house since he lived there. He started to remove it to take it home. "You can't take that, Jack," Nelson said. "That's property affixed to the house!"

Massey was also strangely evasive about how much money he had, as if his status as one of the richest men in Nashville was somehow a secret. From about 1970 on, his bank of choice for personal loans was Commerce Union. (Even though he was the chairman of Capital City Bank, he generally didn't borrow much money from that institution because bank examiners frown on loans a bank makes to its own directors.)

In the early 1980s bank examiners looked over Commerce Union's books and told Nelson that he needed to have a personal financial statement from Massey on file. Nelson called Massey and told him this. "He said that he wasn't going to give me one," Nelson said. "So I made a promise to him that if he would give me a personal financial statement, I wouldn't even look at it, that I'd keep it in my desk and only release it to the bank examiners if they insist. He said he'd think about it.

"A few weeks later the bank examiners came, and I called him and told him that I had to have this. So he called his accountant or auditor or whoever it was and he authorized them to bring it down to the bank and show it to the bank examiners. It was delivered by hand and taken away by hand. I never looked at it."

It was about this time that *Forbes* estimated Jack Massey's wealth at $150 million in a 1984 article. A few days later Massey told *Tennessean* reporter Albert Cason that the magazine was way off on its estimate. Cason asked him whether they overestimated or underestimated. "If you can find that much," Massey told Cason, "I'll give you fifty [million dollars]."[31]

Whenever he was asked, Massey denied that he was a workaholic, pointing out that he frequently vacationed in Palm Beach, played golf, played gin, and socialized. But in truth, all of these things were extensions of his work.

Business associates and people asking him to invest frequently traveled to Palm Beach to meet with him, and he would usually make time for such get-togethers on just about any day of the week. Massey often played golf or went to parties in order to further his business contacts. And he truly believed that gin rummy was a good way to work on mathematical and negotiating skills. Even that wasn't—in his mind—idle play.

"He really didn't have hobbies other than his work,"

nephew Joe Massey said. "His companies, his businesses, and his associates were in a sense what he was interested in doing in his spare time. I remember when he tried to talk me into playing golf. He told me it was good for business. He told me you could make deals on the golf course and you could get to know people on the golf course. He used it as a relaxing thing, but he also used it as a way to get to know people and to work into deals."

Massey never thought twice about calling colleagues or employees at night, on weekends, or even on holidays. Hal Kennedy, who did public relations for Massey in the 1960s and 1970s, said he would frequently get a call from Massey on Sunday telling him to bring his typewriter over to his house. "He'd tell me to come over because we had to get a statement ready for the *Wall Street Journal* or something. I did this sort of thing all the time."

Frank Sheffield, who worked for the Massey-Burch Investment Group starting in 1980, said that "dealing with Mr. Massey was a 365-day-a-year job. . . . I have been over to his house on Christmas Day working on projects. The guy was intense."

If a workaholic is simply defined as someone who works all the time, Massey certainly fit the description. But if a workaholic is someone who works at things he doesn't enjoy, then Massey was not one. In 1986, at the age of eighty-two, Massey was asked whether he was still having fun every day. "Yes, indeed," he said. "I love it; I love working. That's the best thing in life is work. And I won't retire. Ever."

Massey wasn't kidding about not retiring. At the age of eighty-four he was still talking about taking his fourth company to the New York Stock Exchange. He was always working on the next venture. "We'd sit down to lunch, and he'd take out a paper napkin and a pen and show me how his next deal was going to be structured," said Kennedy. "That was a sign of just how fast his mind was working all the time."

Massey did not revel in material things, and he was not flashy. "He could have bought a Rolls Royce, but he didn't want one," said his nephew Joe Massey. "He could put that money in a little company that some people had a dream of starting and see if it would work, and that was more fun for him."

Massey was also not interested in building a shrine to himself, or in seeing his name in lights. To the dismay of the Nashville Chamber of Commerce, neither Kentucky Fried Chicken nor Hospital Corporation of America built a downtown office building. And Massey was never interested in putting his name on bigger companies. When he and his colleagues were looking for a new name for Granny's Fried Chicken, it never occurred to him to name it Massey's Fried Chicken.

So if it wasn't greed, and it wasn't ego, what drove Massey? "At some point the money ceased to be his motivator," said former Tennessee Governor Lamar Alexander. "It was the sport and the challenge of it all—his desire to win."

Yes, Jack Massey was a competitor. "His middle initial, 'C,' might as well have stood for 'competitor,'" his daughter, Barbara Massey Rogers, later said. This was something that just about everyone who knew him noticed. "He loved to play golf and he wasn't a particularly good golfer, but that didn't keep him from being competitive even on the golf course," said longtime HCA board member Carl Reichardt.

Oddly enough, Massey didn't seem to resent it when people started companies that copied his. He demonstrated this trait when Kentucky Fried Chicken was riding high. According to an interview that Massey gave a few years later, he was sitting at a table at the Belle Meade Country Club in 1967 when John Jay Hooker came by his table and first told him the idea that later blossomed into Minnie Pearl's Fried Chicken. Massey wished Hooker the best of luck.

"More power to you, John Jay!" Massey said, according to an interview he gave years later. "It would be great. I have no objection to it. Somebody's going to be our competitor, and I'd just as soon it be a friend. The more business you can do selling chicken is going to make more chicken bought, more chicken eaten."

During the next two years, as Minnie Pearl's Fried Chicken was conceived and grew amid considerable hype, Massey remained friends with its founders John Jay and Henry Hooker. In fact, the three men were all involved in the formation of Hospital Corporation of America, with Henry serving as the original vice chairman of the HCA board. When the Minnie Pearl's chain collapsed, Massey remained friends with the Hooker brothers, although he lent his support to Hooker's opponent, Winfield Dunn, in the 1970 Tennessee gubernatorial election.

HCA had imitators, one of which was Nashville-based Hospital Affiliates International (HAI). And while there may have been hard feelings when Park View physician-owner Irwin Eskind founded HAI, Massey held no grudge. Many years later, when both Massey and Eskind were having orthopedic problems, Massey gave Eskind a call.

"Jack told me he was flying down to see an orthopedic surgeon in Alabama who he had great confidence in, and he wanted to know if I wanted to come along," Eskind said. "So I said certainly, and he picked me up and flew me down to Alabama. And I do remember that I couldn't get off the flight without paying him. The payment was that I had to finish the gin rummy game we had started."

Another notable trait about Massey is that he went out of his way to be friendly and courteous. "Wherever we went, when he met someone, he called them 'sir,'" stepson Bill Armistead said. "I don't care whether he was talking to a waiter; I don't care where we were."

Lenora Johnson, a close friend of daughter Barbara

Massey Rogers, noticed something similar about Massey when Rogers was in the hospital with a back problem. "I spent a lot of time with Mr. Massey at the hospital, and I noticed that he was super nice to the nurses and the people who would come in and clean the room and do things like that—that he would thank them and tell them that they had done a good job and compliment them," Johnson said.

The first rule of management, to Massey's way of thinking, was to never ask an employee to do something that you would not be willing to do yourself. Rule number two was to work at least as hard as everyone else in the company. His willingness to work hard served as an example to everyone who saw his car in the parking lot when they got to work each day.

"I'll tell you one thing," said Dr. Thomas Frist Jr., "when he came back to HCA as our president at the age of seventy, that was very unselfish of him. I wouldn't have done that at his age. He gave up a lot of his life to do that. But the fate of the company meant that much to him."

Massey also exhibited humility in the degree to which he showed a personal interest in people who worked for his companies or, for whatever reason, crossed his path and caught his attention. One of the early examples of this phenomenon was the time he offered a job to a young man he thought did a good job at the dry cleaner Massey frequented. That boy, Max Goodloe, went to work for Massey Surgical and went on to start his own surgical supply business in Richmond, Virginia.

Clarence Edmonds, who went to work as Massey's accountant in 1969, said he was amazed at how self-deprecating Massey could be. "I went in to interview with him the very first time, and he asked me to tell him about myself. And I said, 'Well, you may not want me working for you if I do,'" Edmonds remembered years later. "Then I said that I was a country boy who grew up in a rural, poor family. And he said, 'Me, too.' And I said, 'I'm a Baptist,' and he said, 'Me, too.' And I said, 'I'm a Republican,' which was a bit of a risky thing to admit in those days, and he said, 'Me, too.' So he said, 'Sounds to me as if we are just alike.' And he hired me, and I worked for him for the rest of his life."

Massey wouldn't have thought much of the later practice of doing extensive background checks on prospective employees, because he had his own ways of testing a person whenever he met them. He would ask people about their lives to see if they were interesting and if they could communicate. If he was thinking about doing a deal with someone or investing in their company, Massey might take them out to play golf, where he would keep a sharp eye on them. Massey was not so much interested in whether the other person was a good golfer, but he believed that anyone who cheated at golf would cheat in business.

"I played nine holes of golf with him one time when I was asking him to invest in my company," said Guy Milner, founder of the Norrell Temporary Services Company. "After the game he told me that he wanted to invest in my company. Anyone who played golf as bad as me, he said, must be a good business person.

"He had a good insight into what was happening with you, and he could read you like a book."

Furthermore, Massey would sometimes "test" people he had known for a while but still wanted to learn something about. Years after the fact, Massey told Nashville banker Dennis Bottorff that he encouraged Dr. Thomas Frist Jr. to be chairman of the Middle Tennessee board of United Way for a reason. "[Donald] McNaughton was still CEO of Hospital Corporation, and Massey still wasn't sure if he thought that Tommy was up to it [being CEO]," Bottorff said. "So he encouraged Tommy to do the United Way, and Tommy did a great job there and later of course became head of HCA and did an incredible job."

Jack Massey was also averse to people who didn't have the courage to disagree with him or stand up to him. "Despite all his wealth and power, he admired people who had the strength of character to stand up to him," said Richard Chambers, who, as president of Nashville City Bank, stood up to Massey in 1985 when he wanted to merge that financial institution with Commerce Union.

The first time Jack Massey met John Y. Brown Jr., the two men argued about whether Massey was going to loan Brown sixteen thousand dollars at 6 or 6.5 percent interest. Brown eventually got the loan, but more importantly, he impressed Massey, and thus began a partnership that would turn out to be incredibly beneficial to both men.

A couple of years later Massey took public relations man Hal Kennedy out to lunch at downtown Nashville's City Club in an attempt to negotiate a monthly fee on behalf of Kentucky Fried Chicken. "I told him it was going to cost him a thousand dollars a month, and he wanted to argue about this," Kennedy remembered. "He said, 'Why a thousand dollars? Why not nine hundred?' Well, I told him that's the damn price. And he finally agreed to it and we started working for him." Kennedy would continue to be affiliated with Massey for the rest of Massey's life.

Massey was so enthusiastic about the negotiating process that on at least one occasion he successfully traded for a new board member for his bank. Massey became impressed with Martha Ingram when both were raising money for the Tennessee Performing Arts Center. He asked her to join the board of Nashville City Bank in 1980, but her husband, Bronson Ingram, would not allow it at first. Then, a few weeks later, Bronson called Massey and asked him if he would donate money for a new structure at Montgomery Bell Academy. Massey said he would, but only if Bronson changed his mind and let his wife come on the board of his bank. Bronson Ingram relented, and Massey gave $750,000 to the school.

Of course, Massey's tendency to put people he met through rigorous tests had an unpleasant flip side. "If Massey got down on someone, he really got down on them and he almost never made up with them, at least as far as doing business with them was concerned," said John Neff, who had a close association with Massey from 1967 until 1975.

Bill Tyne, who had almost a father-son relationship with Massey from the time the two men met in 1972, said this about his mentor: "He expected a very high amount of business acumen from the people around him. Not everyone could function at this level. You may have heard it said that 'Some people don't suffer fools gladly.' Well, he really didn't suffer fools.

"Now, some people really enjoy working for someone with high standards like this, but some don't react well. And he was not going to sit around with people who don't get the job done."

Massey was not, however, a micromanager. Had he been, he never would have taken a company to the New York Stock Exchange, let alone three. He believed in hiring people who he thought were talented, hard working, and trustworthy, and then turning them loose to do their job.

"He wasn't the kind of person who pored over reports or who had a messy desk," Winners Corporation CEO Lonnie Stout said. "In fact, he didn't spend a lot of time on anything. Mr. Massey made quick decisions. He would listen to a presentation, and when the person would leave, he'd say to me, 'Lonnie, that sounds like an idea we ought to look into. Would you evaluate that?' or 'I don't think that's a very good idea. Let's just send them a note thanking them for coming by.' He was quick like that and brought other people like me in to do the detail work, at least he did when I worked for him."

Was Jack Massey interested in politics? Sort of. Massey believed in capitalism, democracy, and the two-party system. He voted every chance he got and made certain his children understood that it was their duty to do the same.

However, Massey was always more interested in business ventures than he was politics. The first time he was officially involved in a political race was when he served as treasurer for U.S. Representative Richard Fulton's 1964 congressional campaign.

"I vaguely remember that I talked him into doing that, but I don't remember much other than that," Nashville attorney George Barrett said many years later. "I don't think he did a whole lot except lend his name to the campaign." Massey's support for the Democrat Fulton was not a sign of a liberal streak. At the time there was not a serious Republican challenger for Nashville's congressional seat, and a vote for Fulton was generally considered a vote against the old-fashioned political machine that had dominated Nashville since the 1920s.

Massey voted Republican most of his life. Usually, however, he did it in a low-key manner, unlike some of his friends in the Nashville business community, such as Guilford Dudley Jr., Ted Welch, Joe Rodgers, and Ted Lazenby, all of whom became leading fundraisers for the Republican Party. (In fact, there were so many Republican fundraisers in Nashville in the last quarter of the twentieth century that Ronald Reagan referred to them as the "Nashville Mafia.")

There was one exception to Massey's understated support for Republican candidates. In 1972, a year in which Richard Nixon appeared certain to defeat challenger George McGovern, Massey gave Nixon's re-election campaign $250,000, making him one of the top ten donors to Nixon's coffers that year. After the election was over, Nixon did the logical thing, offering his benefactor the ambassadorship to Spain. Massey turned it down. "I probably would have liked that, Alyne Massey said, "but he never asked me whether I wanted to do it or not. He just told me he didn't want to do it."

Massey, of course, got to meet Nixon and exchange a few pleasantries with him, but other than that, it doesn't appear as if he ever asked the president for any favors. And, although he gave money to Republican candidates throughout the rest of the 1970s and 1980s, he never duplicated that level of support for anyone again.

Massey's main reason for voting Republican was his belief in government non-interference. "I try to support people who are interested in free enterprise and our freedom," he told a reporter in 1979. "We try to elect honorable people to public office, people who understand what really makes this country successful, and people who are reasonable in their views of government."[32]

He was not a member of the religious right, however. Although he voted for Ronald Reagan every chance he got, Jack Massey did not agree with Reagan's stance on abortion.

"He told me he was pro-choice because, back when he was a pharmacist, not a week would go by without a husband, boyfriend, or mother coming in to help a young woman who was hemorrhaging, and he knew what that meant," said Elizabeth Queener, the sister of Massey's second wife, Alyne, and administrator of the Massey Foundation from 1978 until 1990.

Massey's particular flavor of "Barry Goldwater Republicanism" is also reflected in the fact that he made it clear he didn't want Belmont College too far under the control of the more conservative elements of the Tennessee Baptist Convention.

Another thing that must be noted about Massey's political interest is that he mentored two Tennessee governors—after they left office. In 1970 Massey supported Winfield Dunn in his campaign and, after the election, took the governor- and first lady-elect on a vacation to Cat Cay Island in the Bahamas. During the next four years, however, Massey almost never called on Dunn while he was in office. "I cannot recall one time when Jack Massey ever came to me and either offered advice voluntarily or [asked] for any favor that a governor might be able to offer someone," Dunn said years later.

After Dunn's term expired in 1974, he took a job as an executive in charge of government relations at Hospital Corporation of America. He stayed with HCA for ten years, when he left the company to run for governor again. And even though the two men were still friends, Massey actually supported Dunn's opponent, Ned McWherter, in that race.

"He told me then that he would have supported me, but he had promised Ned that he would support him before he knew that I was running," Dunn said. "But that was the way Massey was. Once he had given his word, it was final."

Massey had a similar relationship with Lamar Alexander, Tennessee's governor from 1977 until 1985. Much like Dunn, Alexander saw little of Massey when he was in office. There was one notable exception to this, however. When Corrections Corporation of America was first formed by entrepreneurs Tom Beasley, Doctor Crants, and Sam Bartholomew, the company got a major infusion of capital from Massey-Burch Capital Corporation

A few months later CCA made the bold proposal to take over the entire state of Tennessee's prison system. Jack Massey actually came to the state Capitol to speak on behalf of CCA. His effort was in vain, however, and the company got very little of Tennessee's business.

When Alexander left office, Massey tried to get the former governor to come to work for a company Massey was trying to start called Education Corporation of America (which would theoretically do to education what HCA had done to health care and CCA had done to prisons). Alexander turned down that offer but later accepted a job to help start a leadership institute at Belmont College, a project made possible by a $250,000 gift from the Massey Foundation.

About this time Alexander was also involved in the creation of Corporate Child Care Corporation, a for-profit day care firm in which Massey-Burch made a startup investment. Alexander stayed at Belmont for about a year before he was appointed president of the University of Tennessee.

"Massey tried to talk him out of that," said Wayne Brown, dean of the Massey School of Business at the time. "He told him that if he took that job, the legislature would get him back for all the fights he had had with them when he was governor."

A volume such as this is naturally inclined to emphasize the things a person did, and not make note of the things he didn't do. Nevertheless, it should be stated that Jack Massey was not an avid reader, other than newspapers and business magazines, and that he couldn't write very well, other than business writing. Young Jack Massey's letters are poorly organized and contain many misspelled words and typographical errors.

And just about everyone queried scratched their heads when asked whether Massey ever discussed a book with them. "One time I bought him a new local history book that everyone was talking about, and I thought he would really like it," his second wife, Alyne, said. "Instead, he got his feelings hurt, and I never really understood why."

Massey never kept a diary, which is one of the reasons that it is such a challenge to recount his life prior to his becoming a millionaire. One of the most revealing things he ever said to anyone came in June 1978, when he was giving a long interview to Deborah Cooney, hired by HCA to conduct oral history interviews with several of the company's founders.

"I don't think anybody remembers the exact details of everything that happened," Massey told her. "I don't. I never live in the past. I'm always living for today and tomorrow, and hoping there'll be a tomorrow. And I don't try to remember. I never did try to remember things."

As if hospitals, fried chicken, coal mining, venture capital, hotels, real estate, and Christian book publishing weren't enough, Jack Massey quietly remained in the drugstore business. During the decade following the end of World War II, he disposed of his original drugstore chain, one location at a time, closing the one in the Bennie Dillon Building downtown and selling the other two.

But in 1955 Baptist Hospital built a professional office building with room for a drugstore on its ground floor near its main hospital. Massey and young pharmacist Bob Johnston developed that drugstore as equal partners.

A few years later brothers Ross and John Hickey merged their two drugstores with the one owned by Massey and Johnston, forming a small chain called Century Two. Century Two continued to own a handful of drugstores in Nashville until the *early 1980s. Massey held onto his ownership of Century Two for sentimental reasons.*

"He was always proud of the fact that he was a pharmacist," Ross Hickey said. "I remember when we had the drugstore in Belle Meade, he'd walk in the door and come back into the prescription room and talk pharmacy talk with me.

"I also knew that, even though he was busy with much, much bigger things, such as HCA and Mrs. Winners, that if I ever needed to talk to him, he made time for me to talk to him right quick because he knew we'd be talking about something related to drugstores." Massey also carried his pharmacy license with him in his wallet until the day he died.

Part-ownership of a small drugstore chain also gave Jack Massey something else to boast about. "He used to say that he owned twenty-five percent of a company that owned four drugstores," said Commerce Union Bank executive Ed Nelson. "In his mind, that counted as owning a drugstore."

10

DRESS FOR SUCCESS

Jack Massey got involved in Hospital Corporation of America with the assurance that it would not occupy much of his time. But for the first couple of years it took plenty, as he and HCA's early financial officials, such as John Neff and Sam Brooks, raised money and introduced the company to Wall Street. In 1971 Massey scaled back his involvement in HCA and began to focus on other ventures. He also began to spend more time on his social life with his new wife, Alyne.

However, in 1976 HCA President John Neff left the company, later to become state commerce and insurance commissioner under Governor Lamar Alexander. Neff's departure was not an expected one, and it created a real dilemma for HCA's board of directors. By this time HCA had become a notable force as a public company, and its fortunes were very much dictated by the whims of Wall Street. So it was important not just to find the right successor for Neff, but to find someone in whom institutional investors had confidence. And while there was a young man at HCA who thought he was ready to run the company (Dr. Thomas Frist Jr.), a majority of the board members thought he was too young.

"I wouldn't say that there was a heated debate or anything," said Carl Reichardt, who went on the board of HCA in 1972 and remained there for three decades. "We made up our mind that we really needed someone from the outside, who hopefully was an outstanding leader in the business community, to give the company more credibility, because HCA and the whole concept of running hospitals for profit was still so new. Meanwhile, it was clear to everyone that Tommy [Frist Jr.] was destined to eventually run the company."

Massey decided that the best thing for HCA would be for him to become its full-time president for about two years, after which he would be replaced by an outsider. So, in May 1976, at the age of seventy, Massey moved his office to HCA's new headquarters building adjacent to Centennial Park. It didn't take long for him to make a few changes.

First of all, HCA's corporate culture was too informal for a man who had made it through the Great Depression by working every waking hour. Massey noticed, for instance, that some of HCA's executives had a tendency to show up a couple of minutes late for meetings. He therefore instructed his secretary to lock the door of the executive meeting room at the exact moment meetings were scheduled to begin. Anyone late would have to miss the gathering and send Massey a written memo explaining why.

Massey also gave out unsolicited tips on how to dress, not always good-naturedly. In the mid-1970s HCA's top executives had a working lunch together on Mondays in the company boardroom. One day Massey walked into the meeting and dropped a copy of the book *Dress for Success* on the table. "I have a box full of these books for all of you to read," he said.

"You have got to be the motleyest-looking crowd of people I've ever seen. I want you to read this book and straighten up the way you dress when you are at work."

At least three of the men in the room remembered that day and said Massey was right—although, curiously, everyone seems to remember the awful things everyone else was wearing and not the clothes they themselves were wearing.

"He wasn't talking about me, because I had been the governor and I knew how to dress," said former Governor Winfield Dunn, who was head of government relations for HCA.

Clayton McWhorter, who went to work as an administrator at an HCA hospital in Georgia in 1970 and became vice president in charge of HCA's domestic operations six years later, said, "There is no telling what some of us were wearing. Probably leisure suits. He didn't much care for those."

McWhorter learned that clothes weren't the only thing Massey could get upset about. One day after he started working at the corporate office, Massey asked McWhorter to make a presentation to the board. As Massey later recounted, the talk did not go well. "He put his finger in his ear, hands in his pockets, and was standing on one foot," Massey said. "He just simply could not say what he wanted to say, and I was very glad when he got through and left."

A few days after the speech, Massey called McWhorter into his office. The junior HCA executive could tell his boss wasn't happy.

"I want to talk to you about your presentation to the board last Friday," Massey began.

"What a relief," McWhorter said. "I thought you were going to talk about the way I'm dressed."

"That could improve, too."

Massey said the speech had been dreadful. "If I were proposing you to be president of this company," Massey said, "you wouldn't have received one vote, not even mine. And I like you. Young man, how long did you prepare for that?"

"On the flight up from Atlanta," McWhorter responded.

"Well, the next time you make a presentation on behalf of this company, you had better be prepared. Do you understand?"

"Yes, sir," McWhorter answered.

McWhorter said he felt pretty bad after his boss had scolded him. But, in the end, he said it was one of the best things that ever happened to his career. From that point on he made certain he was better prepared to make presentations, and he even got some help when it came to his speech skills. The incident strangely enough endeared Massey to McWhorter. "Sometimes a screw-up makes you visible," McWhorter said years later. "And he was a friend to me from that point on, until the day he died."

HCA's new boss also had a tendency to ask questions to which he already knew the answers. If the person he queried knew the answers and told him, he was impressed. If he didn't know the answers but admitted that to him, Massey was still impressed; at least the person was being honest. If the person didn't know the answers but claimed he did, Massey was not impressed. "If you wanted to stretch the truth and point fingers or whatever, he could be brutal," said McWhorter.

One person who noticed this tendency and saw it just about every day was Vic Campbell. An Indiana native who first went to work for DuPont after college, Campbell moved to Nashville in 1972 and took a job helping to prepare registration statements for HCA's financial team. The first time Massey was introduced to Campbell was on a private plane. After being told that Campbell was HCA's "so-called Securities and Exchange Commission specialist," Massey insisted that Campbell sit next to him.

"He starts asking me a lot of questions about SEC reporting," Campbell said. "I had most of the answers, but then I got to a big question that I didn't know the answer to. I told him I'd find the answer. Well, after I got back to Nashville I looked it up and sent him a memo with the answer on it. He later called me and thanked me. And I realized later that he always knew the answer; he was just testing me."

The experience Massey gained as the owner of a surgical supply firm and board chairman (of both Baptist Hospital and HCA) gave him great confidence in his ability to know the ins and outs of his company, sometimes too much so.

"He could be very focused on little costs," said board member Bob Anderson. It wasn't always a good thing, though. Around 1977 HCA was trying to convince a large hospital in Palm Beach, Florida, to allow HCA to run it under a management contract. Massey took a special interest in the hospital, since it was close to his vacation home. When Joe Hutts, then chief of HCA's management division, called on the head of the hospital, Massey came along.

"We were having a meeting with the hospital president to talk about us managing their hospital, and he was putting us off and getting more evasive. He seemed dubious about the idea that we could save him money on supplies," Hutts said. "Of course, Mr. Massey really knew that stuff because he came from that end of the business. And I could see that Mr. Massey was getting more intense.

So, he finally asked the guy, 'What do you pay for surgical gloves?' The guy said, 'I don't know that.' Massey said, 'Well, what do you pay for these kinds of syringes?' The guy said, 'I don't know that.' And Massey said, 'Let me tell you what we pay for those things,' and he proceeded to do so. And then he said to the guy, 'I run a billion-dollar company and you run one hospital. If I were you, I'd pay a little more attention to things like that, and your hospital would run better.'

"We may have convinced him that we could do a better job. But we didn't get the contract."

By this time HCA was a mature and established company, but it was in an immature industry. "A major part of our work back then was to try to get analysts to cover the industry, and when we did this, it was a significant achievement," Campbell said. HCA was also suffering from three things that weren't the company's fault. One was increasing interest rates. Another was added pressure from the federal government—the Carter administration in particular—to reduce health-care costs.

But probably the biggest problem was the persistent bear market of the early to mid-1970s. "HCA's stock did very poorly for a long time because small stocks in general were out of favor at that time," said Katie Gambill, an analyst with Equitable Securities of Nashville who followed HCA.

Massey was responsible for, though by no means always the initiator of, HCA's multi-pronged strategy at that time. In part because of rising interest rates, HCA began managing hospitals for a fee, following the lead of cross-town competitor Hospital Affiliates International. HCA began dabbling in foreign markets and managing and owning hospitals in England and Australia. And in its most unusual project ever, HCA completed and operated the King Faisal Specialist Hospital in Riyadh, Saudi Arabia.

Behind the scenes, HCA considered the idea of merging its company with Louisville-based Humana. But the deal fell through because neither Humana nor HCA officials could agree on who would run the merged entity.

As HCA's tenth anniversary neared, Massey emphasized a goal the company had set the night he and several of his colleagues first purchased Park View Hospital. "It was a huge goal for us to have a hundred hospitals in the first ten years," said Clayton McWhorter. "I remember Massey said we were going to have one hundred even if the last one is a two-bed hospital."

By the time HCA achieved that milestone, in 1978, Massey was looking for his successor. Much as it had done back in 1970, HCA looked outside the company, recruiting former Prudential Securities Chairman Donald McNaughton to be the next president.

Massey initially found out about McNaughton when he read about his retirement in the *Wall Street Journal*. After McNaughton met everyone in Nashville, Massey invited him down to his home in Palm Beach. "He didn't even know who we were when I called him the first time," Massey later said. "He'd never heard of us."

As Campbell remembered it, it was Massey's aggressive pitch that made the difference. "I remember that McNaughton kept saying over and over again that he wasn't sure if he wanted to live in the South, this kind of thing," said Campbell. "And then Massey says to him, 'You know why you need to come down here and take this job? Because we are going to make you rich.' And I think that was it."

A few years later, Massey recounted to a reporter something that he said to McNaughton on his last day. "Don," Massey said to his successor, "I want you to know that you're in charge of the company, and I'm not going to look over your shoulder and ever tell you what to do. You are on your own." McNaughton later thanked Massey for keeping his promise.

It was the late 1970s. Many people Jack Massey grew up with, worked with, and knew most of his life were ailing or dead. And there is nothing like the death of a child or sibling to remind us of our own mortality. Both Jack Massey's adopted son, Don, and his brother Joe died in 1979.

Remarkably, however, Jack Massey showed no signs of slowing down. He still came to work every day, had an active social life, spent time on the golf course, and played a mean game of gin rummy. He maintained an active role in the leadership of Nashville—behind the scenes, as a member of a group called the Watauga Club that regularly met to discuss important local issues. Now one of the state's wealthiest men, Massey was also making a name for himself as a philanthropist.

Among the Nashville organizations that had been the recipients of his gifts by this time were Harpeth Hall School, Montgomery Bell Academy, Meharry Medical College, and Belmont College. Massey was in such a good mood, in fact, that he even gave money to his old nemesis Vanderbilt University. The key person that influenced him in this bit of generosity was his second wife, Alyne, a Vanderbilt alumna.

"One day Sam [Fleming] came in, and Jack was here, and Sam said he wanted me to serve on the Vanderbilt Board of Trust," Alyne Massey recounted several years later. "Jack thought that was very nice. And then Sam said that he wanted us to give a million dollars to the Vanderbilt Law Library and that way we could name it for my father, who was a prominent lawyer in Franklin.

"Well, my father graduated from the Yale Law School, not Vanderbilt. So I wasn't sure about that idea. Jack piped up and said to Sam, 'I'll give you a million dollars for it if you will name it for Alyne.' And I said, 'Oh, no, you only name it for people who are dead—and I am very much alive!' But Jack said, 'Well, then I'm not going to give it.' And here I am, a new member of the board, and I didn't want the school not to get the money. So I said OK."

Massey also gave generously to the Tennessee Performing Arts Center, which was being considered for the bottom few floors of a twenty-one-story state office building then in the planning stages. To get TPAC off the ground, organizer Martha Ingram needed $4 million. "Jack Massey invited a few friends to his house one September evening and raised $1 million in his living room," a press account reported. "By December next, the other three million dollars for the center's endowment was at hand."[33]

There were limits to Massey's power and influence, however. About this time Massey pledged his financial support to a grandiose plan to build a convention center, hotels, office buildings, and apartments in the undeveloped train gulch area just west of Nashville's central business district. "Mr. Massey was prepared to sink a huge amount of money in that project," said Ted Welch, a Nashville developer and Republican fundraiser who spent a lot of time trying to promote the gulch. Under the rough blueprint, Massey would finance, Welch would develop, Joe Rodgers would build, and Earl Swensson would design the whole project.

Efforts in this direction were so serious that some of the partners even formed a new construction company, called American Constructors, to build the project. However, the gulch project didn't get off the ground after Mayor Richard Fulton chose to put Nashville's convention center in the heart of Nashville's downtown, about six blocks away.

*J*ack Massey was a consummate deal maker. No matter how much money he had, his brain was constantly coming up with ideas for new profit-making ventures.

In the late 1970s Massey took a trip to Morocco to talk to King Hassan II about the possibility of HCA building a hospital there. On that trip he had breakfast with Armand Hammer, the head of Occidental Petroleum Corporation. HCA executive Bob Crosby remembered the meal well.

"There I was, sitting with Jack Massey and Armand Hammer, two of the most successful and famous businessmen in the world, and to say the least I was pretty spellbound," Crosby later wrote. "The thing that was most fascinating to me is that they were sitting there eating this melon that they served in Morocco, somewhat similar to a honeydew melon, but it appeared to be of a much higher quality and much sweeter flavor. Mr. Massey and Armand Hammer were talking about how good this melon was.

"Before I knew it, the two of them had paper and pencils out, and they were calculating how they could buy these melons wholesale in Morocco and charter ships to take them back to the United States and make a market in the United States and make some money.

"Here were two very wealthy men, and the money they would make from this melon project would be just minuscule compared to their current wealth, but just the challenge of seeing an opportunity and making it turn into a profitable venture was something that they thrived on and always thought about. That, to this day, is still one of the most delightful experiences I have had in my career."

11

GOOD BISCUITS,
BAD STOCK

T HE VOLUNTEER CAPITAL/MRS. WINNERS saga is an interesting
case study about trial and error.

After the Wendy's initial public offering went well, Volunteer Capital Corporation continued to make money. But by
this time, a small profitable public company that garnered little
attention wasn't enough for Jack Massey. The man who hit
home runs with Kentucky Fried Chicken and Hospital Corporation of America was keeping his eyes open for another winning opportunity, a concept that might give him a third company that he could take to the New York Stock Exchange.
That chance came along in 1978.

Massey had known L. Z. Hartzog for years; he had once
been a Kentucky Fried Chicken franchisee and was one of the
largest Wendy's franchisees. Hartzog, who was hard of hearing

and flew a private plane with a giant heart painted on its tail, had started a chain of chicken restaurants in Atlanta called Granny's. Volunteer Capital leased equipment to Granny's and watched its development closely. At some point someone at VCC suggested that the firm buy Granny's with the idea of franchising it and turning it into a national chain. This idea was largely based on the notion that Heublein was neglecting its Kentucky Fried Chicken business, a view commonly held at the time.

It's hard to know who originally came up the idea of the Granny's acquisition. Unlike the Kentucky Fried Chicken and Hospital Corporation of America stories, there was not an overabundance of people claiming credit for the Granny's idea in later years, but rather a shortage of them. However, it is almost certain that the idea came from Massey, Hartzog, or Earl Beasley, or two of the three, or possibly all of them.

Beasley was the president of Volunteer Capital, which meant that he would have been on the lookout for a new idea. Hartzog was probably looking to sell his company. And Massey, of course, was looking for a new venture, and by this time he had already begun to tell people that he wanted to take a third company to the New York Stock Exchange. "I want to get back to being a franchiser," Massey told the *New York Times* after the Granny's acquisition."[34]

In November 1978 Volunteer Capital bought Granny's, and over the next two years VCC's management came up with a strategy for the chicken chain. The first problem was the name. Granny's had been sued for violation of naming rights by a similarly named business out of the Midwest, so VCC set public relations firm Holder-Kennedy to work coming up with a new one. Holder-Kennedy originally came back with the name Winners Fried Chicken, based on the idea of sports.

"We could visualize that the place would be decorated with trophies and blue ribbons and pictures of athletes—this sort of thing," said Kennedy. "But after we told everyone about this, there was a funny reaction from all the women in the office. They were averse to using the name because of the connotation that it would be associated with men watching football, men sitting on the couch, that sort of thing. So we put 'Mrs.' In front of the name, and that was it."

The company also came up with operational concepts meant to differentiate it in the world of fast food. It made homemade biscuits a major staple of its menu. This was a big deal at the time. McDonald's was not serving biscuits, while Kentucky Fried Chicken was serving a roll that was one of the least popular items on its menu. "Mrs. Winners has the best biscuits I've ever eaten," Massey proudly told the *New York Times* at one point.[35]

Volunteer Capital decided that its Mrs. Winners chain would serve breakfast, thus making use of the facility for more hours each day (KFC was not serving breakfast). Volunteer Capital came up with an architectural concept that invited family dining more than KFC, which at the time primarily consisted of takeout units. Mrs. Winners would also focus on suburban markets—places into which KFC had been slow to expand. Volunteer Capital then changed its name to Winners Corporation and got to work expanding the chain and selling franchises. Despite his advanced age, Massey was involved in just about every major strategic decision the company made.

Mark Frost, a young man who worked for Massey-Burch Capital Corporation's in-house broker-dealer, First Nashville Corporation, said he was present at a meeting when some of Mrs. Winners' menu items were being named. "One of the best things that the restaurant was going to be serving was a Chicken Club Biscuit, and we were discussing what we were going to call it," Brown remembered. "And then, all of a sudden, Don Johnston pops up and says, 'Well, gosh, Mr. Massey, you need to call it a "Big Jack."' And there was this hush in the conference room, because you have to remember that none of us called him Jack. To us he was Mr. Massey. We no more called him Jack than you could go on a ship and call an admiral by his first name. So this was quite funny."

Winners Corporation's strategy seemed to make sense, and of course Jack Massey's presence was an immeasurable asset. So Winners didn't have a hard time selling franchises and drawing people to buy its stock. But about the time the company began to expand its chicken chain, there were signs that all was not well. As Mrs. Winners restaurants began to open, they began to report disappointing numbers. Meanwhile, the corporation's Wendy's restaurants were also struggling, particularly in California. In 1980 Massey fired Earl Beasley as president and replaced him with M. V. "Buck" Hussung.

Mrs. Winners grew to sixty-two locations in 1982, then one hundred by the summer of 1983. It also built a $5 million, 60,000-square-foot headquarters in the new Maryland Farms office complex—an office much nicer than anything Kentucky Fried Chicken ever had in Nashville.

The news from new Mrs. Winners locations was not good, however. For one thing, there was the matter of the name. The company probably would have been better off if it had stayed with Kennedy's original "Winners" idea, because at least that could have brought to mind a tangible image. By using the title "Mrs. Winners," however, the chain had named itself after someone who didn't exist and whose name didn't bring to mind an image of any kind. In fact, unlike Kentucky Fried Chicken, McDonald's, Long John Silver's, and Wendy's, the chain never could figure out what its image or symbolic leader was.

In 1982 R. J. Reynolds bought Heublein, and a few months after that purchase the company began remodeling or rebuilding many KFC locations. Meanwhile, McDonald's went through a major resurgence, introducing breakfast to its menu in 1982 and Chicken NcNuggets in 1983.

"When McDonald's came out with their version of the homemade biscuit, that was unthinkable for us," Lonnie Stout,

Winners' chief financial officer at the time, said years later. "We just hadn't believed that they would do this, but they did. And then they put all their marketing muscle behind it."

Even while the chain was still expanding there were still signs that Mrs. Winners was doing poorly overall and horribly in certain markets, most notably the state of Louisiana. The company missed earnings for the first time during the first quarter of 1984. Shortly thereafter, Stout departed.

Nevertheless, Jack Massey believed Mrs. Winners was still, well, a winner, and he was convinced that to succeed, the company needed to expand, raise its profile, and advertise more. This meant raising more capital, and one way to do that was to be listed on the New York Stock Exchange. In the spring of 1984 Mrs. Winners applied for and was granted a listing on the NYSE. The company went public on August 8 of that year, and Massey thus became the first man in American history to take three separate companies to the Big Board. It was this achievement that later resulted in many kudos and tributes, such as his induction into the National Business Hall of Fame in 1987.

A wave of national media attention naturally followed, but most of it was focused on Massey's achievements rather than his new company. "Massey, who turned 80 earlier this month, has just listed Winners Corporation on the New York Stock Exchange," *Forbes* reported. "The company is a run-of-the-drum-stick Southern food chain, but its debut sets a record."[36]

The *New York Times* said that "Jack Massey is no workaholic Puritan. He is an easygoing dreamer of sorts, a financial adventurer who ultimately works the arithmetic and creates a team. He is a gregarious Palm Beach regular who likes golf, the good life, and his friends, several of whom have made big money investing with him. Though he has no college degree, he is also a teacher, a man who likes to share his information, insights, and experience."[37]

But after the hoopla surrounding its public offering, things got worse at Mrs. Winners. The company lost $3.6 million in 1985 and about $2 million during each of the next three years. The stock was punished, falling from $13 at its initial public offering to about $3 two years later.

Mrs. Winners' NYSE listing made it inevitable that the company's failure was noticed in the national media. In December 1986, in a story headlined, "The virtues of quitting while you're ahead," *Forbes* examined the failure of the chicken chain. Massey, whose health had begun to take a turn for the worse by this time, spoke of himself in the third person in the article. "Jack Massey for the last two years has been in and out of the hospital and has admittedly neglected the company," Massey told the reporter.[38]

By this time Mrs. Winners was embroiled in a legal mess. Its Mississippi franchisee had filed suit against the company for failure to live up to its business agreement. The lawsuit was especially troubling to Massey because among the owners of the franchisee were Nashville general contractor Joe Rodgers; Massey's daughter, Barbara Massey; Massey's accountant, Clarence Edmonds; and several investors from Jackson, Mississippi. Barbara Massey and Edmonds refused to take part in the lawsuit, but Rodgers did, and his involvement in it was troublesome to Massey.

"My father and Joe Rodgers had a father-son relationship, and the lawsuit brought tears to Daddy's eyes," Barbara Massey Rogers later said. The suit dragged on for months, and depositions were taken on both sides. It was eventually dismissed.

By this time Hussung had been fired and replaced by the returning Lonnie Stout. As soon as the lawsuit was over, Stout came to Massey and told him that the company needed to dispose of the chicken business. "Many people have often told me that they thought that Mr. Massey didn't want to give up on Mrs. Winners, which is why we held onto it for so long," Stout said. "Well, that is not true. The day that I pronounced it dead, he told me to do what I thought I had to do. You see, we weren't hanging in there for some sort of emotional reason. We were hanging in there because we didn't have a choice. We had to get the lawsuit off our backs before we could move forward, and Massey knew that."

As if the company didn't have enough trouble on its hands, in 1988 it withstood a low-bid takeover attempt by Texas investor Joseph Stillman. Finally, in August 1989, Stout found a buyer for the Mrs. Winners business, selling it to Arby's franchisee Russ Umphenour in Atlanta for about $30 million in cash and the assumption of lease obligations.

In the spring and summer of 1973 two boys began collecting golf balls from the bodies of water on the Belle Meade Country Club, the most exclusive such club in Nashville. Eventually, Bert Denton and Al Thomas gathered more than two hundred balls, and they decided it was time to cash in on all their hard work.

Young Denton retrieved from his father's closet a suitcase big enough to hold the golf balls. Half expecting to be kicked off the grounds, he set the suitcase up along the path that golf carts took between the sixteenth and seventeenth holes.

"Nine times out of ten, the members of the club would chase us out of there," Denton recalled three decades later. But as luck would have it, one of the first carts that came by that day was one in which Jack Massey was riding. And the sight of two boys trying to sell the fruits of their labor was too much for Massey to pass up.

"He took a look at my suitcase full of golf balls and asked me how much I'd take for it," Denton said. "I told him thirty dollars.

"He said, 'How 'bout twenty-five?' I said, 'No, I want thirty for them.' He said he'd pay thirty if I'd throw in the suitcase. I told him that there was no way that I could throw in the suitcase because my father would kill me if I didn't bring it home. And I think he really admired the fact that I stood my ground."

Massey eventually bought the golf balls but not the suitcase. A few days later he invited the boy over to his house and got to know him. During the next few years, Massey helped Bert Denton's parents send him to a private middle school and later to Belmont College.

"The years he helped me, he would require me to come over and visit him and show him my report card from the previous semester," said Denton, who later became a lawyer. "He was a real stickler for that."

12

THE OLD MAN

B Y THE LATE 1970s MORE than four hundred people were
approaching the Massey Investment Company annually
with ideas for new companies or in hope of securing an
investment in an existing one. The vast majority of these people were turned away. But Massey Investment did invest in
dozens of companies each year. Some did horribly, others
treaded water. Occasionally, Massey Investment helped create
a company that did splendidly, such as Intermedics.

Eventually, however, Lucius Burch III believed Massey
Investment Company needed to be reorganized. "For one
thing, it was apparent to me that there was no future after Mr.
Massey's death," Burch said. "But there was more to it than
that. Up to that point, we weren't running a venture capital
company so much as we were just doing deals for Mr. Massey
and his friends—a syndication formed at a cocktail party. We
were finding the deals, structuring the financing, syndicating it,

managing it, and realizing on it, but no one was paying us a fee for all this. We were all on salary from Mr. Massey, and everyone who was investing in it and making money from it was just getting a nice favor from him."

In 1980 Massey Investment Company was reorganized and renamed Massey-Burch Investment Group, an entity owned 50 percent by Massey and 50 percent by Burch. Within a couple of years of its reorganization, the way Massey-Burch Investment Group did venture capital had changed in many ways from the way the old Massey Investment Company operated. Money would not be raised for a particular company, but for a fund that, in turn, invested in one or two dozen companies. Only serious investors could invest in the funds—the minimum investment was usually $250,000.

Massey-Burch Investment Group derived its revenue from two sources. One was management fees paid for by the companies in which it purchased equity (typically two thousand dollars a month). The other was a 2 percent annual fee paid by investors.

With this new structure, Jack Massey's role as the creator of companies grew to another level. Massey-Burch soon counted among its investors not only wealthy Nashvillians, but also Vanderbilt University and the Tennessee Valley Authority.[39] Although there is no point in listing the hundreds of companies, successful and unsuccessful, in which Massey-Burch invested, a short list of some of the more interesting is worthwhile.

SURGICAL CARE AFFILIATES

Andrew "Woody" Miller was one of HCA's first executives, hired by the company in 1969 to be its internal audit manager. He eventually worked his way to the top of HCA's hospital management division. In 1981 he tried to convince the company to build a chain of outpatient surgery centers, but the board scuttled the idea because of conflict-of-interest concerns. Miller decided to do it himself and convinced Massey and other Massey-Burch executives that the idea was worthwhile. He left HCA and moved into an office at Massey-Burch, and within a few months he had convinced former General Care executive Joel Gordon to help him start the business, called Surgical Care Affiliates.

Years later, Gordon explained the logic behind SCA. "Back then, a lot of things that used to take a three- or four-day hospital stay were beginning to be done on an outpatient basis," he said. "They had improved anesthesia. They had come out with arthroscopic technology. Gall bladders used to take a week in the hospital, and now they were doing a gall bladder operation in one day."

SCA required very little seed money. The business got started with $800,000 invested by Miller, Gordon, Massey-Burch, and a few other individuals. Armed with that capital and stock certificates, SCA purchased outpatient surgery centers in Louisville and Lexington, Kentucky, and Fort Worth, Texas, and then began applying for certificates of need to build about a dozen others throughout the Southeast. At that point, SCA raised about $14 million through the sale of a million shares of stock to the public.

"People and institutions who bought that stock certainly weren't buying bricks and mortar or existing cash flow," Miller remembered a few years later. "They were buying the track record of the management team, and they were buying the concept. And Jack's presence as an investor and his presence on our board of directors gave us instant credibility."

After its initial public offering, SCA built a chain of outpatient surgery centers, each of which was partially financed by surgeon investments in the communities in which they were built. "A large part of what Joel and I did was go around convincing doctors to buy investment units," Miller said. "Every one was structured so that the doctors owned forty-nine percent and the company owned fifty-one percent. Surgical Care had a management contract to run the center."

Surgical Care Affiliates remained an independent company until it was acquired by Birmingham-based HealthSouth in 1996 for $1.2 billion.

SOUTHLIFE

After Houston-based American General took over Nashville-based NLT in 1982, several NLT executives were either forced out or left voluntarily. Ted Lazenby was a part of that exodus, and in 1983 he and Commerce Union Bank Chairman Ed Nelson had the idea of putting together a chain of insurance companies, making them more efficient, and eventually selling them.

"There were a number of small, family-owned companies that could not compete in today's economy and regulatory environment, plus they didn't have a big enough portfolio to avoid investment risks," Lazenby said. "We took this idea to Massey-Burch, and Jack saw that we were onto something immediately."

Lazenby and Nelson asked Massey-Burch for a hundred-thousand-dollar investment. Massey and Burch loved the idea, so much so that they invested five times that amount of their own and their clients' money. Lazenby and Nelson raised another half-million dollars through about a dozen Nashville friends. They called their venture Southlife.

The initial capitalization of a million dollars carried Southlife through two acquisitions: Public Savings Life, purchased through a sale of preferred stock and bank debt; and Coastal States Life of Atlanta, purchased through bank debt. With those two acquisitions under its belt, Southlife went public and made two more acquisitions by 1987.

In 1989 Southlife was acquired by Capital Holding Corporation (later Providian) for $160 million. "And all this came from that five hundred thousand dollars in seed money," a grateful Lazenby said a few years later. "And if Jack did not very quickly see the opportunity, we might not have been able to get Southlife off the ground."

CORRECTIONS CORPORATION OF AMERICA

In 1980 Tom Beasley, chairman of the Tennessee Republican Party, attended a cocktail party for U.S. Senator Howard Baker. The *Tennessean* had only a day or two earlier published a story about overcrowded state prisons, and the conversation made its way to that topic. "They'll never solve that problem until they figure out a way to get the private sector involved," Beasley heard someone say.

Beasley began talking up the idea of a new private prison company, which he began referring to as Corrections Corporation of America. As is the case with many startups, connections and timing were a big part of getting the venture off the ground. Beasley mentioned the idea to John Neff, who at the time was the Tennessee commissioner of commerce and insurance. Neff told Beasley that Lucius Burch had told him only a few days earlier that he was thinking about finding someone to start just such a company, and Neff put Beasley in contact with Burch.

"We had already been studying the idea of a business that would do in prisons exactly what HCA had done in the hospital business," Burch said. After only one meeting, Massey-Burch agreed to raise half a million dollars for the company in exchange for 50 percent of its stock.

CCA was the best publicized and most controversial Massey-Burch company ever. In 1985 the company made an all-out effort to take over the Tennessee prison system. Governor Lamar Alexander supported that notion, but it was rejected by the legislature, in part because of criticism revolving around the number and identities of people who had received insider stock.

CCA began to report consistent growth for the first time a year later, when it successfully got a contract to own and operate four large prisons in Texas. About this time Massey talked on a Nashville television program about how excited he was about the company.

"If HCA can build hospitals, then they can build prisons for people in prison," Massey said. "The first unit was built and filled and profitable, and I'd say in the last ninety days they have more than doubled their business, and probably in another ninety days they will double it again, if they can handle it. It's just growing so fast. Almost every state in the union has called wanting to talk to them about it."

During the next year the company signed contracts in New Mexico, Louisiana, Oklahoma, and Texas.

PHYCOR

Jack Massey's health had begun to decline by the time Phycor came along. In 1988 former HCA executive Joe Hutts was toying with the idea of a company that would buy large physician clinics. He happened to meet up with Massey-Burch's Don Johnston, who only a few days earlier had spoken with Lucius Burch about the same thing.

"Lucius talked about how his father, a doctor, had spent years and years building up his practice, but when he sold it, all he got was a value equal to the assets at a discount," Johnston said. "Well, that lingered in my mind, and pretty soon we were talking about the idea of a company that would do for physicians what HCA did for hospitals."

Massey attended most of the early Phycor meetings and was very enthusiastic about the idea; after all, fifty years earlier he had learned a lot about how to run doctors' offices through his surgical supply business. Massey-Burch invested $3.5 million in Phycor as a startup, then invested in two other private offerings before the company went public in 1994.

Phycor did quite well during the next two years. In 1996, its stock nearly reached forty dollars a share, and the company held the assets to five clinics with thirty-eight hundred doctors. But about that time, the entire physician practice management industry fell upon hard times, in part because of reimbursement pressure from the federal government, and in part because the very idea of a chain of multi-specialty clinics had cultural problems. By 1999 Phycor was losing money and facing a wave of lawsuits. The company eventually filed for bankruptcy.

Surgical Care Affiliates, Southlife, Corrections Corporation of America, and Phycor represented a fraction of Massey-Burch-related companies in the 1980s. These companies did a lot for the Nashville economy, and Massey-Burch funds generally outperformed other investment yardsticks. Nevertheless, by the end of the decade Massey was not happy with the course of events at the venture capital company that bore his name.

Much of his dissatisfaction had to do with ways in which the business had changed over the years. By this time Massey-Burch was a complicated company that answered to a list of institutional investors. Jack Massey no longer controlled it the way he had a decade earlier. He may have felt that the investment business had been more fun back when the investors consisted of himself and a handful of his friends, and when he himself negotiated and closed many of the deals.

There were other arguments, no doubt, disputes which might have seemed important at the time but don't seem so in hindsight. In any case, Massey decided to split from Massey-Burch, and in 1989 the octogenarian ordered his lawyers and accountants to split his assets from Massey-Burch. He began making plans to start and operate a new venture capital company that theoretically would be run by his new protégé, Bill Andrews.

"We had been partners for twenty years," Lucius Burch III said later. "It made absolutely no sense for him to go into business and purchase us out, especially at his age. But I think that's what led him to do it, his old age."

There were also other business ventures in the 1980s that were unrelated to Massey-Burch. In the 1940s, 1950s, and 1960s, Jack Massey was affiliated with Nashville's Third

National Bank. His focus shifted when he bought a large chunk of stock in Nashville City Bank in 1968, and in 1981 his focus shifted again.

Nashville's Commerce Union Bank was originally started in 1916 by Nashville businessman Ed Potter. Potter and his brother Justin (Jet), who made most of his money selling coal, controlled the bank for two generations. But in 1976, the last of the Potter brothers died, and within a couple of years the Commerce Union board was looking for someone to buy the block of stock owned by the Potter family, which constituted 20 percent of the bank's shares.

In 1981 that stock was purchased by brothers Gustavo and Ricardo Cisneros, two members of one of the wealthiest families in Venezuela. Three years later, however, the Cisneros brothers had to sell their stock suddenly because of exchange rate matters. They called Commerce Union President Dennis Bottorff and told him they had agreed to sell the stock to First Tennessee Bank of Memphis. Bottorff was stunned.

"I knew that if they sold twenty percent of the bank to First Tennessee, then they were basically selling the whole bank to First Tennessee, and none of us wanted that to happen," Bottorff said. "So I called and talked to Ricardo."

Cisneros told Bottorff that they had to sell the stock and sell it fast. He gave the Nashville banker forty-eight hours to find a person, an institution, or a combination of people and institutions that would take First Tennessee's place.

Bottorff immediately began working on a plan to divide the Cisneroses' stock into four or five portions and sell them to different national banks (at the time, an out-of-state bank could legally own just five percent of Commerce Union). He had made quick presentations to a couple of financial institutions when Jack Massey called.

"He said he wanted to have lunch with me, and I told him that as much as I wanted to right then, it really wasn't a good time to do so," Bottorff said. "But he was persistent, so I agreed."

Bottorff was aware of the fact that Massey already owned about $4 million in Commerce Union stock, which he had purchased when Ed Nelson was president of the bank a couple of years earlier.

The next day Massey told Bottorff that he was interested in buying a large part of the Cisneroses' Commerce Union stock. "He said he'd take it all, if he had to, but in any case he'd take whatever anyone else didn't take," Bottorff said. After word got out in New York that Massey had committed, selling the stock became easier, and three financial institutions stepped forward to invest.

"Everyone else got to thinking that if Massey wanted to buy it, then he must know something," Bottorff said. "So, quite honestly, he saved Commerce Union from going to First Tennessee."

When combined with his earlier investment, Massey ended up with about 9 percent of the stock in Commerce Union, an investment worth about $25 million to $30 million at the time.

With his foot in two Nashville financial institutions, Commerce Union and Nashville City Bank, Massey naturally began to think out loud about engineering a merger between the two. According to people who were involved in these discussions (which never made the newspapers), merging the two banks was something Commerce Union's directors were interested in and some of Massey's colleagues on the Nashville City Bank board would like to have done as well.

But Calvin Houghland, who owned four times as much City Bank stock as Massey did by that time, didn't like the idea, nor did bank President Richard Chambers. "While Jack was a significant shareholder, Calvin was a much more significant shareholder, and at the end of the day Calvin didn't have to do it Jack's way," Chambers said many years later. "There was always dynamic tension between Jack's interest and Calvin's interest."

One disagreement between Massey and Houghland did make the papers, however. In the fall of 1985 Houghland considered selling his Nashville City Bank interest to Robert Bass, a Texas developer who at that time was developing an office tower in Nashville that was later called the Nashville City Center. Under the deal, which was never consummated, the bank would agree to be the anchor tenant in Bass's building.

Massey came out in the newspaper against the proposed deal, calling it bad for shareholders. "If they wanted to come in and do business in Nashville, they should have offered something to every shareholder," Massey said. "Instead, they just wanted to get working control of the bank and then get the bank to move into their building. I think it's unfair."

In spite of Massey's objections, Houghland signed an option to sell his shares to Bass. About that time the Nashville City Bank hired Kidder, Peabody & Company to look for a larger bank for it to merge with. In the summer of 1986, a few months after a regional interstate banking compact made the purchase of one bank by another across state lines legal in Tennessee, Dominion Bankshares of Roanoke, Virginia, purchased Nashville City Bank.

Massey did not go on the board of Dominion as a part of that transaction, which meant that, for the first time in forty years, he was not on a bank board. Under the many banking mergers of the next two decades, Dominion became a part of First Union and later U.S. Bank.

But when it came to real estate ventures, Jack Massey lost his Midas touch. In the 1940s he had purchased four houses on West End Avenue between Twenty-first and Twenty-second avenues, with the anticipation (which turned out to be accurate) that Nashville's physician community would abandon downtown for the Vanderbilt-West End corridor. One of the first physicians who followed Massey to West End was his friend Thomas Frist Sr., who in 1947 bought one of Massey's houses and set up his practice there.

Eventually, Massey and Frist began looking to do something different with their West End land, and as early as 1972 they started talking about putting a hotel there. But the project did not get off the ground until it was placed in the hands of developers Joe Rodgers, Jim Caden, and Chip Christianson. By that time, Massey's and Frist's parcels were combined with a few others, one of which had once contained the Tennessee governor's mansion.

In 1982 the trio, doing business as CRC Holdings, announced plans to build a $40 million hotel and office building on the site which would be called Vanderbilt Plaza. They chose architect Earl Swensson, who had made a name for himself as the primary architect for the Opryland Hotel & Convention Center. Massey invested $6 million—more cash than he ever invested in any of his startup companies, including HCA. He also spent personal funds decorating the hotel with such amenities as paintings and oriental rugs. Frist pitched in $2 million, and CRC solicited investments in $20,000 increments from about 140 prominent Nashville residents.

Many of those were physicians who had previously made money through their ownership of Park View Hospital stock. Others included former Tennessee Governor Winfield Dunn and Massey's accountant, Clarence Edmonds. Largely due to Massey's prestige, Mellon Bank of Pittsburgh agreed to be the construction lender.

Because of key tenants such as Dean Witter and Earl Swensson Associates, Vanderbilt Plaza's office side was about two-thirds occupied when it opened in 1984. But after its opening, the Vanderbilt Plaza Hotel had occupancy rates well below projections. Simply put, the hotel charged rates that were too high for Nashville at the time. With the hotel losing money, attorney Brad Reed tried to negotiate a lower interest rate with Mellon Bank, but it was to no avail.

In 1986, the organization that owned Vanderbilt Plaza filed bankruptcy—it was Jack Massey's first major project to be associated with that unhappy word. Two years later, the court turned the property over to trustee Travelers Insurance, which later sold the hotel and office building to Loews. In the end, Vanderbilt Plaza's owners got about 10 percent of the money they had invested.

Another disappointing Massey-related real estate venture was on the outskirts of Nashville, at the Maryland Farms property. The City of Brentwood rejected the first master plan for Maryland Farms because of concerns it would increase the burden on the existing taxpayers. "[Developer] Al [Johnson] scared them to death with his first master plan because it had a lot of apartments in there, and the last thing that Brentwood wanted was apartments," Maryland Farms investor John Neff said. "They didn't want any children, because they didn't want to hire more teachers and build schools."

The developers eventually ended up with a plan that consisted predominantly of office buildings, and by the mid-1970s two of them had already been constructed, along with roads and utilities. Every bit of this early development was financed by bank loans; none of the partners was spending any real cash yet.

By this time there had been a shift in the ownership group. After the infrastructure costs soared, Johnson sold his interest to accountant Clarence Edmonds. The partners also sold stock to Ken Larish, a former employee of Third National Bank's real estate department. He was brought in to be chief executive officer of the project.

Office users began filling up Maryland Farms in the early 1980s; among the more notable corporate entities that moved into the development were Comdata and Winners Corporation As buildings were developed, a new business entity was formed with each new piece, which meant that the Maryland Farms development consisted of dozens of individual real estate ventures, most of which were made up largely of Neff, Edmonds, Massey, Larish, and others. But as the project became more successful, some of its investors took the fateful step of leveraging their ownership in it to finance other developments (one, for instance, was a large parcel of land in Lexington, Kentucky; another was in Murfreesboro, Tennessee).

When the real estate market collapsed in 1989, some of the side ventures simply failed to materialize. Meanwhile, rent at Maryland Farms had to be reduced from around $15 a square foot to about two-thirds that amount because of what was happening elsewhere in the Nashville market. "I consider this to have been as much my fault as everyone else's," said Neff, who, along with Edmonds and Larish, declared personal bankruptcy as a result of the Maryland Farms collapse. The Massey Foundation eventually took control of the entire development and was able to ride out the financial storm.

There is one other notable real estate transaction Jack Massey took part in during the last decade of his life. This one was not important because of its size, but it was amusing because of the personalities involved.

In the early 1970s Massey purchased an oceanfront home in Palm Beach, Florida. Next to the house lay about four hundred feet of undeveloped beachfront property, and directly across from the beachfront property lay Mar-a-Lago, the estate of cereal heiress Marjorie Merriweather Post. Post's property included not only the mansion but also the vacant land across the road from it. The mansion's value in part depended on its ocean view, which of course would have been diminished if the beachfront land were ever developed.

Post died in 1973. Her will called for the vacant land to be sold (with the proceeds going to her foundation), while the mansion was to be turned over to the federal government as a presidential retreat and guest house for international dignitaries. Since Massey lived next door to the beachfront property, and since he had plenty of money to invest at this point, he bought the four hundred-foot stretch of vacant land for $348,000.

In 1980, having decided that Mar-a-Lago was going to cost too much to keep up, the federal government gave the mansion back to the Post Foundation, which tried to liquidate it. Prospective buyers of Mar-a-Lago knew they would have to buy Massey's property as well to protect the value of the mansion. In 1985, Scotsman O. W. Smith, the owner of a gold refinery, offered $12 million for the mansion and furnishings and $2 million for the vacant land, which at the time was appraised at about half that amount. Massey apparently took a liking to Smith, but the offer eventually fell through.

By that time international deal maker Donald Trump had sensed a bargain, and he made the foundation an $8 million offer for the mansion and furnishings. The foundation, quite anxious to get the transaction over with, agreed to sell. Meanwhile, Trump approached Massey and did his best to talk the old man down from his $2 million sale price. Massey didn't come down one penny.

A couple of years later, in his book *The Art of the Deal*, Trump crowed about how he got a bargain when he bought the Mar-a-Lago mansion. He also boasted about how he financed 99.97 percent of the transaction. "But Trump doesn't say that, as a part of the deal, he paid Massey two million dollars for a piece of land appraised at half that value," the *Palm Beach Post* reported.[40]

*H*al Kennedy started doing public relations for Jack Massey in 1966. Four decades later he still described Massey as one of the best friends he ever had.

"One time I told him that my agency [Holder-Kennedy] was in trouble and that we needed to borrow ten thousand dollars from him to make payroll," Kennedy said. "He looked at me and told me to show him the numbers, and I did. And he looked at them and said to me, 'You don't need ten thousand dollars—you need fifty thousand.' So he wrote me a check and told me to pay him back when we got everyone else paid off.

"It took me a while. And finally, two or three years later, I told him we'd paid off that note. He said, 'What note?' You see, to him it was an inconsequential amount of money, but to us it was a lot. If I remember correctly, he didn't charge us any interest at all, or maybe prime, I can't remember for sure. But that's the kind of friend he was."

13

SUNSET

I T DOESN'T MATTER IF YOU are pharmacist; it doesn't matter whether you organized a hospital; it doesn't even matter if you started a chain of hospitals. No amount of knowledge can prevent the decline of your body. And money can't buy good health.

Jack Massey did everything he could to keep his deteriorating shell from stopping him. In November 1986 the eighty-two-year-old Massey was diagnosed with osteoporosis, a painful disease characterized by the loss of calcium in the bones. The condition was rapidly approaching the level at which even the most basic movements could break bones, which is why Massey went on round-the-clock nursing care from that point on.

"We had to watch him constantly," said Lydia Grubb, who left her position as a nursing instructor at Vanderbilt to be head nurse at the Massey home. "When he'd start to reach for something, you'd have to be there because you wouldn't want him to twist so far, because one twist and he could get a broken back."

For the first time in his life, Massey had to slow down. He could no longer play golf; he could no longer climb stairs; he had to get a chauffeur because he could no longer drive. The chauffeur wasn't his idea; it was a gift from his daughter, Barbara. Nevertheless, Massey continued to be as busy as most men in their prime, helping to run City Bank, Massey-Burch, Winners Corporation, and Thomas Nelson. "I still found his mind to be sharp, up to the very end, so long as you caught him at the right time of day," said Lonnie Stout, president of Volunteer Capital.

Determined to hold off Father Time as long as possible, Massey became a model patient, swimming and walking regularly—although he did, despite doctor's orders, still smoke cigars when wife Alyne wasn't around. He even maintained his required exercise regimen in spite of board meetings and other such important business.

"I remember one time he was sitting in an important board meeting of some kind and it was time for his walk, and I had to open the door and get him," Grubb said. "I opened the door and he saw me. With the greatest of dignity, he said, 'Gentlemen, if you'll excuse me, I have to go for my morning walk now.' He was very cooperative."

On bad days Massey would complain about the tremendous physical pain he was enduring. And for the first time his life, he began to feel sorry for himself.

"The day he found out that he had to go into the wheelchair, he told Alyne and me that he was going to walk back in the woods and not come back, the way a dog goes off to die," Barbara Massey Rogers said. "It took us a full day to talk him into participating in life from a wheelchair." A few weeks later, Massey's daughter arranged a surprise gin rummy party for him that was attended by some of his closest friends.

Eventually, Massey's sense of humor came back. About this time, Nashville banker Dennis Bottorff came by for a visit and asked him how he was doing. "My engine's working, but my fenders are falling off," Massey told him.

Another person who saw some of Massey's humor at this stage was former Tennessee Governor Lamar Alexander. "When his back was hurting so much that he had to stay at home, I went out to visit him," said Alexander, who at the time was involved in a Massey-affiliated company called Corporate Child Care. "I was talking with him about this and that, and as I stood up to leave he told me there was just one other thing he wanted to ask me. I said, 'What's that, Mr. Massey?' And he said, 'Do you suppose I could get a little more of that child care stock?'"

Massey tried to put into perspective the fact that his business career, which had always been so successful, was drawing to a close with a few unsuccessful ventures, such as Mrs. Winners, Vanderbilt Plaza, and Maryland Farms. "Did the losing streak bother him?" asked Clarence Edmonds. "It did, but he tried not to show it. But if you knew him as close as I did, you knew that it bothered him."

Having a few investments and companies do poorly was something Massey could deal with, but the notion of retiring galled him just as much as ever. In the late 1980s, with his health clearly declining, Massey continued to talk about taking a fourth company to the New York Stock Exchange. Appropriately, the company he intended to take was American Retirement Corporation—the assisted living and nursing home firm he and Dr. Thomas Frist Sr. had co-founded in 1978.

"We have a company called American Retirement Company which builds retirement homes for older people," he told a television reporter in 1986. "Of course, all of them are younger than I am. . . . This company is not a public company today, but we hope within a year or two it will be, and we certainly hope to take it to the New York Stock Exchange."

ARC was profitable, but only marginally so, and it wasn't ready to go public. Under the leadership of new CEO Bill Sherriff, the company maintained a steady course in the 1980s, a time when too many retirement homes were developed. After the real estate collapse of 1986, ARC would start growing again, largely by acquiring distressed properties.

"Even at that time, while he was in a wheelchair, and he might doze on you a little bit at a board meeting or something, he would still have an incredible mind if you could catch him when he was focused," Sherriff said. "And he could still quickly grasp things, could still distill a problem down to its core.

"I guess the thing that I will always remember more than anything else was his extraordinary insight into people. Whether it was in meetings with outside parties or in board meetings, he was always very acute, and his timing was excellent as to when he would speak, how he would speak, and what he would say. He just had a way of determining whether a person had character and whether they were good folks to do business with, and he put a lot of emphasis on that."

Sherriff was aware of the fact that Massey wanted ARC to make it to the New York Stock Exchange. "But he wasn't putting pressure on us to do it before the time was right, and he knew that the time wasn't right. He let me know that we should always think about the Big Board, but he did it in an encouraging way. He wanted me to build a foundation so that we could get there one day."

Never the kind of person to be rude or dishonest with a reporter, Massey gave several interviews during this period that were laced with fascinating anecdotes and great advice. Reporters often started off conversations with him by asking him the secret to making a fortune. His stock answer: Work hard, have fun, and find a niche no one else has found. The money will take care of itself.

"A man came to see me in my office right after World War Two," Massey said in one such interview. "He told me that he was going to be a millionaire in a year. And I said, 'More power to you.' Well, a year from then he was broke. And I always thought about that. If he'd taken his time and done all the hard work that had to go with it, rather than just trying to make a deal to make money, he might have been a millionaire."

Meanwhile, Massey continued to show a real interest in meeting young people. "It seemed like every time I brought someone over, he wanted to meet them and find out about them," stepson Bill Armistead said. Some of these young men ended up with rather amusing Jack Massey anecdotes.

Headley Bell, a classmate of Massey's stepson, Bob Armistead, said he once lost $150 to Massey in a gin rummy game. "I didn't have it in cash, so I wrote him a check for it," Bell said several years later. "For the next few weeks I waited and waited for him to cash it, because I wasn't sure if I had enough money in the bank to cover it. But he never cashed it."

Another young man heavily influenced by Massey in this manner was Frank Garrison, who frequently played gin rummy and backgammon with Massey. Massey gave Garrison several stock tips which helped Garrison pay his way through law school. Years later, Garrison owned a small private equity business in Nashville, and said Massey had a profound impact on his life.

"It's hard for me to know the degree to which he changed my life, but it is true that being around him made me believe that it would be great to be a venture capitalist and financier," Garrison said. "I don't think that doing this is something that I would have thought of on my own."

Nothing made Massey happier during his declining years than his association with Belmont University. Decades earlier Massey had begun giving substantial amounts of money to Belmont. The first large donation, in 1967, was $250,000 for a new arts building and auditorium, which was christened Massey Auditorium. While that structure was still going up, Massey and Belmont President Herbert Gabhart talked at length about the direction the school should take.

"We discussed many things that the school could teach—the furtherance of the music program, the idea of a nursing school—there are a lot of things that we discussed, but somehow we settled on the need for an undergraduate business school," Gabhart said. (It should be noted that Vanderbilt was trying to raise money for a graduate school of business at the same time, a cause to which Massey gave no money.)

A few months later Massey asked Gabhart how much money it would cost to start such a program. It took Gabhart about a month to come back with a figure of between $1.3 million and $2 million. By coincidence, Jack Massey's first wife, Elizabeth, died a few days after Gabhart gave him the proposal. "At the time I had no idea what her death would mean to the idea," Gabhart said.

A couple of weeks after her death, Massey came to visit Gabhart and told him that the night before she died he and Elizabeth had discussed the idea of a major gift to Belmont. Massey decided to give a million dollars—half for a building, half for faculty salaries—toward the new business school. A few weeks later, he increased the gift by two hundred thousand dollars, to acquire the land for the business school. Massey announced his gift at the opening of Massey Auditorium a few weeks later, concurrent with the launch of a fund drive intended to match his donation.[41]

As the building was nearing completion, a reporter asked Massey why he thought business education was so important. "Everyone should study accounting and other basic business courses, no matter what he's interested in," Massey said. He told the reporter that he had known many high-ranking management people who could have benefited from a better business education. But he said even a housewife could benefit as well.

"Let's assume that you made a great deal of money and then died," he told the reporter. "Would your wife know what to do to manage it, or would she be at the total mercy of the bank? The banks are going to be legal, but everything they do is going to be in their best interests, not necessarily your wife's.

"It takes a fundamental knowledge of the functions of the stock markets and other investing avenues in the business world to handle one's money properly. If a man or woman doesn't get it in college, when they get out into the business world they're going to be lost."[42]

When asked about his enthusiasm for a business school, Massey frequently pointed out that Nashville had no educational institution of that type. He was quite right in that regard. Many young people left Nashville in the 1950s and 1960s to go to business schools in other parts of the South, and they often didn't come back. One such institution was located about fifty miles north of Nashville, at what was then called the Bowling Green Business College and which later was merged into Western Kentucky University.

Another hint of what Massey was thinking when he donated money for a business school came from the way he mentored people at work. "He always insisted that his executives have courses that helped them in speaking, negotiating, and working with others," said Bettye Daugherty, secretary to the board of Hospital Corporation of America, and herself a graduate of the Massey School of Business. "And he would always insist that they have opportunities to take those courses because he thought it would help them and consequently help his business."

Although he liked to play cards for money and was no teetotaler, Massey seemed comfortable giving his money to a relatively conservative Baptist college, especially in light of things happening on college campuses elsewhere in the country in the late 1960s and early 1970s. Massey also had tremendous faith in Gabhart, who was the closest thing to a spiritual advisor that Massey had during the last few decades of his life.

The business school opened in August 1972. Just four months later Belmont's main academic building was struck by lighting and destroyed by fire. Belmont replaced it with two rather plain four-story structures—one for science and the other for the humanities. Massey helped out with those two buildings as well, by loaning Belmont money.

Not long after that, Belmont needed a student center. Massey set up a lunch with Gabhart and Shoney's chief executive, Ray Danner. Danner's son had attended Belmont, and Danner owed Massey a favor over the awarding of the Kentucky Fried Chicken franchise in Louisville.

"Friend, it is time for you to do something for Belmont, and it is time for me to do something again for Belmont," Massey said to Danner. A few weeks later, Danner told Massey he would contribute three hundred thousand dollars toward the student center if Massey would match the amount. He did.

A man who always seemed to enjoy spending time with young people, Massey got a kick out of Belmont. Regardless of how busy things got at HCA, Massey-Burch, or some other business venture, he managed to keep track of things at his pet college. Massey believed strongly in an emphasis on business ethics, and so he felt that a business education on a Baptist campus was an appropriate combination.

He liked meeting students—especially the ones working their way through college, to whom he felt he could relate. And he was very conscience of Belmont's image in Nashville. In 1978 a student at Belmont College ran a funny ad in the *Tennessean* asking for someone to send him money to help him "survive another year of high tuition, long hours of work, study, and cafeteria food." Massey was not amused and sent the young man a letter. "Many successful people have worked their way through college by being innovative, motivated, and by using their God-given faculty to be successful with honor," Massey wrote. "To me, begging has an entirely different connotation."

A few years later Massey took to lunch a student named Ashley McAnulty, who was attending Belmont on a scholarship named for Massey and endowed by several of Massey's friends. "We talked about all sorts of things," McAnulty said. "He talked about Colonel Sanders and about the stock market and about how he had bought the land on which the hotel sat many years earlier. You can imagine the impression all this made on me. I also remember that he wanted his fries to be very crispy and his tea not to be too strong. And when his lunch arrived he took his spoon and gave me some of his fries because he didn't think mine would be as good as his."

An undergraduate business program was only part of Belmont's strategy to differentiate itself in Nashville's crowded field of universities. It put together a small school of restaurant management that was largely financed by Shoney's. It developed a nursing curriculum to replace the Baptist Hospital School of Nursing, which closed in 1970.[43]

Another major thrust was a music/business curriculum, which was originally the brainchild of Belmont faculty members Bob Malloy and Jay Collins and three leaders in Nashville's music industry: Frances Preston, Bill Denny, and Joe Talbot III. "Back then there wasn't a source of people who knew anything about the business side of the music business, and the idea was to build a feeder of people for management positions," Denny said. "Vanderbilt wasn't interested in it, and Belmont was a godsend for taking it on. I think it worked out very well."

Belmont was growing and finding its niche, but by the late 1970s it was obvious to Massey and to others that the school needed to have a graduate business program in addition to its undergraduate curriculum. "It seemed to me that there were many people in Nashville who needed to take a graduate class in business who didn't have the opportunity to go to a place like Vanderbilt or some other business school because they needed to make a living for their family," Massey said.

A businessman who had seen many young executives in need of training during the course of his career, Massey visualized a school that would offer a master's of business administration degree through night classes. Such a school, Massey thought, would compare favorably with Vanderbilt's Owen Graduation School of Management, which in its early years had developed a reputation for impracticality.

But Belmont had a problem. Under the program statement of the Tennessee Baptist Convention, none of Tennessee's three Baptist universities was allowed to offer graduate education. In 1981 the convention voted overwhelmingly to reject Belmont's request to offer a graduate degree. Massey did not give up, however, and when thirty-two-year-old Bill Troutt became Belmont's president, the reversal of that decision became his top priority.

"When I first became president, I went out to see him," Troutt said many years later. "He put his hand on my shoulder and said, 'Bill, you are going to be a great man in his town.' It was one of the great affirming moments of my life." A couple of years later Massey strong-armed the selection of Wayne Brown, a former director of the Tennessee Higher Education Commission, as dean of the business school.

Troutt and other Belmont officials traveled the state and met at length with the leaders of Tennessee's two other Baptist colleges. In 1985 the Tennessee Baptist Convention authorized all three schools to offer graduate programs. Massey and other members of his family, including brother Harry Massey and daughter Barbara Massey Rogers, then made a series of large donations, and by the fall of 1986 Belmont had enough faculty members to begin offering an MBA degree. Massey also continued to lobby his business colleagues to support Belmont, an effort which eventually netted former HCA and HealthTrust executive Clayton McWhorter.

"He called me up after the creation of HealthTrust and basically told me that he wanted me to do something for Belmont. That's how my relationship with the school got started," said McWhorter, who also followed Massey's footsteps into the venture capital business with the formation of a firm called Clayton Associates. "I asked Massey what he wanted me to do, and he said that Bill Troutt would call me. So Bill calls and we have lunch, and I gave twenty-five thousand dollars to do room dedications [endowments] in the Massey building. That is how I got involved, and of course from that point on, Bill Troutt never let me off the hook, and things just kept getting bigger and bigger."

Massey also played an active role in the formation of Belmont's business curriculum. "He didn't meddle," Brown said. "But he did have some general curricular concepts that he wanted emphasized. He didn't want us just to teach marketing, accounting, finance, and management. He wanted us to put an emphasis on oral and written communication skills, on computers, on leadership, and on ethics. And he didn't want me to hire a PhD who didn't have business experience—and that wasn't easy."

In 1988 Belmont broke ground on a new building primarily for the graduate school of business. Architect Earl Swensson, who was at about that same time designing Nashville's BellSouth Tower, came up with an unusual octagonal-shaped building for Belmont's business school, but it wasn't much to Massey's liking. "I had it all thought out from a functional standpoint, and when I showed Mr. Massey the design, I was all excited about it and used all sorts of architectural terminology," Swensson remembered years later. "He looked at it and looked up at me and said, 'Earl, I'm not going to put my name on an oil can.' I said, 'Yes, sir,' and I went off and redid the whole thing."

Swensson then designed a new building that blended in and connected with the chain of large buildings built around the original Belmont Mansion, a historic home from which the institution got its name. "It was a major project, because we renovated the old building while we built a new building to look like the old building, and when it was all over it looked like one big building," Brown said.

Massey attended the groundbreaking ceremony in a wheelchair. "I'm so pleased to see so many people who have an interest in this institution," he said. "Today is probably the highlight of my life."[44]

This was one of a handful of special days for Massey during the decline of his health. Another occurred in 1987, when he was inducted into the National Business Hall of Fame, an entity sponsored by *Fortune* magazine and Junior Achievement. Massey was one of six men inducted that year; others included former Pepsi executive Donald Kendall, developer Trammell Crow, aircraft pioneer Igor Sikorsky, Chicago Bears owner George Halas, and Firestone founder Harvey Firestone.

"What can a man say? What can a man do?" Massey said while accepting his award. "Anyone who has the privilege of standing here and receiving this great award is extremely fortunate. The only thing I know to do now is to say thank you, go home, and go to work."

Never one for pomp, Massey was somewhat embarrassed about all the honors being bestowed upon him. He still preferred a game of gin rummy to a formal dinner, still preferred to invest fifty thousand dollars in a new company than to buy something he really didn't need, still preferred a smelly cigar to a nice glass of wine. He also got so used to being asked about his business achievements that he downplayed them.

"So tell us about taking three companies to the New York Stock Exchange," an interviewer once asked him on a local television show. "I never think about that," he said. "That's happenstance. We were lucky. Really were."

In late 1989 Massey invited a reporter from the *Nashville Scene* to his house in Belle Meade. For some reason, he had a lot of say that day:

> "We need a lot of leadership in Nashville right now. I'm a little too old to get involved in it. The folks around my age a long time ago quit that kind of business. It's time for the young people to take over. There are a lot of young folks, a lot of young men, who ought to be participating.
>
> "We need to get the fellows from thirty-five to fifty and let them grow into developing a series of programs to solve some of the problems that we have in this city. And we have a lot of problems. We're not growing. We're losing business. We think we're growing, but we're not.
>
> "We used to have a different kind of business than what we have now. What we have now is branch offices, whereas we used to have headquarters here. We still have some, but not like we did have, and not like we should have. Charlotte, North Carolina, is taking them all. We need to find out what Charlotte is doing.
>
> "I think part of the problem with leadership is, there's a little age gap in there. There's one group in there my age who were active, and there's this gap until the next one takes over. But there are a lot of men who could do it.
>
> "I remember a project like TPAC. It was Martha Ingram, Pat Wilson, and myself. We went to

the governor and asked him if we just couldn't lift up the state building and put the performing arts center underneath it. We finally sold them. But they told us they would only do it if we raised four million dollars. We started the day after Labor Day, and by December thirty-first of the next year we had four million dollars. There was the leadership to do it. You have to have people to get it done. The three of us got it done; we had to do a lot of crying and fussing to do it.

"Everybody's satisfied. The older people have made enough money to get by. They don't have to go out and dig for it. They're just satisfied and complacent about it. I think they have a responsibility. Somebody's got to lead."

A few days later Massey attended a Winners Corporation board meeting. "We were coming out of all our legal troubles and our Wendy's locations were doing well and it was a pleasant meeting," CEO Lonnie Stout said. "We were talking about alternative businesses, one of which I remember was a microcomputer company. Mr. Massey was excited about the prospects, and for the first time in a while, the company was doing well. The bad stuff seemed like it was all behind us."

Longtime friend Tom Cummings also said he spent some time with Massey that month. "By chance, I dropped by around Christmas that year and he was at home," Cummings said. "We had about an hour and a half of the best time that we had had in a long time. We talked about everything and nothing. It was just a couple of old friends talking and reminiscing about whatever just came up."

Massey spent that Christmas in Nashville, then went to Palm Beach a couple of days later. He attended a New Year's Eve party there and a few days after that became ill. "I will never forget it, because here we were at this party and this doctor came up to us and even told us that there were several people at the party who had the flu, and so we left a few minutes later," wife Alyne Massey said a few years later.

Massey got sick the next day. And, as sometimes happens to the very old, flu deteriorated into pneumonia. After a few weeks his body appeared to be fighting off the virus, and then, in February, he took a turn for the worse. On February 15, 1990, Jack Massey died. The immediate cause of death was a respiratory problem caused by pneumonia.

14

THE LEGACY OF JACK MASSEY

J ACK MASSEY DID NOT DO many of the things which, for better or worse, often thrust the wealthy into the public spotlight, in life and in death.

He did not get into legal trouble, something that can turn an obscure businessman such as Enron's Ken Lay into a household name. He did not run for public office, the avenue by which many Americans learned about Ross Perot and Malcolm Forbes. Unlike Donald Trump, Massey did not make a celebrity of himself or try to become a television star. Unlike Dave Thomas, he did not make himself the centerpiece of his company's marketing campaign. Unlike George Steinbrenner, he did not shift his investments into something disproportionately covered in the media, such as a professional sports franchise.

He did not build a sinfully large and luxurious house a la Clarence Sanders, the Piggly Wiggly founder whose home—the

Pink Palace—was so flamboyant that it was made into a museum after he lost it in bankruptcy. Massey also did not publish a book about his life or his philosophy.

Perhaps most importantly, Jack Massey didn't put his name in the title of any company he controlled, except for Massey Surgical Supply, the small firm he started in 1937. There easily could have been a Massey Towers in downtown Nashville and a Massey Office Park on the outskirts of town. Mrs. Winners could just have easily been called Massey's Fried Chicken. But Jack didn't want it that way.

Because of all these things, Jack Massey quickly became one of America's most forgotten business legends after his death. By 2004, the hundredth anniversary of his birth, there wasn't very much in Nashville—with the notable exception of the Massey School of Business at Belmont University—honoring the person who was quite likely the most influential businessman in the city's history.

Massey had a tendency to be overlooked by the media as well. Whenever referring to Hospital Corporation of America, reporters often pointed out that the company was founded by Dr. Thomas Frist Sr. and Dr. Thomas Frist Jr. They were less likely to mention the role played by Jack Massey (and less likely still to mention the name of co-founder Henry Hooker).

Perhaps the most egregious "etching out" of Massey's name from the history books took place at Kentucky Fried Chicken. As this book was being written, KFC had a very short history of its company posted on its Web site.

"By 1964, Colonel Sanders had more than six hundred franchised outlets for his chicken in the United States and Canada," the history stated. "That year, he sold his interest in the U.S. company for two million dollars to a group of investors including John Y. Brown Jr., who later was governor of Kentucky, from 1980 to 1984." Television documentaries that discussed the history of fast food or of Kentucky Fried Chicken also failed to mention Massey's name.

Nevertheless, it is startling how many things, physical or otherwise, Massey changed or may have changed in his lifetime, especially in Nashville. Had it not been for Jack Massey, Belmont College might not have survived. Nashville might not have had a Baptist Hospital. There might not have been a Corrections Corporation of America, or a Thomas Nelson Inc. based in Nashville, or a Vanderbilt Plaza Hotel, or a Maryland Farms office park.

On the national level, the franchising industry might not have turned out the same had it not been for Jack Massey. The Frist family probably would not have become as prominent as it did, and Bill Frist (Tommy's younger brother) might never have had the resources to make a transformation from surgeon to U.S. Senate Majority Leader.

Then there is the health-care industry. In 2004 health care was dominant in Nashville. A Chamber of Commerce-affiliated organization called the Nashville Health Care Council estimated that there were three hundred health-care companies in Nashville operating on a multi-state level or larger. Those companies operated a total of twenty-four hundred facilities outside of Nashville and employed 310,000 people outside of Nashville and 86,000 inside the city.

Health care also had indirectly created several other notable employers in Nashville. Gresham Smith & Partners, which for years did almost nothing other than build hospitals for HCA, eventually grew into one of the South's largest architectural and engineering firms. In 2004 it had 625 employees, fourteen offices, and about $85 million in annual revenues. Meanwhile, Rodgers Construction, which also had HCA as its only client for years, also grew into a large Nashville employer, until it was eventually purchased by Dallas-based Centex Corporation.

What individual should get the most credit for this? One of the most qualified people to answer that question was Dr. Irwin Eskind—who hardly knew Jack Massey. However, he was one of the sixty-five Park View physician-investors who, on that memorable night in May 1968, voted to trade his shares of stock in Park View for a new company called Hospital Corporation of America.

Within a few months it became obvious to Eskind that HCA's organizers were onto something. He talked his partner, his brother, and his brother's brother-in-law into starting a similar company called Hospital Affiliates International. During the next few years HAI grew nearly as fast as did HCA, in large part because of the many talented people who worked for the firm, among them Jack Anderson, Richard Ragsdale, and Phil Bredesen, who became governor of Tennessee in January 2003.

Because it didn't have access to as much capital as HCA, HAI focused on managing hospitals rather than buying them. This may have been a blessing in disguise, because there were many hospitals willing to farm out their management but that never would have considered selling. When interest rates skyrocketed in the late 1970s, the business of managing hospitals made more sense than did the business of borrowing money to buy them, and HAI was already the established leader in that field.

HCA bought HAI in 1981. After that acquisition the same people whose money had started HAI invested in a startup HMO called HealthAmerica. That company was later bought, and its executives started other companies. Other companies, in turn bred other companies. And so on, and so on. By the year 2000, Nashville's health-care industry was so interconnected that the Nashville Health Care Council produced a complicated "family tree" of sorts. HCA was at the top of that tree, with HAI beside it.

All of that made Irwin Eskind one of the founding fathers of Nashville's health-care industry. Asked in 2004 about Jack

Massey's significance to his home city, Eskind didn't bat an eye. "If it hadn't been for Jack Massey, then I don't think we would have had a health-care industry in this town," he said. "Period. Exclamation point."[45]

Another way of looking at Massey's influence comes from Dennis Bottorff, who by 2005 was running a Nashville venture capital company called Council Ventures. "You certainly can't give Jack all the credit for all the HCA spinoffs, because there are a lot of people who were involved in all those companies," Bottorff said. "But if it hadn't been for HCA, there wouldn't have been all those companies to spin off."

In 2004 Don Johnston was president of Massey-Burch Capital Corporation, a company still going strong even though no one named Massey or Burch worked there. Amid the mounted fish and deer heads that adorned his office, Johnston heaped praise on the man for whom he had once worked. "When I moved here from Dallas, the first thing that was obvious to me was that HCA was to Nashville what Texas Instruments was to Dallas," he said.

"Both companies led to other companies that were leaders in industries that, for most part, they pretty much created. And now you can see generations and generations of companies formed from the people who came out of those companies, both of which have very distinct cultures."

Nashville's health-care world also had a sister industry that possibly meant as much to Nashville. By 2004 Music City seemed to have a disproportionate number of venture capital companies, with names like Salix, Clayton Associates, and Capital Advisors. These companies made Nashville one of the finest cities in America in which to start a health-care company. And many of these venture capital firms were started by people with a direct link to Jack Massey.

Nashville venture capitalists such as Johnston, Townes Duncan of Solidus, Clayton McWhorter of Clayton Associates, Dennis Bottorff of Council Ventures, and Larry Coleman of

Coleman Swenson Booth all have different ways of explaining the ways in which Massey influenced their industry. But perhaps this is the best summary of what they all said: If you are hard-working enough, and smart enough, and lucky enough to see a company in which you have invested and worked make you rich, then don't bury the money in your backyard. Get back out there and invest it again. You owe it to yourself, and you owe it to your community.

"As [Massey] succeeded and made money," banker Sam Fleming said, "he was not afraid to reinvest that money back into other enterprises and other things that he thought had potential. On the contrary, so many people I have known who had money wanted to put it in government bonds, or put it in a cookie jar.

"It's sort of like the Parable of the Talents—in fact, Jack and I talked about this. He thought it was his duty to take what he had and try to make more out of it rather than bury it and protect it. He wanted to do something else for his fellow man— to leave this earth knowing that he had made a difference."

A similar perspective came from Andrew "Woody" Miller, the former HCA executive who in 1981 left to start Surgical Care Affiliates. In 2004, Miller was the head of a venture capital fund called Health Mark Ventures. When asked the identity of his mentor, Miller immediately invoked the name of the pharmacist from Sandersville, Georgia.

"Jack was my mentor at HCA from day one, and to this day, when I invest money, I follow what I call the Jack Massey Model," he said. "He was very interested in me personally and gave me a lot of advice over the years. But I think the main thing he did for me was offer me personal support when I was starting Surgical Care Affiliates. I had never started a company before, and I needed it."

The mentoring motif comes up again and again. If there is one thing Nashville had in abundance fourteen years after Jack Massey's death, it is people who claimed they were mentored by him. Among the more obvious ones were Tommy Frist, Clayton McWhorter, Lucius Burch III, William Andrews, Vic Campbell, Bill Troutt, and Lamar Alexander. And there were many more. In fact, some of the people who say that Massey was their mentor have a tendency to exaggerate the closeness of their relationship with the man. That alone says something about how highly he and his legacy are regarded.

Curiously enough, one of the first and most famous students was someone with whom Massey had a falling out. Back in 1963, when they first met, Jack Massey and John Y. Brown Jr. got along famously. "We became like father and son," Brown said. "I sort of fit in perfectly for what he needed in his life and he fit in perfectly for what I needed in my life. We just liked each other. He liked to play golf and play gin rummy. And we enjoyed each other's company."

Massey and Brown benefited tremendously from knowing each other; both made fortunes working together. Massey went on to co-found HCA, and Brown went on to become governor of Kentucky. However, Massey and Brown hardly spoke to each other after Heublein bought Kentucky Fried Chicken in 1972.

Interviewed in 2004, Brown insisted that the only fight he and Massey ever had concerned moving the corporate headquarters. "We never had a single argument in eight years, except for the fact that I wanted the business in Kentucky and he wanted it in Tennessee," Brown said. However, it seems likely there was more to the Massey-Brown squabble.

In a 1978 interview, Massey said he had negotiated the sale of KFC to Heublein behind Brown's back, and that he had done so because at the time the two men were not getting along at all. "John Brown would not sell it if he knew I had anything to do with it, because he's very jealous of my position," Massey told the interviewer.

During that same conversation, Massey gave an account of what happened at Kentucky Fried Chicken that Brown later described as "illusionary." The dispute largely centered on exactly who did all the work at the company. According to Brown, Brown did most of the work: "Jack wasn't interested in running anything, and Jack didn't. When we were in Nashville, Jack would come to the office one day a week." Meanwhile, Massey gave a completely different account: "I did everything there was to do. Everything!"

Nevertheless, Massey and Brown did have some nice things to say about each other after the KFC experience. "He [Brown] is the best salesman I've ever known; he did most of the acquisitions, he went out and acquired companies," Massey said. "He has great qualities, but being chief executive officer wasn't one. He was the most wonderful person to be associated with. We had a great time, and it was just a wonderful partnership."

Brown, meanwhile, concluded a long interview with the following statement: "Let me tell you something: I had a great affection and love for Jack. He gave me my chance, and I will always appreciate it. I am proud of what we did— regardless of whether I was lucky or good or somewhere in between."

It also should be pointed out that the incident worked out best for both men. Brown, of course, took the company back to Kentucky and was elected governor in part because of its success. Massey cashed out and shifted his focus to hospitals, something he probably wouldn't have done had he remained focused on selling drumsticks.

"In a way John Y. Brown did him a favor," said HCA co-founded Henry Hooker. "That whole incident with Massey getting upset at [Brown} led him to turn his attention to HCA, which was much better for him and for Nashville anyway."

It should also be pointed out that not all of the people who admired Jack Massey and were inspired by him became millionaires. Take Jackie Gorman, for instance.

Gorman was a thirty-year-old single mother when she got a job as the receptionist at Massey-Burch in 1983. For seven years Massey would talk to Gorman, ask her about what was happening in her life, and give her advice. He was, in her words, "like a father" to her. He frequently made dollar bets with her on trivial things, such as what temperature it was according to the digital readout on his Cadillac. He was nice to her young daughter when she came in one time wearing a Halloween costume. Eventually, as Massey lost his ability to get around by himself, he became dependent on Gorman instead of the other way around. And on at least one occasion he was generous to her—though no more than he was to everyone else who worked there.

"He gave everyone some stock—I can't remember which company it was in—but even I got some," Gorman said. "Unfortunately, a couple of years later, I had to sell it because I was moving back in with my mother and needed to do some work on her house, and also because I needed to buy a new car so I would have a safe car for my kids. And he didn't like that very much. He called me when he heard that I had sold the stock and read me the riot act, because he told me that that stock was for my kids' college education."

Gorman had a front-row seat to the transformation of Massey from a healthy, proud man who walked upright and by himself to a man who needed help to go to the bathroom. She also saw the inevitable transformation of Massey the charmer to Massey the amusing curmudgeon.

Through it all, Gorman developed a deep affection for Massey. And after he died in February 1990, she missed the sense of security she had previously gotten from bouncing ideas off the old man. So, a few months later, she started making occasional trips to Nashville's Mt. Olivet Cemetery to talk to his marker. "When it was time to go to interviews or something that was big in my life, then I would go to the cemetery to sit and ask his advice," Gorman said.

Many people who knew Jack Massey say that if it weren't for his business partnership, or leadership in their company, or his investment in their venture, or support of their campaign, they wouldn't have accomplished as much as they did. Gorman, who in 2004 was the manager of the conference sales division for the Fairfield Resorts office in Crossville, Tennessee, proudly said she should be included in that list.

"I don't know exactly how it happened, but he gave me the strength that I needed to accomplish something in my life," she said. "It wasn't something that he said; maybe it was his aura. Maybe it was just being a part of a team that was his team. But before I went to work there I hadn't had good jobs, and that ended up being the first stop on the path to a better life. I never would have thought in a million years that one day I would be the manager of a department."

Shortly after Massey's death, the third company he took to the New York Stock Exchange disposed of its unsuccessful Mrs. Winners restaurant chain and changed its name back to Volunteer Capital Corporation. For a couple of years VCC kept watch over the Wendy's restaurants it had owned since the mid-1970s, keeping an eye open for a new business opportunity. That chance presented itself in the form of a sit-down restaurant in Nashville that the company began growing into a chain in the mid-1990s.

"We wanted to give it a good American name, and we were originally thinking about calling it Alexander Hamilton's," said company Chief Executive Officer Lonnie Stout.

"But we weren't sure about that, and then we started thinking about simply calling it 'Alexander's.' Well, we called our trademark lawyer and he did a search, and wouldn't you know it? Someone beat us to it.

"And then someone suggested the idea of putting a 'J' in front of the name in honor of Mr. Massey. Well, I thought it was a great idea because it would be a way of naming it after Massey in a very subtle way, which is the only way in which he would have allowed it."

J. Alexander's thus became the name of the restaurant chain, and J. Alexander's Corporation became the name of the company. And, after a few years of struggling in the late 1990s, the company began consistently reporting profits in 2002, growing to a chain of twenty-seven upscale eateries in the process.

"J" would have been pleased.

APPENDIX I

Excerpts from articles written in the days
after Jack Massey's death in 1990:

"He [Massey] was one of the most alive-eyed persons I have
ever known. He could see in a minute what it would take others hours to see. He would look in every direction and then
proceed. He had depth and height perception in a world that is
bleary-eyed; yet, he had 20/20 vision when it came to looking
straight ahead."
— Dr. Herbert Gabhart,
Nashville Banner column, Feb. 16, 1990

"Mr. Massey started his career as a drug-store delivery boy. In
Horatio Alger fashion, he rose from that insignificant position
to become one of the nation's top businessmen. And always,
along the way, he kept his integrity, sense of humor, and sense
of caring for others. For those reasons, among others, Mr.
Massey's life will be celebrated for years to come by people
whom he has influenced for good, and by those yet to be benefited by his many gifts of time and money."
— Editorial, *Tennessean*

"Over the years Mr. Massey was instrumental in starting and financing many businesses, making public offerings of the shares of more than a dozen private companies and providing capital for three dozen others that remain private. . . . Of his appetite for financial adventure, Mr. Massey once said, 'Lots of people make more than I do, but not many have as much fun. The fun is in the accomplishing.'"

— *New York Times*

"Last month, the most improbable thing happened: Jack Massey retired. He passed away on the morning of February 15, leaving behind a legacy that is of mythical proportions and only likely to increase as the months roll on. . . . Jack Massey was the embodiment of the American Spirit, an amalgamation of sophisticated business acumen and frontier expansionism. He was a liberal giver, of both money and advice, but Jack Massey was no saint. He was known as a ruthless negotiator, who could, as one acquaintance put it, 'talk you out of your last penny.'"

— Editorial, *Advantage* magazine

"Jack Massey was my friend of nearly sixty years. He could and did walk with kings, but he never lost the common touch. He was enormously successful and not afraid to re-invest his gains in new and sometimes venturesome projects because he knew that if he lost, he had the ability to recover."

— SAM FLEMING,
as quoted in the *Tennessean*

"Jack Massey was a unique driving force—a person who seemed to gain more energy and excitement with each year. He was a very tough negotiator who liked winning but enjoyed even more playing the game of business."

— EDWARD G. NELSON,
as quoted in the *Tennessean*

"His achievements in numerous business enterprises are legendary, and his ability to capture and move forward an innovative concept may be his greatest legacy. . . . He was truly a business genius."

— DR. THOMAS FRIST JR.,
as quoted in the *Tennessean*

"While his accomplishments are significant, and in fact legendary, the building of industries, businesses, and civic resources should not be characterized as Jack C. Massey's greatest legacy. Rather, the intangible qualities that made him the ideal of a community leader, entrepreneur, and friend are an endowment that will continue to inspire those whose lives he affected."

—Volunteer Capital Corporation
annual report

"He was one of those rare persons who had an extra feel for things financial, and he could determine whether a situation was good or bad as quick as anybody I ever knew."

— ANDREW BENEDICT,
as quoted in the *Tennessean*

APPENDIX II

Jack Massey's statement before the U.S. Senate Subcommittee on Antitrust and Monopoly
February 24, 1970

I must say that I am proud to be here to represent the Hospital Corporation of America and the corporate groups of taxpaying, investor-owned hospitals of which Hospital Corporation of America is a recognized leader.

We at Hospital Corporation, and I am sure those in management of the other proprietary hospital groups, are convinced that free enterprise, using private capital in investor-owned hospitals, with physicians participating in management, can provide superior patient care while helping to halt the spiraling costs of health care in this country.

We believe that there is a need for participation of the private sector in the construction and operation of hospitals for the benefit of the people of this great nation.

The health-care field is the fastest growing area of activity in the United States today. Costs within the health-care field are rising at a rate much greater than the overall cost of living. The need for facilities is becoming almost impossible to fund, despite the billions of dollars that have been provided by the federal government and the substantial sums that have been furnished by state and local governments.

With all of this public expenditure, there still remains a large number of communities which need hospitals, or which need additional or replacement hospitals, and which have been totally unable to finance them.

Hospital Corporation was organized to help fill some of this great need, to help solve some of the problems confronting the health-care field today. Our company was formed to build a nationwide group of high-quality medical hospitals, with private capital, with the efficiency of business management, with patient care under the direction of professional administrators and boards of leading physicians.

We have made some progress toward that objective. We are now operating twenty-three excellent hospitals with more than twenty-seven hundred beds, located in seven states. We have ten others under construction—three of them scheduled to open within sixty days—and ten more committed for construction, with land already optioned or acquired, in a $90 million building program which is currently underway.

We are studying other desirable acquisitions, and we are looking constantly at other sites for new construction. We are invited to build new hospitals in a great many more communities than we are in a position to undertake. There is a large and generally recognized need for privately financed hospitals.

Let me give you a couple of examples. A little town called Erin, Tennessee, had two doctors, but no hospital, serving some twelve thousand people in its immediate area. The doctors and the community had attempted to build a hospital but failed in their efforts to raise the necessary money. One doctor announced that he would leave the community because he had no facility in which to care for his patients. The second doctor said that if the other left, he would go, too, because he did not want twelve thousand people knocking on his door at night.

We built a hospital for Erin, only a thirty-six-bed one, but it is a modern facility with the latest equipment and complete services appropriate for a community of that size. The two doctors stayed to look after the people of Erin, a board-qualified surgeon has joined them, and a fourth physician will move there in June. That community for the first time has acquired medical care because of Hospital Corporation of America.

The twin communities of Blacksburg and Christianburg, Virginia, home of the eleven-thousand-student Virginia Polytechnic Institute, had one small, antiquated hospital. Hill-Burton funds had been applied for and denied, and a valiant public subscription drive had fallen far short of the money necessary to build a critically needed new hospital. We are constructing a modern, new hospital for the communities, without cost to them. The thirteen thousand permanent residents and eleven thousand students will have access to the highest-quality health care, because of Hospital Corporation of America.

These are only two examples, of course, but they are typical of the type of contribution we are attempting to make, and the type of service we are trying to provide the people of communities in which additional facilities are needed—without adding to the tax burden, without competing with existing institutions, without unnecessarily duplicating services.

We are providing those services which are needed in each community where we operate. In the smaller communities where we are the only hospital, we are providing all services practical for that size hospital, including emergency, obstetrics, and pediatrics.

In larger cities where additional facilities of those or other specialized types are needed, we are providing those in harmony with the other hospitals and in consultation with health planning agencies. In New Orleans, for example, we are building a small obstetrical hospital, because this is needed. Miller

Hospital in Nashville has a very active emergency program, partially due to the need for it to serve the section of town where it was located. Park View Hospital in Nashville, on the other hand, does not compete with the very fine emergency facilities which exist a few blocks away at three hospitals. We try to be reasonable about the inclusion of services, and fit them into community needs. It is just about that simple.

We generally try to avoid the more exotic and extremely infrequently used facilities, such as open-heart surgery, heart transplants and such, which should be provided in large university hospital centers. These tend to add a major burden to the overhead, penalizing the ordinary patient with a premium payment, whether in an investor owned or non-taxpaying hospital.

You will notice I prefer to use "non-taxpaying" rather than "non-profit," because I think they all have to make a profit to be able to stay in business.

It is important to emphasize that in cities where we are the only hospital, we treat everyone who needs care, regardless. Certainly, we do not encourage the so-called indigent patients to come to HCA hospitals if other, more appropriate, facilities are available. We pay large amounts of taxes to the federal government and to the states and counties and cities in which we operate. These taxes help to support the tax-supported hospitals which are in business to care for the non-paying patient, and were established for this purpose. We think that this is where they should go. But we never turn down a patient.

And there is a rapidly decreasing number of indigent patients today in reality. With Medicare and Medicaid, local welfare programs, foundation grants, and various forms of health insurance, there is a source of payment for most patients that are admitted. Tax-free hospitals have ready access to those sources and can fund their care of the non-paying patient from one of them. Actually, fifteen out of sixteen people in America today have some type of third-party coverage.

And, of course, the very fact that we are building hospitals with private capital that would otherwise be built with someone's tax money, federal or local, frees available public money for such purposes.

To be quite specific, this year we will pay approximately $3.5 million in federal and state income taxes, not to mention substantial amounts of state and local ad valorem taxes at all twenty-three locations. Our existing hospitals represent an initial cost of more than $31 million, with another $9 million in equipment. To replace these hospitals today would cost another $90 million. And, as I told you, we have presently committed more than $90 million to new construction.

Had these twenty-three hospitals been built with Hill-Burton funds, or by local government, they would have cost at least that much; or, to replace today, would cost $90 million to construct and equip, and they never would have paid a penny of taxes. In fact, they would most likely have required continuing subsidy from tax funds to keep them in operation.

But that is only a part of the story. From the outset, we have been concerned with providing the best possible patient care, at the lowest possible cost. Dr. Thomas Frist, our president, is one of the most conscientious physicians I have ever met. He has been involved in management of hospitals, both voluntary and proprietary, for many years. I helped build Baptist Hospital in Nashville, and served as its president for twelve of the last twenty years. We knew what needed to be done.

The goals of top-quality patient care and economical operation are not at all inconsistent. In fact, management decisions usually accomplish both at the same time.

Our satellite concept, for example, makes sophisticated professional services available from one large metropolitan hospital to a group of smaller hospitals surrounding at very low cost to the small hospital and to the patient. Electrocardiograms are transmitted by telephone from the small hospitals in Nashville, read by experts, and a report returned by phone within minutes. Laboratory specimens are picked up daily at the small hospitals and brought to Nashville for more elaborate tests than can be handled locally.

Our home office provides a central personnel resources pool which makes available the services of ADA dietary personnel, pathological and radiological specialists, inhalation therapists, medical librarians, specialists in coronary care and other fields—to all hospitals. Centralized utilization of such personnel not only holds down costs but provides types of consultants which would not otherwise be completely out of the reach of smaller hospitals.

We are achieving major cost savings in centralized purchasing of equipment and supplies, which help to control costs in individual hospitals. Group purchasing of standard items for twenty-three hospitals results in substantial savings. Buying insurance coverage for the hospitals as a group saves many thousands of dollars a year.

Support services which would otherwise have to be bought locally at considerable expense are provided from headquarters at great savings: such services as legal, audit, public relations, personnel, employee communications, data processing, and architectural.

A staff architect and standard prototype plans for new hospitals result in immense savings in construction costs. Building new facilities on a critical path method enables us to buy materials for several hospitals at once, at much better prices, with resultant economies of major proportions.

We have already proved that corporations such as ours can build hospitals more economically and operate them more efficiently than any other type of management, for the benefit of the patients, the taxpayers, the physicians, and the communities were serve.

We hope that such programs as Medicare will find a means to recognize such efforts to reduce costs and will develop an incentive reimbursement program that will motivate all hospitals to work for closer cost control. As long as such programs base reimbursement on cost, the incentive is to increase cost.

We would welcome the opportunity to participate in a pilot program, such has been proposed by the Federation of American Hospitals, to develop a more acceptable form of reimbursement. If this is a proper time, I would like to request such an opportunity and hope that this committee will encourage the Social Security Administration to undertake such a program, as one step toward controlling rising health-care costs.

That is one of our primary objectives. We feel we are doing a good job and making an important contribution to the solution of one of the nation's most serious problems.

We have nothing to hide from this committee or the people of America. We are proud of our achievements and of the service we are rendering. We are proud of our employees, who have devoted their lives to the care of the sick and injured.

We are proud of the physicians who make time in their busy schedules to serve on management committees and participate in decisions affecting the administration of hospitals, without compensation for these extra duties.

We are in the hospital business because we feel there is a great need for businessmen to be in the hospital business. We are not in the drug business, or the surgical supply business, or the insurance business, or the nursing home business. Our only subsidiary is a food service equipment dealer which provides specialized services for our dietary departments.

We do not see anything wrong with taxpaying hospitals earning a fair return on investment. Other companies make profits in building automobiles and bombs that kill. Doctors and laboratories and clinics make profits on treating the sick. We are not ashamed to be profit-oriented. In the great American tradition of free enterprise, we feel that investors are entitled to a fair return on their capital. I must strongly emphasize that the company has not paid, and has no intention of paying, any dividends to our stockholders. We plan to continue to reinvest our modest earnings in more facilities and equipment.

We are more than ever convinced that heavy involvement of private enterprise in the operation of hospitals, with the efficiencies I have described, can help control the costs of medical care. We believe that the investment of private capital in a substantial percentage of the nation's hospitals can fill a serious gap, can make good hospitals available where they are needed, and can help to eliminate some of the need for government financing and other participation in the field.

In addition, our company offers a pragmatic and concrete vehicle to demonstrate the partnership between the public and private sectors which has been enunciated in federal legislation. We are willing and able to do our part in the partnership for health care.

We hope that a strong, healthy private hospital industry, working in cooperation and partnership with the other types of hospitals—namely, government-owned and -operated city-county hospitals—can compliment each other in an effort to render the highest quality of service at the most economical cost. We are grateful for the opportunity to be a part of this effort and believe that we offer to the people of the country a means to achieve high-quality hospital care.

APPENDIX III

Speech by Jack Massey on the Venture Capital business
Given sometime in the late 1970s

Not long ago one of the nation's business magazine's devoted twenty columns to lament the death of innovation and the entrepreneur. The magazine expended thousands of words in an effort to document its thesis that the entrepreneur has passed from the American scene.

If the magazine's editor had taken time to look beyond the Hudson River, he most certainly would not have placed himself on such a weak limb. Innovation in our society has never been as vigorous as it is today.

The narrow thinking expressed in the article is nothing new, of course. Undoubtedly the same opinion has been voiced since man began evolving as a technological creature. And that article will not be the last. I am certain, before the year is out, hundreds of so-called experts will express similar ideas in speeches and articles.

The life of the innovator, to be sure, is not an easy one. It never has been. The setbacks of the innovator are many, and many will fail. But those who succeed will become very wealthy individuals, and in the next decade the number of successes will be staggering. Additionally, their successes will provide investors with lucrative returns. The opportunities are too numerous to list, and there is no specific field or area where they will be discovered.

My view of the entrepreneur is clear. For it is the entrepreneur upon whom I depend for my livelihood. I consider myself an entrepreneur. I have formed companies of my own and know the problems that confront anyone who is trying to market a product, a service, or a concept.

One of my companies, Massey Investment, specializes in nurturing the entrepreneur. The company—eight people strong, which includes four clerical workers, three professionals, and I—sees as its market the entrepreneur. We do not restrict our interest to any industrial or technical segment. If it's a good idea, run by the right people, it makes little difference what the product might be.

Massey Investment, let me emphasize from the offset, is not philanthropy. To the contrary, the company is strictly in business to make money, and happily Massey Investment has a done a creditable job for the past ten years.

Returning to the alleged demise of the entrepreneur, I must say that those doomsayers are well shielded from the real United States. Glancing over our records for the past twelve years, more than four hundred people have made contact with Massey Investment. All had ideas and products they thought were destined for market success. Of course, there were charlatans among them, but as a rule, those contacting us were sincere individuals who had spent long hours working on projects they felt would be market successes.

Obviously, Massey Investment cannot participate in as many ventures as are offered, but we have a wide range of potential investments from which to choose. In recent years, our participation has ranged from fast-food companies to hospitals, golf carts, electronics, and mining equipment.

New opportunities appear for the investor daily. Naturally, there is risk involved, and it is my recommendation that the shy keep their money in the bank. There are no guarantees that you will make one dime, and you could lose millions. But I am absolutely awed by the number of innovations that this country will see in the 1980s. National problems, like energy, present opportunities for the aggressive entrepreneur. Likewise, changing lifestyles offer the investor great potential, as does inflation, and even government regulation.

For the investor, the coming years promise to be a bonanza. Most entrepreneurs, if I had to develop a profile, are young and all share several traits. First, they are extremely confident (an attribute of the young). Second, they know that their idea is a winner. And third, they are capital starved. Most entrepreneurs that Massey Investment sees don't come to us from the proverbial basement with their invention in hand. Generally, they are already in business, having started a plant and established a market. When they arrive at our door, they usually tell us that, "We're first in our market, but we're broke."

Success for these innovators is within their grasp, but without some quick help and astute guidance, many will fail because of their success. Business, in other words, is so good that bankruptcy is imminent. Banks like to lend money to companies like General Motors, ITT, Procter & Gamble, but they balk when the entrepreneur seeks a loan. Most bankers, I feel, suffer from what Theodore Levitt described as "marketing myopia." Massey Investment thrives on and specializes in the entrepreneur. Obtaining a high return on our investment is the company's objective, and through the years we have realized this goal.

Massey Investment, for those who know little of the company, had its beginning in 1968. The first client was a small restaurant chain, Shoney's. The company was headed by an eager and aggressive businessman named Ray Danner, who had first made his mark in the outdoor movie business. Our job was that of consultants. Specifically, our assignment was to make the detailed arrangements for Shoney's to go public.

Shoney's at the time could not afford the normal consultant's fees for our work. What was worked out with Shoney's was a system that subsequently has served as a basis for operations of our company.

When we took Shoney's public, we agreed with the company's management to take warrants for stock at the offering price. This suited Shoney's in that the stock would be sold anyway. Several years later we exercised the option, at a considerable profit of millions of dollars. This, I feel, is a pretty fair return on the work we performed.

Our experience with Shoney's provided us with the foundation of Massey Investment. First, Massey Investment does not seek out entrepreneurs or advertise our services in the classified sections of newspapers. We don't go out with a fistful of money. Entrepreneurs must come to us and both need and want our help. We routinely turn down anyone who needs us but is reticent to accept our help. Our second commandment of business, and one that undoubtedly causes Harvard Business School types to shake their heads, is that we act on instinct.

Massey Investment's most important criterion is the person or persons involved in the venture. I remember one group that called and wanted assistance. He said, "There are four of us, Mr. Massey, and we have an excellent product but are underfinanced." I listened more and finally agreed that we should have a meeting. The morning of the meeting one of the group called to confirm and remarked that "the three of us will be there." At this point, I interrupted and reminded him that earlier he had said four. "Bring the alcoholic, too," I said, "or we can't have the meeting." To my relief, the fourth man was not an alcoholic, and eventually he headed the company. My point is that a good investor must know the people, all of them who will be taking his time and money. The fourth could just as well have had drinking problems, and he could have dragged the company under.

While it is, of course, necessary to go over the financial condition of any company with a fine-tooth comb and to study the market, the human factor is critical. I can hire accountants to study the financials and marketing experts to judge the potential market. But only Massey Investment can evaluate the people who want its participation. The first two factors can be fine tuned and adjusted, but the characteristics of the people are firm and can't be changed. Thus, if the human factor doesn't meet the company's standards, my advice is to get away from the venture quickly.

Once the human factor has been totally analyzed, Massey Investment then scrutinizes the product or service and the capital needs that will be required. Usually the entrepreneur has no idea of how much capital he requires, and generally he underestimates the needs. This is where financial expertise comes into play. But, while we participate in management decisions after financial arrangements are made, we maintain a wide berth in keeping out of the entrepreneur's way. A true innovator cannot operate if he is stymied at every juncture. If you don't have the stomach for this type of operation, the bank is the best place for your money.

Another failing of the investor when he seeks to enter the economy is the tendency to consider only high-technological innovations on the road to a sound investment. Entrepreneurism does not always surface in the form of technology. Innovation appears in many forms. Some of the soundest investments Massey Investment has made have been with innovators of new marketing systems.

One of the best illustrations of this point is the case of a young Texan who came to me several years ago. He had developed a pacemaker that he felt was obviously superior to others on the market. Pacemakers were not new at all, but what he had developed, perhaps unknowingly, that differentiated it from the competition was a distribution and marketing system that was unique in the industry. He met the human factor test, and as a result we made a substantial investment in his enterprise. His problem was that his marketing system was selling more pacemakers than could be produced, and the banks would not lend him money to expand his manufacturing plants.

In quick order we agreed to take an option for shares of stock and then arranged with a New York bank to provide his company with a $10 million line of credit. This was $7 million more than his estimate. The truth was, however, that $3 million would have done little to relieve his manufacturing problem and probably would have only compounded his problems. Massey Investment made a handsome profit on the venture.

One of the more frustrating results of being an entrepreneur in the early stages is that the more successful you are, the harder up you are. Success translates into increased sales, and this means more money for manufacturing, which involves capital, often times a lot of it.

In other words, there is no orderly growth to success. If there were orderly growth, there would be few companies publicly traded. The Fords would still own Ford, and the DuPonts, DuPont. Their early successes caused them to have to share their companies with investors of their day.

In my own experience, such was the case with Colonel Harland Sanders and Kentucky Fried Chicken. The Colonel's small chicken business was growing too fast for its creator. For $2 million, the company was purchased. Six years later, the company was sold for $239 million. But bear in mind that it wasn't a risk-free gamble I took when we paid out $2 million. In fact, I took a tremendous risk. The Kentucky Fried Chicken franchise system was in shambles; distribution was in chaos. Not only was order brought to the distribution channels, but in six years the company was completely rebuilt from the ground up. It wasn't a sure thing, and it took a lot of hard work. The company I sold was a far cry from the company I bought.

The success of KFC spawned scores of imitators, and food units proliferated throughout the country. The would-be entrepreneur thought that just opening one store, franchising units, and going public was all that was required for instant riches. Of course, it wasn't long before the big fast-food collapse came. The survivors are few, but those who have provided a service and satisfied the public survived and are still on the scene.

Many said that the fast-food bust came because the market was saturated. This is a false assumption. The fast-food market is still a rich area for investment. One case in point is Wendy's, a hamburger chain. Who would think there would be room in the marketplace to sell hamburgers with McDonald's on one side, Burger King on the other, and a score of lesser companies around? Well, Dave Thomas did, and with Massey Investment's help, Wendy's is now the second largest in the industry. Its primary ingredients were the man, Thomas, who met my human factor test, and a product that was different enough to carve a niche in the hamburger market.

Another of my companies, Volunteer Capital, today is Wendy's largest franchisee, and I feel that both the chain and Volunteer have just started to grow.

As Massey Investment has grown and prospered, the company has been able to assume more risk, but at the same time we have positioned ourselves for greater rewards. Recently, we entered into a venture with a group that had invented a new, high-technological method involving opto-electronics. As with most, the young company had the technical expertise but lacked the capital to carry through with its plans.

Massey Investment raised the necessary capital for the company and in return received from the company a block of shares of stock at a cost basis of about one dollar per share.

For years thereafter, the company struggled to develop a market, and our investment looked poor indeed. However, a lucrative market was developed, and last year the company was acquired by Honeywell. Massey Investment received thirty dollars per share for the stock.

Many investors, I fear, look only for the breakthrough product or the established me-too product. These, of course, offer potential. But another potential area for the investor is the service economy. And service is the fastest-growing segment in the United States and promises to be even bigger in years to come.

The service industry has provided us with perhaps our greatest achievements. The demographics of this country are rapidly changing, and it became apparent to anyone who studied census data that the number of elderly people will increase significantly in the coming years. One basic need of this group is hospital care. While hospitals are noted for inefficiency, I determined that these institutions could be both efficient and profitable. And it was on this assumption that Hospital Corporation of America was founded. And, again, I return to people. With the right people, hospitals can be made profitable. With the wrong people, they run deficits and fail to meet the needs of the communities that they serve.

The service industry is benefiting from increased discretionary income. The potential for investment in this industrial segment is overwhelming, and the opportunities are varied.

Although Massey Investment is involved in many different businesses, it is my belief that there really is no difference in business. The same principles apply in a drugstore as in a factory. You must have good people. You must find a need and a way to satisfy that need profitably. And business consists of two things: people and money. If you have the idea, and it is sound, and you have good people, capital can be obtained.

There are many venture capital firms looking for high-potential investments in new businesses. We are looking for other situations in which we can turn a $2 million investment into $239 million, a $1 investment into a $30 stock. A recent magazine article about our activities was entitled "Anyone can buy General Motors." Anyone can buy blue-chip stocks and receive dividends and, if all goes well, eventually sell the stock for more than they paid for it.

Massey Investment prefers to become involved with investments with some risk but with a much greater potential for reward. But they must have the people. We are an investment company with very little interest in active, day-to-day management, although we have one or more members on their boards of directors.

Massey Investment seeks situations where the investment will grow, and where it can be leveraged into a much greater success, with a fair return to all investors. But it also likes to be in a situation where it can make other contributions to the success of the company, through advice to management and the use of our contracts in other businesses and in the financial community.

There are plenty of opportunities for entrepreneurs today, and plenty of qualified, highly motivated people finding solutions to the needs of society. Our schools are producing more high-quality, well-educated people today than ever before; there is more money around than at most times in the past; and the world's appetite for goods and services is at an all-time high.

With these conditions and the new technology so abundant, the day of the entrepreneur is far from dead.

NOTES

1. In addition to being the location of Massey's first drugstore, the Tulane Hotel is the birthplace of recorded country music in Nashville. In 1945 three WSM engineers rented a second-floor suite in the Tulane Hotel and turned it into the Castle Recording Studio, Nashville's first professional recording studio.

2. Dr. Dorothy Brown died while this book was being written, on June 13, 2004.

3. *Forbes*, Jan. 23, 1978.

4. Massey's West End Avenue drugstore building was, at the time this book was written, a Fuddruckers restaurant.

5. So little is known about this original Baptist Hospital that its existence wasn't even mentioned in a history of Baptist Hospital published in 1998. The only evidence that the author found to prove that it existed is an announcement of its formation in the October 8, 1924, *Nashville Tennessean*.

6. Sullivan's account of the origins of Baptist Hospital come from two sources: a written version called "Beginnings of Mid-State Baptist Hospital," and an interview with the author in 1997. The high points of both accounts tally; however, there are differences in details between the two accounts. For example, in the written account Sullivan said that Massey stood to lose $30,000 if the hospital went under. In the interview, he said that the amount was $40,000.

7. Curiously, the most prominent Baptist in the Nashville business community, General Shoe Company President Maxey Jarman, did not become a Baptist Hospital trustee.

8. Baptist Hospital closed its nursing school in 1970.

9. Virtually all Baptist Hospital expansions made during the Massey era were designed by the Nashville architectural firm Hart Freeland & Roberts and built by Charlotte-based contractor J. A. Jones.

10. John Ed Pearce, *The Colonel: The Captivating Biography of the Dynamic Founder of a Fast-food Empire* (Garden City, N.Y.: Doubleday & Co., 1982), p. 121.

11. One amusing tidbit: in his personal appointment books, Massey at first referred to John Young Brown Jr. as "Young John Brown."

12. Jack Massey recounted in later interviews about how Sanders first offered to hire him to be president of Kentucky Fried Chicken. It should be pointed out, however, that John Brown said in a 2004 interview that he found that story hard to believe. "As far as the Colonel offering Massey a job," Brown said, "that just doesn't sound right to me. He could have said that but not meant it."

13. It is unclear when the bank meeting took place. This seems like the most logical time, but Brown seemed to recall that there was still a question about the $2 million price when the bank meeting occurred.

14. Massey's original cash investment was supposed to have been $240,000, but he had to raise that amount to $265,000 after Kenny King decided at the last minute not to invest.

15. Sanders was not a member of that board, nor would he be so

as long as Massey controlled the company. According to Massey's notebooks, he originally intended for Sanders to be on the board, but by the time the deal closed he had changed his mind about that.

16. Pearce, p. 141.

17. Pearce, p. 201.

18. *New Yorker*, Feb. 14, 1970.

19. *Business Week*, June 24, 1967.

20. Dave Thomas later went on to start Wendy's. Baker later owned a pizza chain called Mr. Gatti's, which he sold in 1981, and by 2004 owned a chain of fast-food restaurants called TacoTico.

21. John Hill was at this time chief executive officer of Hospital Corporation of America.

22. Among the people who said in 2004 that they didn't know the story behind the Massey/First American story were former First American Chairman Andrew Benedict, former First American President Ken Roberts, and attorney Brad Reed. Bass, Berry & Sims attorney James O. Bass Sr., 94 at the time this book was being researched, told the author he would rather not comment on the relationship between First American's board and Jack Massey.

23. If you look at a map you can easily see that Macon, Georgia, is not on the way from Nashville to Atlanta. So it looks like the HCA executives were anxious to take the people from Mutual of New York to the groundbreaking.

24. To be absolutely accurate, Lucius Burch III went to work in 1968 for John Neff & Associates, which was a money management company. Two of its clients were Massey Investment Company (a business name for Jack Massey's personal investments) and Capital Investment Services (a partnership between Massey and Neff that advised companies). When Neff went to work full time for HCA, John Neff & Associates was closed and Burch, Hibbetts, and Beasley went to work for Massey Investment Company

25. *Forbes*; Jan. 23, 1978.

26. *Forbes*; Jan. 23, 1978.

27. *Forbes*; April 1, 1976.

28. *Forbes*, April 1, 1976.

29. *New York Times*, Sept. 19, 1982.

30. *Forbes*, Jan. 23, 1978.

31. *Tennessean*, Sept. 21, 1984.

32. *Chattanooga Times*, Oct. 17, 1979.

33. *Chattanooga Times*, Oct. 17, 1979.

34. *New York Times*, Feb. 2, 1979.

35. *New York Times*, Sept. 4, 1984.

36. *Forbes*, Sept. 24, 1984.

37. *New York Times*, Sept. 4, 1984.

38. *Forbes*, Dec. 15, 1986.

39. Massey-Burch's Valley Venture Fund was a $30 million account that came about as a result of a lawsuit that the Tennessee Valley Authority won related to the price of uranium. The court ordered the $30 million fund created and invested entirely in start-up companies that were located within the TVA service area. Massey-Burch successfully bid on the business of investing the fund.

40. *Palm Beach Post*, June 18, 1989

41. Belmont's original business school building was later converted to a library.

42. *Tennessean*, May 14, 1972.

43. As this book was being researched and written, Belmont was building a new life sciences building for its school of nursing, to be named for Nashville philanthropist Gordon Inman.

44. *Tennessean*, Oct. 21, 1988.

45. Dr. Irwin Eskind died while this book was being written, on March 28, 2005.

INTERVIEWS
AND SOURCES

Rather than pepper the text with footnotes, the only direct quotes that I have chosen to specifically attribute are the ones that came from written sources, such as books, magazine articles, and newspapers.

Direct quotes that are not amplified with a footnote came from in-person interviews, most of which were conducted by the author during the course of researching this book or his first book, Fortunes, Fiddles and Fried Chicken: A Nashville Business History. However, it should be noted that the author never met Jack Massey, so every direct quote from him came from an interview conducted by someone else. Anyone should be able to obtain a taped copy or written transcript of every one of these interviews at the Massey School of Business at Belmont University. Here is a complete list of those interviews:

In 1978 Hospital Corporation of America conducted an oral history project, and as a part of that project Deborah Cooney interviewed Jack Massey on July 22, 1978. The author would like to thank Dr. Thomas Frist Jr. and Vic Campbell for sharing with me a transcript of this very fascinating interview.

HCA conducted a similar project eight years later, and Marc K. Stengel interviewed Massey again on Sept. 26, 1986. Again, thanks to Frist and Campbell for loaning me a copy.

The Massey School of Business at Belmont University has several videotaped interviews of Massey which were conducted by either Bill Troutt or Wayne Brown.

In 1986 Massey was a guest on a short-lived television show called Nashville Business Edition. Barbara Rogers Massey loaned the author a copy.

A copy of Jack Massey's statement and testimony before the U.S. Senate Subcommittee on Antitrust and Monopoly can be obtained at the Jean and Alexander Heard Library at Vanderbilt, U.S. Government Documents division.

IN-PERSON INTERVIEWS

Lamar Alexander	Dr. George Carpenter
Dr. Ben Alter	Richard Chambers
Bob Anderson	Yvonne Christopher
Bill Armistead	Larry Coleman
Thomas Bainbridge	Donald Cowan
Gary Baker	Tom Cummings
Lee Barfield	Dewey Daane
George Barrett	Ray Danner
Tom Batey	Betty Daugherty
Earl Beasley	Bill Denny
Tom Beasley	Bert Denton
Headley Bell	Joe Diehl Jr.
Stanley Bernard	Bruce Dobie
Dennis Bottorff	Walter Dube
James C. Bradford Jr.	Jane Dudley
John Y. Brown Jr.	Townes Duncan
Wayne Brown	Winfield Dunn
Bob Brueck	Clarence Edmonds
Rogers Buntin	Kitty Moon Emery
Lucius Burch III	Dr. Irwin Eskind
Dr. Fred Callahan	Clarence Evans
Vic Campbell	Dr. Thomas Frist Jr.
Richard Cannon	Mark Frost

Richard Fulton
Wilford Fuqua
Herbert Gabhart
Matt Gallivan
Katie Gambill
Frank Garrison
Doyle Gaw
Jackie Gorman
Batey Gresham
Lydia Grubb
George Harsh
Marilyn Herbert
Ross Hickey
Henry Hooker
Marvin Hopper
Ruth Hovey
Joe Hutts
Al Johnson
Lenora Johnson
Victor Johnson Jr.
Don Johnston
Will Johnston
Sydney Keeble
Hal Kennedy
Dr. Morse Kochtitzky
Dorothy Kottler
Ted Lazenby
Buck Lyon
Merry Maney
Alyne Massey
Joe Massey
Sidney McAlister
Ashley McAnulty
Bill McKnight
Clayton McWhorter

Andrew (Woody) Miller
Guy Milner
John Neff
Edward G. Nelson
Dr. Tom Nesbitt
Stirton Oman Jr.
Elizabeth Queener
Richard Ragsdale
J. Bradbury Reed
Carl Reichardt
Tandy Rice
Bailey Robinson
Joe Rodgers
Barbara Massey Rogers
Dr. Frank Royal
Omega Sattler
Dr. Herbert Schulman
Frank Sheffield
Bill Sherriff
Reuben Smith
Lonnie Stout
Earl Swensson
Dewitt Thompson
Dr. Kirk Todd
Bill Troutt
John Tudor
Judy Vechionee
Jimmy Webb
Bill Weaver III
Fred Webber
Ted Welch
Mrs. David Williamson
David K. Wilson
Hunter Woods

Consulted Sources

Jack Massey's childhood
Sandersville Progress: March 31, 1908; April 7, 1908; June 9, 1908; Dec. 31, 1954.

Wedding announcement
Nashville Tennessean: Sept. 28, 1930.

Massey Drugs
Nashville Banner: Nov. 13, 1930.

Nashville Tennessean: Sept. 14, 1930.

Park View Hospital
Nashville Banner: Dec. 18, 1961.

Tennessean: Feb. 9, 1961; Oct, 3, 1965; Aug. 15, 16, and 21, 1967; May 19, 1968; June 25, 1968.

Kentucky Fried Chicken
Business Week: June 24, 1967; June 27, 1970; Sept. 30, 1972.

Nashville Banner: March 6, 1964; Dec. 15, 1967; March 24, 1969;

Nashville Tennessean: Dec. 27, 1962; Jan. 27, 1964; Jan. 12, 1965; June 2, 1966; Aug. 3, 1966; Nov. 9 and 18, 1966; Jan. 8, 1967;

New York Times: June 9, 1968; Jan. 5 and 17, 1969; March 24, 1970; April 3, 1970.

New Yorker: Feb. 14, 1970.

Wall Street Journal: March 18, 1966; April 12, 1968; May 9, 1968; Oct. 15, 1968; Feb. 26, 1970;

Early HCA
Tennessean: May 19, 1968; June 25, 1968.

Mrs. Winners
Forbes, Dec. 13, 1988

Wall Street Journal, Aug 15 and 21, 1989.

Wendy's
Business Week; Sept. 20, 1976.

Forbes; April 1, 1976.

Nashville Banner, Oct. 16, 1991.

Intermedics
New York Times; April 2, 1977; March 20, 1979; Sept. 11, 1982; Jan. 2, 1987; April 23, 1988; June 17, 1988.

Capital City Bank/Nashville City Bank
Nashville Banner; Nov. 18, 1959; March 14 and 21, 1960; Jan. 15, 1963; Nov. 20, 1970; May 20, 1971; Aug. 6, 1974; March 20, 1975; Nov. 22, 1985; Feb. 2, 1987.

Nashville Tennessean; April 25, 1968; March 11, 1969; Oct. 8, 1970; Oct. 8-9, 1985; Nov. 23, 1985; June 22, 1986; March 22, 1987.

Radnor Lake

Nashville Banner; June 19, 1973; Aug. 2, 1973

Tennessean; Jan. 3, 11, 21, and 22, 1972; Feb. 15, 1972; Aug. 8, 16, 17 and 20, 1973;

General Profiles

Forbes; Sept. 24, 1984.

Fortune; April 13, 1987.

Belmont University

Note: The author thanks Jane Thomas at the Bunch Library at Belmont University for her assistance. He is also indebted to whoever operated Belmont's newspaper clipping service, because whoever it is did a complete job. The following articles are only a partial list.

Nashville Banner; Aug. 31, 1959; July 18, 1963; Dec. 10, 1965; Jan. 6, 1973; Nov. 1, 1974; Sept. 8, 1984; May 28-30, 1986.

Tennessean: Aug. 8, 1952; Dec. 4, 1959; Aug. 22, 1960; Nov. 13, 1960; June 26, 1963; Sept. 10 and 17, 1964; April 22, 1968; May 23, 1968; Sept. 8, 1968; May 14, 1972; Sept. 3, 1972; Dec. 30-31, 1972; July 5 and 22, 1973; Aug. 8 and 10, 1977; Oct. 20, 1982; May 7, 9 and 26, 1986; Oct. 20, 1988;

HCA under Massey's presidency

New York Times; April 1, 1974; June 17, 1975; March 11, 1976; Sept. 24, 1976; March 11, 1977; May 12, 1978; May 29, 1983.

Wall Street Journal; May 12, 1976; July 21, 1976; Aug. 16, 1976; April 29, 1977; Oct. 13 and 27, 1978;

Commerce Union Bank

Nashville Banner; June 28, 1985.

INDEX